1,000 YEARS OF HUNGARY

EMIL LENGYEL

1,000 YEARS OF HUNGARY

THE JOHN DAY COMPANY, NEW YORK

© 1958 by Emil Lengyel

Library of Congress Catalogue Card Number: 58-7470

Manufactured in the United States of America

TO LIVIA

CONTENTS

1,000 YEARS OF HUNGARY

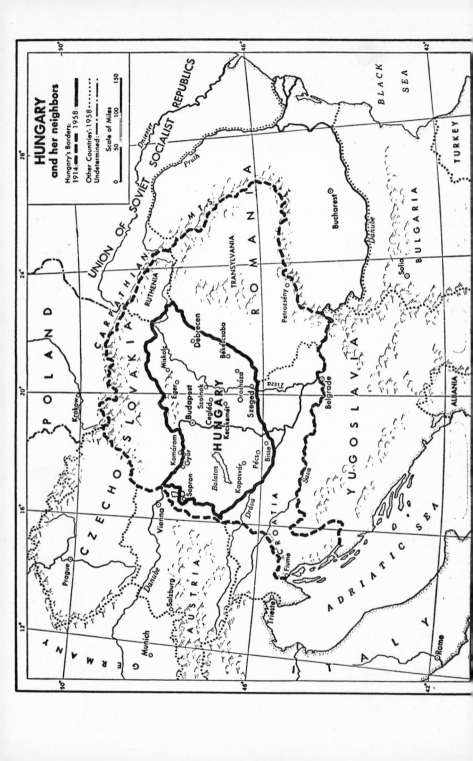

CHAPTER **1**   **THEY CAME FROM THE EAST**

A BRONZE STATUE in a public park of Budapest represents a
writing monk, his features concealed by the cowl of his robe.
The inscription on this unusual monument reads ANONY-
MOUS, which is also an uncommon designation. Here, then, is
a writing monk, the name and face of whom are unknown.
This unknown man wrote a chronicle in Latin about the early
Hungarians' deeds, and it is known as *Gesta Hungarorum*—
The Hungarians' Deeds. The author is described as "King
Béla's Unknown Chronicler"—*Anonymus Belae Regis Notar-
ius*. Scholarly research guesses that he probably served in the
capacity of *notarius* at the court of Hungary's King Béla III,
who died at the end of the twelfth century.

Thus Hungarian history begins—with a mystery wrapped
in the enigma of an unidentified chronicler. Who then, are
these Hungarians, who call themselves Magyars, and whose
country is Magyarország—Magyarland?

They seem to be standing alone in the heart of the Danubian country, in east-central Europe, and they are flanked by

all the three main groups of Europeans—Germans, Latins, and Slavs. Are the Magyars related to any of these groups, are they distant kin, or are they total strangers? Where do the Hungarians come from, and what language do they speak?

In the northeast Indian hill station of Darjeeling, within sight of the Himalayas' tallest peaks, a Hungarian explorer looking for the answers to these questions died in 1842, and there his grave still stands. His name was Sándor Körösi Csoma, and a highly respected name it is in the world of science. He was a scholarly explorer and a remarkable linguist who set out to seek the Magyars' ancient home, wherever the tracks might lead him. In the writings of medieval Arab scholars he detected references to the esoteric Magyar race. His contorted tours of exploration led him first to the Arab lands in what today we call the Middle East, in search of authentic documents. Thence he penetrated into Central Asia, into the land of the steppes and of the valleys in front of the high mountains. The chroniclers spoke about the Uigurs, a word that sounded like *Ungar, Hongrie*, Hungary; and there he was looking for his kinsmen's forebears. Then he sought Hungarian kinship in Dzungaria, the remote land that lies northeast of Tibet's Lhasa, whose name may have been the origin of *Hungaria*.

He found many interesting things, exceptionally strange languages, but he did not find the Magyars' original home. In his age, he was the most notable man in search of the Hungarians' origin, and he was followed by others. The difficulties they encountered were great. It is very well to look for the ancestral home of a settled people, who built towns and forts and left their mark on their environment. But where is one to find the traces of nomads? Where is one to find the marks of the whirlwind of thousands of years ago? Archeological exploration is of no use in such cases. Where are the scholars to find their clues?

There are the inevitable legends, of course. Folklore speaks

about Nimrod the giant, who had two sons, Hunor and
Magor. The former was the ancestor of the Huns, and Magor
was the progenitor of the Magyars. The first chronicler of
Magyar deeds, Anonymous, derived the Magyars' origin from
the Magog of the Bible, the son of Japheth. Medieval writers
—and most of them were men of the church—were inclined
to attribute the ancestry of people to famous Biblical figures.
What shall we think of such "scholarship" or of the legend
of Nimrod?

Much of the speculation about the Magyars' origin is based
upon their language. In the course of time several theories
have emerged. An earlier scholarly speculation held that the
ancestors of the Hungarians first gained their separate identity
in the gap between the Caucasus and the Urals, on the border
of Europe and Asia. A cataclysmic event displaced them
from their steppes some four thousand years ago, according
to this version, and flung them onto the slopes of the Altai
Mountains, in Central Asia, where the Soviet Union and
the Sinkiang of the Chinese meet today. That historic event
was the irruption of the Aryan-speaking people—Indo-Europeans—from their European center into their Indian habitat. Still according to this scholarly guesswork, they had
established themselves in the region between the "sea of
amber," the Baltic, in Europe's north, and the Black
Sea, in the south. It was a branch of these Aryans that
crossed the mountains and descended upon India, where
they founded the Sanskrit-speaking cultures.

The same theory says that the Magyars' ancestors held
their own in Central Asia until the second century of the
Christian era. Then they were lifted out of their Asian habitat
by another ethnic tidal movement. This time Asia began to
pour into Europe. The Magyars were deposited on the peripheries of that continent, and were engulfed and then dis-
gorged by other groups. This was part of the tremendous
westward movement of the people from their desiccated Asian

steppe land into Europe, where there was more rain, therefore more grass, and therefore life.

Another View About the Magyars' Origin

There is a more recent theory about the Hungarians' origin,
also based upon a study of languages. According to this view,
which is accepted by most scholars today, it was on the western slopes of the Ural Mountains, separating Europe from
Asia, that the Magyars gained their separate identity. They
are therefore a "European" and not an "Asian" people. It
was on the Ural slopes that their historical wandering began.
Whatever their earlier habitat had been, they had left it in
the course of that great convulsion of the human race known
to us as the *Völkerwanderung*, caused by the drying up of the
steppes. It may have been fear of the consequences of this
process of desiccation that induced the rulers of China to
build those fantastic walls. "The building of the Great Wall
of China was an event fraught with the greatest consequences," wrote the Hungarian scholar C. de Ujfalvy,* "and
one may say without exaggeration that it contributed greatly
to the downfall of the Roman Empire."

The walls restrained the famished nomads and diverted
them toward the west.

We have a dramatic illustration of how rapidly grass land
can be turned into dust land in the creation of the "dust
bowl" of the United States in the thirties of the twentieth
century. It was, indeed, drought that propelled waves upon
waves of nomads westward from Asia to Europe centuries
ago, in the view of the noted American anthropogeographer
Ellsworth Huntington, of Yale University, who wrote about
this phenomenon dramatically in *The Pulse of Asia*.

As the Hungarians were dislodged from their grazing
grounds, they were forced to join the jostling crowd of other

* *Les Aryens au Nord et au Sud de l'Hindou Kouch*, 1896, p. 24.

hungry nomads in search of grass and, perhaps, tilled soil. Farming people are at a disadvantage with nomadic people, because their superior civilization, coupled with greater comfort and less mobility, enervates them, according to A. C. Haddon in *The Wanderings of the People* (1911), and therefore they are ill prepared for a show of force. Neighboring brigands attack the settled peasant, then retreat into their barren steppes with their loot, to be propelled into the sown area again by the whip of hunger. These hungry robbers then fasten themselves on the vanquished people, sometimes completely displacing them, settling, becoming the victims of bolder marauders.

More and more of the hungry nomads were crowded into Eastern Europe, moving westward in bold outbursts of enterprise under adventurous leaders. What is history to us must have been to them a fabulous saga about the glories of the two Romes, the First Rome facing the Mediterranean, and the Second Rome, Constantinople, on the Golden Horn. The story of the wealth of the two Romes must have reached the famished nomads in a vastly exaggerated form, telling of great urban centers gorging themselves with food, glittering with gold. The attraction of the western world became irresistible.

Then, as now, the horizontal structure of Europe revealed two sharply different worlds. Then, more than now, the difference must have been vast. There was the western world, the climate of which was regulated by the clouds from the west. That was the world of the oceanic climate, and its rain was more than sufficient for farming. The prevailing winds lost much of their rain content in their eastward travel. Gradually, the climate became continental, with little rain, not only less than in the east but far less reliable. Should it fail one year, the land of the steppes was filled with vultures feasting on household beasts and their human masters. Then the land was white with the bones of animals and men.

So the Magyars were among the nomads who heeded the call of the rain from the west.

What Was Their Language?

Since it was the language that helped Hungarian researchers to trace the origin of their people, the question must be asked: What is the tongue of the Hungarians like? The world which the Hungarians occupy is crowded with Indo-European people. They live on the margin of a monstrously bloated Slavic world, which covers almost the entire northern part of the Eurasian continent, from the Bohemian mountains to the Pacific Ocean. The Slavs inhabit also the areas to the south of the Magyars, from the head of the Adriatic to the Black Sea.

To the west of the Hungarians live people speaking Germanic languages practically from the back door of Budapest, the Hungarian capital, to the North Sea; and these people comprise the Austrians, the Germans, a large part of the Swiss, the Dutch, the Scandinavians, and the English.

Finally, to the east of the Hungarians lives a people which indicates its presumed origin by its very name, the Romanians, descendants of the Romans, and speaking a language related to Latin.

Are the Hungarians then related to the Slavs, the Germans, or the Latins? In looks they are not much different from them, blond and brunette and dark, like their neighbors. A somewhat more prominent cheekbone in some cases seems to be the most obvious difference.

Yet the Hungarians are not Slavs, nor Germans, nor Latins, and this difference is an important factor in their history and fate. The Hungarians are not only not related linguistically to their neighbors, but they are not even Indo-Europeans, the vast group of people that have given the world what we call western civilization.

The Hungarians are a Finnish-Ugrian people, descendants

of the Ugrians and related to the Finns. Who were the Ugrians from whom the Hungarians appear to be descended? History does not help us here, either. Old Russian chronicles speak of an ancient "Ugra" type, which survives now only as a linguistic group. Most of these Ugrian people are nomads raising reindeer, and they are also fishermen. Occasionally they are members of primitive peasant groups fighting the frigid forces of nature in Europe's far north.

In the distant past the Finns and Magyars may have been tied together in blood brotherhood, wandering nomads in search of food, probably also hunters and fishermen. In the course of history they were flung apart, and the Finns were tossed into the most extreme part of northwestern Europe. There they fell under the influence of the adjacent Scandinavian cultures. The Magyars, on the other hand, made their way into the mid-Danubian basin.

The Finnish-Ugrian language which the Hungarians speak is believed to be a subfamily of a larger group that spans most of the top of the Eurasian continent—the Ural-Altaic group. The speakers of these tongues range all the way from Turkey to Manchuria. They include also the Mongolians and even the Japanese.

Although Finnish and Ugrian are basically related, they do not sound at all alike and they are almost as far apart as English and Persian, both of which are Indo-European tongues. Yet all Finnish-Ugrian languages have certain traits in common that are absent from the Indo-Aryan tongues.

Before mentioning some of these, however, let us call attention to the peculiar situation of the Hungarians. They represent an island in Europe, not even distantly related to any of their neighbors. Unable to speak the languages of their neighbors, they have remained an alien body, jealous of their distinct personality and looked upon with suspicion by their alien environment. It was inevitable that their small nation should fall within the gravitational pull of more powerful nations; the surprising thing is that they did not absorb it. The Finns have also retained their national identity. However, they had a great advantage over the Hungarians in that they occupy a cul-de-sac of Europe, a blind alley, abutting on the empty northern seas and occupying a glacially corroded part of the distant north. The Hungarians, on the other hand, have only to invoke the testimony of the map to show that their country on the mid-Danube is in the fulcrum of great international highways, a strategic area. The strategic value of this region is attested by history, century after century. There have been few major wars in which Hungary was not in-volved, and there have been a few in which she played the leading role.

A Strange Language

Visitors to Hungary in the past may have gained the impres-sion that the language of the people of Budapest was German. A considerable number of people spoke some kind of German there. But what else was one to do? A few score miles from Budapest, Hungarian was not understood. The better-educated people therefore felt compelled to learn German, the most im-portant of the "world languages" in that area. The writer of this book was completely monolingual in his youth, speaking nothing but Hungarian. However, when he started looking for a job, the first question invariably was: "Do you know some German?" He did not, and so he had to learn it. For the same reason he learned other languages too. A member of a small nation becomes multilingual by necessity—not by choice.

The Hungarian language is agglutinative, and that marks a basic difference from the Indo-European tongues. Language parts in Hungarian, and in other members of the same family, are "glued" to the main stem, so that the preposition becomes a post-position. This makes the learning of the first foreign language particularly difficult for a Hungarian.

As an illustration of the basic nature of Hungarian, let the

writer cite a word which has a history. It is a long word, because of the agglutinative nature of the language, and it was
scribbled on the walls of the seaport town of Fiume, at the
head of the Adriatic Sea, before the end of the First World
War. Fiume was then attached to Hungary as a semi-self-
governing body. The law of Hungary provided that public
officials in Fiume must master the Magyar language before
they could be employed as such. However, most of the candidates for these positions were Italian-speaking. Medieval Venice had left her mark on that coast.

To show how utterly impossible it was for a foreigner to
master Hungarian, and also to show how impossible was the
requirement, this was the Hungarian word Italians of Fiume
scribbled on its vacant walls:

"*Legeslegmegengesztelhetetlenebbeknek.*"

This is one word indeed, although a rather unnatural one,
and it means,"To the most irreconcilable ones"—referring to
the irreconcilable nature of the ruling Hungarians. Also it is
an illustration of the "gluing" nature of the tongue.

Another peculiar trait of the language is that it places the
family name first (which is not illogical), followed by the
Christian names, and finally the person's titles. To provide
one illustration, the name of President Dwight Eisenhower
reads in Hungarian "*Eisenhower Dwight Elnök úr*" (E. D.
President Mister).

Languages of this group have no gender, nor any word to
express the idea "to have" as an auxiliary verb. Finnish, to give
one more illustration, has no fewer than fifteen declensions.
On the other hand, Hungarian and related languages have
the advantage of being beautifully phonetic; they are written
mainly as they are spoken. Also, these languages can be very
concise, expressing in one word what Indo-European tongues
take several words to express. In Hungarian, for instance,
"I love you," is "*Szeretlek.*" It was because of these qualities
that Hungarian was recommended as a universal language by

one of the world's greatest philologists, Jakob Ludwig Karl Grimm.

How was the earliest history of the Hungarians reconstructed from their language? In their circuitous wanderings the Magyars have picked up many foreign words and embedded them in their own tongue. Thus it has been conjectured that the Magyar nomads must have come into contact with Persians near the Caucasus region. From them they acquired such basic words as *vár*, fort; and *vásár*, market. In contacts with Turkic people, to whom they were collaterally related, the Magyars picked up other words. When they turned from the earlier hunting and fishing stage to farming, they acquired Turkic words connected with the tilling of the soil: *búza*, wheat; *árpa*, barley; *eke*, plow; *szöllő*, grape; and many others. The Hungarians adopted additional Turkish words centuries later, when the Turks occupied a large part of their country.

In a more sophisticated age the Magyars brushed against the Slavs and learned from them words relating to religion, politics, law and crafts. There is a large number of Slavic words in Hungarian. Then, in the course of time the Magyars were exposed to the Romance languages, French and Italian, referring to the arts, fashions, and above all abstract concepts. For many generations the country's official language was Latin, and the Hungarians adopted many words of that tongue. The word of greeting to a friend even today is *szervusz*, the origin of which is of course the Latin *servus*, servant, I am your servant.

Tracing the acquisitions of the language into more modern times, we find that Hungarian has absorbed many terms of philosophy and psychology from German. Technical terms have been taken or derived from both German and, recently, English. The most important alien contributions to Hungarian have been made by the Romance, Slavic, and German tongues, in that order. However, basic Hungarian is old

Magyar, which is rich in the imagery characteristic of the nomads but rather poor in abstract concepts.

What has Hungarian given to other languages? Very little. The best-known words of Magyar origin are "coach"—*kocsi* (so named after the village of *Kocs* in Hungary) "hussar," * and "goulash"—*gulyás*.

On the Way to the Danube

There were many footloose tribes in Eastern Europe at the time of the migration of the peoples, and the Hungarians were not among the largest of them. Because of the large number of these itinerant tribes, all the stopping places of the Magyars cannot be enumerated, nor would they be of special interest. Their social organization must have been functional—to fulfill the tasks imposed upon a group of nomadic people. Ideology played little role in their lives. They worshiped the things they feared, the forces of nature—they were fire-worshipers, nature-worshipers, fetishists. They had a totem sign, which was the legendary hawk they called *turul*. Their tribes could not have been large without becoming too unwieldy, nor small without becoming too ineffective.

Out of the melee of many tribes looking for that "greener grass" on the other side of the rainbow, the Hungarians began to emerge by the middle of the ninth century. They were roaming then in the Don River region, not far from the Black Sea, in an area which the Byzantine writers described as Lebedia, presumably a chieftain's name. A good place was a dangerous one in that era, and this seems to have been a good one. Consequently, the Magyars were being pushed around a lot, particularly by the Petchenegs, who were to become their nemesis. The Magyars called them Besenyő. (The Hungarian "s" is pronounced as "sh.")

* And now some Hungarian etymologists are casting doubt even upon the Magyar origin of *huszár*. They think the word is derived from "Khazar," the Turkic people with whom the Magyars were in contact during their early wanderings.

Because of needs of self-defense and better organization the Magyars split into two sections. One of these sought grass for their animals beyond the Volga River, while the other one tried to establish itself on the grazing grounds in the "Land Between the Rivers," which they called Etelköz, the southwest Russia of today.

It was a daily struggle for survival. The spotlight now shifted to the Magyars between the rivers, on the periphery of the Balkans, in southeasternmost Europe, and not very far from the gravitational influence of Byzantium, the Eastern Roman Empire. Trying to strengthen their hands, the Magyars made pacts with the foes of their own foes. "The enemy of my enemy is my friend." Their enemy then was an arrogant person, Simeon I, who ruled over much of the Balkans, called himself the Czar of Bulgaria, and also "Autocrat of the Greeks." By assuming the title of "Czar" he indicated his ambition of becoming the Caesar of his age. The Byzantine empire was already in that decline which saw its destruction centuries later. Simeon clashed with Leo the Wise, the Byzantine Emperor, who demonstrated his wisdom by holding onto an unsteady throne for a quarter of a century. The Magyars made their pact with Leo.

Further to strengthen themselves against Simeon the Bulgar, the Magyar chieftains entered into a blood compact—vérszövetség—by cutting their veins and mixing their blood. These events were recorded in primitive chronicles, fact and fiction, so that definite dates cannot be established. It is believed that the blood compact was entered into close to 890 A.D. The leader of his Magyar confederation was Árpád, destined to play a historical role. He was the son of Álmos—"The Dreamy One"—so-called because his mother had dreamt that mighty rulers were to issue from his seed.

The son of Árpád was Levente—the word means "The Doughty One"—and it was he who clashed with Simeon whom he defeated. Simeon thereupon leagued himself with the Petchenegs, an awesome people, the cruelty and valor of whom froze their enemies' blood, if the chroniclers may be trusted. Like the Magyars, they seem to have descended from the Urals in that tragic search for greener grass, and they fell upon Árpád's people between the rivers, the land of the good grass. This became the turning point in the Magyars' history.

Forced out of their grazing ground, they undertook a major operation. They climbed the Carpathian mountains, which they crossed at the Verecke Pass, and moved into the area that was to be known as Hungary. The year is presumed to have been 895, known to the Hungarians as that of the *honfoglalás*, conquest of the homeland.*

The leader of the conquerors was Árpád. What the *Mayflower* is to Americans, the "conquest" is to Hungarians. The number of those who claim that their ancestors moved into Hungary via the Verecke Pass is large. The authentic history of the conquest is scanty and some historians suspect that many of its presumed facts might qualify as fiction.

The Danubian Thoroughfare

The Magyars descended into the mid-Danube region. What did they find there? Had the region been bare of civilization, an area without history? On the contrary, it had been one of the earliest sites of Western culture, or so one school of historians holds. Historic Hungary had been part of a larger region which had been the launching site of Central Europe's Bronze Age. It was the area that provided the tin which, alloyed with copper, made the bronze after which the age was named.

* The millennial celebration of the conquest, however, took place in 1896. The Hungarian government had called upon a committee of leading historians of the Scientific Academy to determine the date of conquest. The scholars could not agree on an exact date. They did agree that the conquest could not have been begun before 888 and must have been terminated by 900. Several historians suggested 895 as the most likely date for the crossing of the Pass and the government accepted their "guesstimate." However, the celebration could be held only in 1896 for technical reasons.

These minerals were found in Bohemia, to the northwest of the land taken by the Magyars. The mines had lured adventurous people from the Near East, from the eastern Mediterranean, and especially from Troy. The Danube was not only one of the routes by which the neolithic culture reached northwestern Europe, wrote C. Gordon Childe in 1927 in a significant essay, "The Danubian Thoroughfare and the Beginnings of Civilization in Europe": "It was also a channel in the diffusion of the arts of metallurgy northward and eastward from the Ancient East."

The land the Magyars beheld had been fought over in the titanic struggle between East and West in early Christian times. The Romans penetrated to the Danube in an attempt to find the natural barrier of their empire to protect it against the barbarians lurking in the darkness of the unfathomable East. They established settlements along the river, including Vindobona, which was later to become Vienna, and Aquincum, the future Budapest. Eventually, the Romans penetrated farther east, and under Emperor Trajan they pierced the walls of Transylvania and maintained themselves for a time in Dacia, the picturesque land on both sides of the eastern Carpathian range.

Subsequently waves upon waves of barbarians had broken upon Mid-Danubia before the Hungarians came. These barbarians had been enterprising German tribes, such as the "people with the long beards," the Longobardi, who were to give their name to the land of the Po River, Lombardy. Then there had been another Germanic tribe, the Gepidae, who had tangled with the Huns, who crushed them in 567, centuries before the Hungarians' arrival. These Turkic people had been the builders of an ephemeral empire spanning Eastern and Central Europe, from the Elbe to the Volga. Then came the Slavic tidal wave. The Slavs seem to have been pushed into their western outpost position—which has been retained to this day—by the Avars. After having accomplished this historic feat, the Avars were wiped off the map.

The West had made an attempt to encompass the East. It was the tradition of the defunct Roman Empire that all the then known world should be embraced by one empire. The memory of the *Pax Romana* lingered on but now it was combined with a religious concept. As there was one God in heaven, where eternal serenity reigned, there was to be one ruler on earth, and perennial peace. This was the idea of the Holy Roman Empire and the ambition of Charlemagne, and under his rule all Europe was to pay homage to the divine dispensation embodied in the imperial power. The great ruler's influence irradiated for a time the northern regions of what was to become Hungary.

The Carolingian realm was sustained by the titanic strength of one supremely confident sovereign and the belief that peace could be won only through unity. After the death of Charlemagne his empire fell into faltering hands. At the time the Magyars made their bid, the King of the East Franks was his great-great-grandson, Arnulf, nephew of Charles the Fat. Arnulf lacked his great ancestor's drive and dispersed his forces by trying to hold together too vast an empire riven by centrifugal forces.

The situation the Magyars found in the land they were to conquer was this. In the north they found the mighty realm of Great Moravia, which included Bohemia, southern Poland and Silesia, too. It reached its greatest height under Duke Svatopluk, a somewhat misty figure. The east and southeast of the land was a perennial battlefield among Bulgarians, the Turkic Khazars and, perhaps, the Vlachs, presumed ancestors of the modern Romanians. The west of future Hungary appears to have been a satellite region of the East Franks.

The Magyars appeared in Mid-Danubia just at the right time, when it was not under a strong central rule and marginal regions of trans-mountain realms were engaged in suicidal jurisdictional disputes. The Mid-Danube region was thus a typical power vacuum. The Magyars destroyed Great Moravia in a series of wars, routed the Khazars and Vlachs, chased the Bulgarians further south. The Bulgarian ruler, Simeon, aimed at much bigger things than the barbarous lands to the north of the mountains. More than ever he was attracted by Constantinople under the spell of which he fell. Relative to Bulgaria in the east and the Frankish realm in the west, the Danube valley was a marginal land; and the Magyars moved into it with alacrity.

Again was shown the truth of the axiom that in an age of turmoil settled people were at a disadvantage against desperate nomads.

The Mid-Danube Region

The country into which the Magyars moved was transitional not only from the diplomatic but also from the meteorological point of view. It was a natural unit, this millennial Hungary (as it became known, since it endured for over a thousand years, to the end of the First World War). It was all but encircled by mountains: the arc of the Carpathians in the north, then the Eastern Carpathians and the Transylvanian Alps in the southeast.

This crescent enfolded the Danubian plains from the Vienna Gap, in the northwest, where the river breached the chain of hills, all the way to the Iron Gate, where the stream smashed its way across a solid rampart of mountains. At the Iron Gate itself the mountains of the Balkans formed the southern boundary of millennial Hungary. The protective arc continued with the Dinaric Alps which, in turn, were linked to the eastern Alps of what was to become Austria.

Across all these mountains were passes, which determined horsemen, such as nomads, could breach. It required great determination, however, to face this difficult terrain, which the defenders could employ as natural forts.

Historic Hungary was thus largely closed to the east, north

and south, but was open to the west, and thereby hangs her
tale and was determined her orientation. The Vienna Gap
itself was a natural gateway along the continental highway,
running parallel with the Danube. At Vienna it was bisected
by the ancient Amber Road, linking the amber-rich Baltic
with the Adriatic.

The rest of the western boundary of Hungary leaned against
the rugged Alpine land. It was nature itself that induced the
Magyars to turn toward the West, both offensively and de-
fensively. It was also natural for them, in centuries to come,
to be exposed to the cultural influence of the West, situated
as they were close to the intersection of the Continental Highway and the Amber Road.

Hungary, too, was a transitional land between East and
West. Because of the forces of nature it was easier for her to
follow the Western lead. Also it was in the very nature of
her location that she could become the rampart of the West
against the East.

The climate of Hungary is also transitional. Three great
climatic influences have been struggling for supremacy in
Hungary, according to the historian Gyula Szekfű, one of
them having a preponderant influence. The western part
of Hungary has adequate precipitation, under the influence of
the seas in the west. The Mediterranean climate represents a
fringe influence, and it blends into the Atlantic influence.
The dominant wind is western in Hungary, as it is elsewhere.
From the east come the scorching winds of the summer and
the numbing cold of the plains in the winter. From there
comes also drought, which in the past meant famine and
which even now means lean years.

In the past the influence of the climate on Hungary was
far more important than it is now. Where rain was abundant,
there were also swamps and malaria. Where the rain was inadequate, there were large patches of steppe land—*puszta*, "the
arid," as the Hungarian calls it—and occasionally there was

also drift sand, *futó-homok*. Still most of Hungary was then, as it is now, a rich farm land, partly covered with what the Russians call *chernozem*, the black soil, humus, the bottom of a shallow sea in geological times, one of the major breadbaskets of Eastern Europe and Danubia.

The Magyar Danger to the West

Beyond the Vienna Gap anarchy prevailed at the time the Magyars arrived in what was to become their home. The empire of Charlemagne was in ruins and the reign of Otto the Great was yet to come. This was, then, a transition period; chaos in the wake of the cataclysmic collapse of an organization pivoted on the heroic personality of Charlemagne. The Magyar frontiersmen were faced with a region lacking the clear-cut outlines of authority. What was more natural than that the Hungarians should continue their westward drive toward lands where the rain was more abundant, and where the treasures piled up by an established peasantry invited their greed?

Western history has preserved the memory of cataclysmic perils from the East. The Occident has not yet forgotten the Huns, inhuman monsters in human form, under the leadership of Attila, whom the world was to know as the Scourge of God. Later centuries witnessed the West being menaced by the destructive fury of the Tatars, who sought to find life for themselves in the death of others. Still more centuries later, it was the Turk who imperiled the continuity of Western civilization. In all these cases the East challenged the West; a terrible epidemic of destruction tested the fiber of the Occident. In the tenth century it was the Magyars who represented the greatest danger to Western culture. They were the modern Huns, and the forerunners of Tatar and Turk. In the face of this danger the Western world fell on its knees: "From the Magyars' wrath deliver us, oh God!" The experience the Magyars left with the Western world was

so traumatic that even generations later people from the West
saw the Hungarians as apocalyptic monsters. Bishop Otto of
Freysing spoke of the exterior of the Hungarians as "ferocious"
at the time of the Crusades. "Their eyes are sunken, their
stature is short, their behavior wild, their language barbarous,
so that one can either accuse fate or marvel at divine patience
for having permitted these monsters the possession of an
enchanting land." To the people in the far west of Europe,
the Hungarians appeared as monsters, and it is supposed that
the word "ogre" was derived from the Byzantine "Ogōr"
—a name for the Magyars derived from the same root as
"Ugrian."

Lord Macaulay described this danger to the West in the
Edinburgh Review, January 1840: "The Hungarian in whom
the trembling monks fancied they recognized the Gog and
Magog of prophecy, carried back the plunder of the cities of
Lombardy to the depths of the Pannonian forests."

Again the Magyars had a great advantage over the settled
people. They were a people on horseback, moving under the
irresistible momentum of their march across the hills and
plains. Leaving behind holding forces, the Hungarian horsemen erupted from the Vienna Gap and turned their faces to
the west. Beyond the Gap they branched off in different
directions. History repeated itself as these presumed kinsfolk
of the Huns repeated the performance of those abominable
nomads. Now it was the Hungarians who ranged far into the
west and south. These campaigns lasted for many years—
from 899 to 954. In one year the Magyar marauders were in
what is northern Italy today and the next year they were in
Burgundy, much farther west. In other years they followed
the Danube and the Rhine, reaching rich Rhenish lands
which they traversed and laid waste. In one of these years,
924, they were making a race to Rome, while in another
campaign they swept along the Adriatic coast of the Apen-
nine peninsula, heading toward the distant south. They scored

victories and established tributary regimes. For a time the
end of the world seemed to the West to be imminent.

However, the Magyar challenge found its Occidental response. The Hungarians represented an anachronism, no-
madism coupled with paganism, against the western idea of
agriculture coupled with Christianity. The churches of the
West were the centers of established settlements as well as the
strongholds of a new culture. They imbued the defenders of
the faith with an ideological fanaticism that the attackers did
not possess.

The defense of the West was organized by Otto I, known
also as Otto the Great, the German king considered the
founder of the Holy Roman Empire. Global unity was the
purpose of that realm: one God and one Emperor. Otto
united the German and Italian lands, and made his peace
with the Pope. Against this formidable combination the
Hungarians could not prevail. The crucial battle was fought
at Lechfeld, near the town of Augsburg, in Bavaria, in 955,
and there Otto the Great defeated the Magyars. Weakened
and sobered by a decisive setback, they retreated behind their
mid-Danubian mountain barrier.

In their forays into the West the Magyars became acquainted with the ways of a world that stood on a much
higher level of civilization than they did. They saw the great
towns of the West, the cultivated fields where far fewer
people died of famine than in their Danubian homes. They
also saw the churches. History records many instances when
defeated enemies assumed the victors' ways.

After their settlement in Hungary the Magyars had divided
the land among themselves. To head off jurisdictional disputes they separated the tribal domains by an elaborate set
of no man's lands. Semisettled, the Magyars could hope to
survive only if they made peace among themselves and with
the Western world. That peace was to be transmitted to them
through Christianity.

CHAPTER **2**   BUILDING A NATION

THE WORLD AROUND the Hungarians either had embraced or was embracing the Christian creed. It was the great-grandson of Árpád the Conqueror, Chief Géza—or Geyza—who took the final step. But the question was yet to be answered: Which Christianity should it be? Much depended upon the answer.

There were two types of Christianity contending for supremacy in those days, and each of them considered itself universal, which idea they expressed in synonymous terms— *Catholic* and *Ecumenical*. When the differences were crystallized, they pivoted partly around ritual and partly around dogma. From the historical perspective these differences do not appear to have been basic. But the struggle was very real and extremely bitter.

It is easy to say that the decision of Hungary was of the utmost importance to Constantinople and Rome. The former irradiated the eastern land, and its greatest conquest was that of the Russian steppes—Kiev, Muscovy, and their successor the Russian realm. The sphere of influence of Rome was in the west and deep in Central Europe. Hungary was on the border line, not only in climate but also in geography. Should Hungary decide to join the East, the stock of the Orthodox Church would be raised; should she join the West, that of Rome. From Hungary's point of view the decision was just as vital. By joining the Eastern Church Hungary would become an Eastern country, and by joining the Western Church she would become an outpost of the Occident.

What governed Chief Géza's decision cannot be even conjectured because historic evidence is lacking. He sent word to the Emperor and German King Otto II to dispatch missionaries to him. He and his family were baptized in the Western rite in 973—a landmark in Hungarian history. The Hungarians thus decided to join the West. It was all the more remarkable because most of their neighbors to the east and south made common cause with Byzantium. Was this basic decision made because of geography—because of those mountains that sealed off Hungary to the East and kept her open to the West? Was the decision the whim of one key man? History teaches that whims of key men seldom decide the fate of nations. It is more likely that the decision of the Chief reflected the wishes of the Hungarian "creative minority," the people who in turn mirrored the views of effective public opinion.

Naturally, Christianity did not win completely at the first try. To many of the chieftains the Magyars' tradition was the traditional way of worship and Christianity was an outlandish abomination. It took generations before the old ways were eradicated.

The Rule of St. Stephen

The pagans were combated by the first of the great Hungarian rulers, King Stephen I (969–1038), who is also known as St. Stephen. He invited missionaries from the West to assist him in his work, and one of these was a Venetian, Gellert or Gerard, who distinguished himself with his Christian zeal. Infuriated by his ardor, a group of pagans seized him, thrust him into a barrel lined with spikes, and rolled him down the craggy hillside into the Danube at Buda. To this day the hill is known as St. Gellert's Mountain.

St. Stephen made an attempt to introduce a certain amount of centralization into the country. Again he followed a western method and organized Hungary into counties, each headed by a count, according to the French pattern. The counts collected the revenue in the King's name, sat in judgment, and organized the armed forces at royal command. The county organization remained an essential part of the Hungarian government throughout the centuries.

King Stephen realized that the Magyars lacked some essential skills. He also saw that they were as yet crude country folk; furthermore, the land appears to have been sparsely settled. He expressed some very liberal ideas about immigration, which he sought to convince his people would enrich the country. He himself married a Bavarian princess, Gisella, and his daughter, Maria, married Otto Orseolo of Venice.

The King had democratic notions about the ruler's duties toward his people. "Humility alone exalts the man," he wrote in his famous "Admonitions" to his son, Emeric. "Haughtiness and hatred humiliate him . . . Monarchs who really rule are lovers of peace, while the others are mere tyrants. Be forbearing toward all, be they influential or poor."

The church in Hungary needed a close-knit organization, and Stephen turned to Pope Sylvester to help him accomplish this work. He also petitioned him for the right to use a royal title. The Pope was only too ready to help. He was a man of great erudition in a variety of fields, which included the natural sciences, mathematics, and theology. He worked with other learned men, and some of them had a broad field of activities in Hungary. His contemporaries called the Pope the "miracle of the world," *stupor mundi.*

Sylvester did bestow the title "Apostolic King" upon Stephen, and the rulers of Hungary wore it until the end of the First World War. At the same time he sent Stephen a crown, two bent bands of gold surmounted by a cross; these formed the upper portion of what later came to be the Hungarian crown. Later the lower portion was added, a broad round band of gold, which the Byzantine Emperor Michael Lukas sent to Hungary's King Géza I. The two crowns, fashioned into one, became the most sacred of all Hungarian relics. Until the end of World War II it was kept under the constant supervision of a Crown Guard in a separate structure. In order to keep the crown out of the hands of the Soviets at the end of the war, it was spirited out of the country and fell into the keeping of the American occupation forces. It is still in the possession of the United States. There is a copy of the Hungarian crown in the Vatican Museum of Rome.

The Hungarians called this the Holy Crown of Hungary, and its presumed magic force induced historic personalities to take great pains to prevent its falling into rivals' hands. It was sometimes concealed or transported from place to place. In the fourteenth century, in connection with a furtive transfer, the cross on top of the crown became tilted. The Magyar freedom fighters of the mid-nineteenth-century revolution temporarily removed the crown from its sanctuary in an attempt to keep it from the Habsburgs.

The Hungarian crown is thus not merely a symbol but also part of the Magyar *mystique.* Since there was only one crown, there could be only one ruler of the land, and this was important in feudal times particularly, when authority was fragmented.

In time a body of doctrine emerged in Hungary which attributed legitimate powers of sovereignty to the Holy

Crown. "The Hungarian people," wrote Ákos von Timon, professor of law at the University of Budapest and most eloquent exponent of this doctrine, "regard the State as a society organized in the interests of the whole, an organic entity incorporated in the Holy Crown. . . . Public power is present in the Holy Crown by a mystery. Each factor of State life is in immediate touch with the Holy Crown and obtains its function from it. It is the source of all power and right."

Even more than that, the crown was presumed to be the owner of land, and thus the root of all property rights. Thus it may be said that it was not the king himself that represented the highest authority in Hungary, but the "jurisdiction of the Holy Crown of the Kingdom," and the power inherent in it was to be exercised by the "legal" nation, the nobility and the sovereign.

The role of the crown in Hungary has been the subject of as many commentaries, proportionately, as the Constitution of the United States. Many sought to place the rule of the Magyar magnates on firmer foundations by giving added weight to their part in the mystical power of the crown as the legal nation, in conjunction with the sovereign, who was the wearer of the crown. Without coronation, it was eventually believed, there was no legitimate rule.

Hungary's Time of Troubles

The long rule of King Stephen laid the foundations of the Hungarian state. He was the first Hungarian to be canonized; and St. Stephen's Day, August 20, became one of the nation's great national holidays, when the shriveled "sacred right hand" of the sainted sovereign was carried in solemn procession in the old town of Buda, the Vár.*

* When the Communists took over in Hungary after World War II they retained August 20 as a national holiday but called it Constitution Day, in honor of the document they produced on that date. This shows the great traditional value of St. Stephen's Day.

The son of St. Stephen entered world history in a round-about way. He was Prince Imre—Emeric, whose Latin name was Emericus. Because of his Bavarian mother, Gisella, the East and the West did meet in the young man's veins. Legend has been far more articulate about this prince than has history; many miracles and saintly deeds were attributed to him. He never became Hungary's king, but died in his father's lifetime at the age of twenty-four, and his grave in the trans-Danubian town of Székesfehérvár became a place of pilgrimage. He was canonized by Pope Gregory VII.

St. Emeric's name was very popular in mid-fifteenth century Florence, when Amerigo Vespucci, son of Nastaggio the notary, was born. Amerigo is the Italianized form of Emeric; and thus, according to some scholars, the name of America is of Hungarian origin.

The House of Árpád, which ruled now, was named after Árpád the Conqueror, but several of its members were men of little distinction. Behind those mountain walls that encircled Hungary, the world was still in turmoil and spasmodic irruptions from the East were not yet at an end. Across the mountain passes tribes of Turkic speech continued their inroads, foremost among them the Cumanians or Cumans, and the Petchenegs whom we have already encountered. The Eastern Roman Empire was weakening, but it gathered strength occasionally under dynamic rulers. One of these was Manuel I (1143–1180), whose ambition was immense. He was obsessed with the idea of reconstituting heaven on earth in the form of the Holy Roman Empire of the East. He conceived the plan of mating the churches of the East and West, and in the adventurous Emperor's projects Hungary was to serve as a bridge between the Orient and Occident. To accomplish his aim he used the well-tested device of divide and rule. At one time he supported the candidacies of three pretenders to the Hungarian throne. Under St. Stephen the state had been getting stronger, but now it began to fall apart. In order to strengthen themselves, the candidates for the throne—there was no clear-cut line of succession within the Árpád dynasty—conveyed large grants of land to the leading nobles in order to win them over to their side. This increased the magnates' power at the cost of the crown and strengthened the atomizing influence of feudalism, which was already triumphant in the West.

Disturbing trends in Hungary were noted by the Bishop of Freysing, already mentioned here. He noticed that the arrant magnates had their chairs taken to meetings with the king, and that they remained sitting in his presence. However, the old supremacy of the sovereign wearer of the crown was not obliterated, and the same prelate observed that even the lowliest of slaves had the right to place the mightiest of nobles under arrest if he dared offend the king. These were contradictory trends indeed, and certain phases of them were disturbing.

The Hungarians' place in world history was not yet established. Would they be one of those fly-by-night peoples who made their mark on history and then vanished? Or were they to develop the staying power to enable them to take more permanent residence in Mid-Danubia?

Subsequent events were to show that the Magyars knew how to adjust themselves to their environment, generate strong leadership, and submit to the common will. Also they knew how to beat back the desperate attempts of nomads from across the chain of mountains to dislodge them. They were successful, partly because of their own qualities and also because of certain defects in their enemies, especially the chronic inability of the nomads to organize themselves.

Not only did the Hungarians manage to hold on but they also expanded their rule into regions where the fragmentation of ethnic groups had not been followed by consolidation. One of the most effective rulers of the Árpád dynasty was the king whom history knows as Könyves Kálmán—Bookish

Kálmán or Coloman (1095–1119)—who expanded Magyar authority into the southwestern regions adjacent to the Illyrian coast of the Adriatic Sea, where Eastern and Western Romes were engaged in a feud. Bookish Kálmán found anarchy in the area, which was peopled by Slavs, and replaced it by Hungarian rule, that lasted into the twentieth century. During most of those centuries the inhabitants of the area, mainly Croats, led an autonomous life under their chief official, the ban, following their own traditions.

Often the bookish king had to turn from his volumes and set his face against the savage hordes that sought to batter down his country's ramparts. Most persistent of these were the Cumans, another group of Turkic speech, who described themselves as people of "abominable manners" (and they do not seem to have been exaggerating). Contemporary accounts speak of them as sadists, with no spark of human kindness, who reveled in shedding human blood. They were also said to have gorged themselves on carrion, and in periods of famine they may have reverted to cannibalism.

Kálmán took both the sword and the cross to the Cumans. He crossed the mountains into Moldavia, whence the Cumans had staged their savage forays. King Kálmán must have studied the elements of human psychology such as this: "Kindly talk is stronger than the sword." According to the testimony of the "Illustrated Chronicle" Kálmán thus addressed his nobles: "Forbear to slay all these people. Let us take them prisoners so that they may be converted and live in amity with us." He also established the first bishopric in Moldavia.

Eventually, the "savages" were settled in Hungary's coreland, where their name is perpetuated in a large number of towns and patronymics containing the word *Kun*, Hungarian for Cuman. They kept on speaking their own tongue for centuries, but gradually they were absorbed in the Hungarian element. They may be responsible for the dark skin color of some Hungarians, thus modifying the German and Slavic ethnic influences.

These "Easterners" also adopted the Hungarians' Western ways. It seemed that then, too, as throughout their history, the Hungarians had a deep nostalgia for the the West. Hungarian would-be scholars were constantly attracted to the famous sites of learning in the Occident. Several of them made their way to Paris, where they sat at the feet of noted masters at the Cathedral School of Nôtre Dame and also learned from the world-renowned Pierre Abélard, who had established a school at the Mont Ste. Geneviève in Paris, which was to be the birthplace of the Sorbonne. One of the graduates of the Paris school was the Archbishop of Esztergom, Hungary's highest ecclesiastical authority, Lukács Bánfi. And if scholarly speculation about his identity is correct, the author of the chronicle about the early Magyar deeds, the historian "Anonymous," may have had much of his education on the banks of the Seine.

The Golden Bull

Feudalism was an attempted solution of the political, economic, and social problems of many parts of the world. It came into being at a time when the centralized authority of Rome had collapsed and the new patterns introduced by the barbarians had not taken form. In course of time, Hungary, now attached to the West, followed many features of Western feudal ways.

This entailed a process of fragmentation both in landholdings and loyalties in Hungary as well. The king conveyed land deeds to the strong so as to assure for himself their aid in times of need. In the picturesque language of the Hungarians, these major nobles were *kiskirályok*, little kings. Naturally, the strengthening of the magnates took place at the expense of the less powerful free people, the lower nobility, and even more at the cost of the unfree peasantry who formed the bulk of the country's population.

In Hungary, as in England, this development took the people to the very verge of anarchy. In order to put an end to it, the nobles forced King Andreas II to sign the "Golden Bull" in 1222, one of the major documents of what has been called the Hungarian Constitution.

Hungarian historians have attempted to show that the similarity between the Golden Bull and the Magna Carta, only seven years older, was due not merely to coincidence, that some leading Hungarians were in contact with leading Englishmen. Thus the Hungarian primate at that time was in touch with Stephen Langton, Archbishop of Canterbury, one of the barons who secured Magna Carta. Also, the bishop of the Hungarian town of Eger, Thomas, had contact with English barons at the siege of Egypt's Damietta in crusading days.

The Golden Bull of Hungary attempted to unify the nobility by creating what medieval Hungary called *una eademque nobilitas*, one and the same nobility. This was also an attempt to create a measure of "democracy" within an aristocratic system, so that the major nobles should not crush the minor ones. However, in doing this the Golden Bull did sharpen the cleavage between the nobles and the common, unprivileged people, who came to be known as *misera plebs contribuens*, miserable tax-paying people. These creatures were stripped of protection that might have been provided by the ramparts of folk solidarity.

The Golden Bull provided, above all, that members of the nobility were not to pay taxes. This immunity continued to the middle of the nineteenth century, and no amount of persuasion, no appeal to their patriotic sentiment, could persuade the nobles, major or minor, to relinquish their "Constitutional" right. This was one of the reasons why the sharp cleavage between the noble and the "ignoble" continued in Hungary into modern times.

The basic document also provided that the king had no right to quarter himself or his retinue in the noblemen's houses without their invitation. Only when the enemy was within the boundaries of the country was the nobility to defray the costs of war; the king was to pay when the foe was outside the frontiers. Under the Golden Bull nobles were not to be arrested and jailed without valid judgment. It provided that royal court must be held each year on St. Stephen's Day in the town of Székesfehérvár. A very important provision was that, should the monarch violate the nobility's basic rights, the latter had the right to rise, even against the anointed king wearing the Holy Crown.

The Mongol Invasion

A Hungarian Dominican monk, Father Julianus, was engaged at the beginning of the thirteenth century in a work that elicited the attention of many Hungarians for centuries—the mystery of their origin. He was looking for the Magyars' original home in eastern lands when he learned about an incident that was to change world history—the approach of the Mongols from their distant Asiatic steppes.

This nomadic people had many faces and names, one of which was Mongol, presumably derived from the word "brave"—mong. They came like the whirlwind out of Asia, whipped by hunger, and soon they were to engulf much of the world. Their leader was Jenghiz Khan, a monster and a genius, whom no earthly power could restrain. The success of the Mongols was due to the fact that they learned the advantage of specializing for war. They also won campaigns because of the panicky fear they evoked in their victims.

The branch of the Mongol horde headed for the Danube was under the command of Batu Khan, grandson of Jenghiz. So terrible was the reputation of this advancing plague that the populace of entire towns chose suicide by preference. Batu's forces quickly overran the seminal settlements of what was to become Russia, and they overwhelmed Kiev in 1236.

Hungary's ruler was King Béla IV (1206–1270), son of the signer of the Golden Bull. In sign of the mortal danger to the country, King Béla had a bloody sword carried around —a call to arms for the nobility. The magnates were suspicious that this was an attempt by the King to subject them to his supreme command, and their response to his call was unimpressive. Several members of the higher clergy, however, saw the danger that threatened not only Hungary but all Christendom, and they helped to set up an army.

By that time the Hungarians had been established as a Christian people. Should they fall under the hoofs of the horses of the Mongols, the rest of Christianity would be endangered. The King, therefore, also appealed to the West for urgent help. It paid him scant attention, since its energies were absorbed by a fratricidal war between the two branches of Christendom. The issue was which branch was to prevail, the Holy Roman Empire or the Holy Roman Church. The opposing leaders were headstrong men, Emperor Frederick II and Pope Gregory IV. They were also men of great intelligence, who must have been fully aware of the dangers the Mongol invasion represented to Christendom, especially if Hungary were put to the sword. But each was mainly interested in wiping out his Christian opposite number. Both of them promised aid to Béla, but neither of them gave it.

The Mongols had vaulted the mountains and were swarming down into the plains. As a stopgap, the King called upon the Cumans, under their able leader Kuthen Khan, to help brake the enemy's onward march. King Béla had an armed force estimated at 60,000 to 65,000 men. The adversaries engaged in a bloody battle. At a crucial moment a tragic mistake was made by the Hungarians. Suspicious of the Cumans, and particularly suspicious of their leader, they cut him down. Large contingents of the enraged Cumans joined the Mongols. The scene was the town of Mohi on the River Sajó, and it was less a battle than a carnage. The Hungarians were decisively defeated.

The roads were strewn with corpses all around. Several high church dignitaries, including two cardinals and several bishops, were lost. The King just managed to escape on a swift horse but was pursued by the Mongols. That winter was exceptionally harsh, and the Danube between the twin cities of Buda and Pest was frozen. On the east bank of the stream the Mongols reduced Pest to ashes, then they crossed the river and did the same to Buda. From there they fanned out, one advancing army taking the "Hungarian Rome," Esztergom, by assault.

King Béla managed to make his flight good. Racing across country, he did not stop until he reached the Adriatic coast. There he tried again to alert Christendom, and in an urgent appeal he turned to the House of Babenberg, ruling dynasty of adjacent Austria. The ruler, Frederick the Quarrelsome, was ready to help, but only if Béla paid him 10,000 silver marks and deeded to him three of Hungary's western counties.

Hungary was in ashes, the King gone: would the country survive, or would fate catch up with her? Would the name "Hungarian" remain only a historic memory, like Avar or Petcheneg, one of the countless attempts to take roots? As this question hung in the balance, the unexpected occurred. Word was relayed to the victorious Mongol leader, Batu Khan, that his uncle, Ogdai Khan, was dead and the struggle for the succession to supreme power had begun. He promptly started home, as the contemporary reports recount, with a train of "a thousand prisoners" destined to be his slaves. However, the mountain passes were exceptionally hard to cross with such a retinue, and Batu issued orders to have the prisoners slaughtered. This was the Mongols' farewell gesture to Hungary.

The Mongol invasion of Hungary was one of those traumatic experiences that people were never to forget. Ever since, the Hungarian language has been enriched with an expression, *tatárjárás*, Tatar (Mongol) invasion, to connote the last word in destruction. Truly, Hungary was now a charnel house.

King Béla, however, was not a sovereign to be daunted. He undertook the work of reconstruction promptly. To enable the land to withstand similar invasions, he gave encouragement to the nobles to fortify their castles. These private forts served their purpose a score of years later, when a weaker detachment of Mongols attempted another invasion under Nogaj Khan. The fortification of the castles had also an adverse effect, in that it encouraged centrifugal tendencies, the atomization of power, and the creation of new centers of strength in the magnates' burghs.

Béla also encouraged the creation of defense pivots in the natural defenses, and these eventually became trading centers and towns. Following the example of illustrious ancestors, he encouraged the immigration of people from other lands, including the German countries. The German immigrants, mostly Swabians and Saxons, possessed uncommon skills. Many were placed near the country's protective perimeter where they were to serve as bulwarks against invaders. In many cases, the inhabitants of longer standing remained in the better-protected and therefore more desirable locations, where the soil was good.

Béla was the last strong ruler of the native Árpád House. One of his successors is known as Kun László—Leslie the Cuman (1272–1290), whose skin was swarthy and whose mother was a Cuman. László made himself unpopular by adopting uncouth Cuman customs. In international relations he took an important step when he sided with Rudolph I, founder of the Habsburg dynasty, in the latter's feud with

Ottokar II of Bohemia, and thus helped to establish the success of the dynasty that was eventually to rule over much of the world, including Hungary.

László's ways were debauched, and as his hands weakened a wave of anarchy was set off. The magnates took advantage of this opportunity and kept on grabbing more power. The lesser nobles thereupon formed their own leagues for self-protection, since they could expect no help from a helpless King. László liked the Cumans above all, and it was an irony of fate that he was cut down by them. When his successor Andrew III died in 1301, the age of Hungary's native House of Árpád was at an end.

The Rule of Alien Dynasties

The Hungarian crown now fell to alien dynasties, which ruled over the land until the end of the twentieth century's First World War, except for the brief reign of the Hunyadis in the fifteenth century.

With the reign of the House of Anjou Hungarian life was woven into the fabric of medieval social life. This dynamic house originated in western France, and it came to rule over a large number of regions, including other parts of France, Naples, Hungary, and Poland, Jerusalem at least nominally, and collaterally even England. Under the prevailing system, strong dynasties strengthened themselves not only by right of conquest but also by marrying royal women with rich dowries of land. It was by way of a dynastic marriage that the Anjous of France became Hungary's rulers, as Charles II of Naples married a daughter of King Stephen V of Hungary, who wore the crown only for two years.

Two of Hungary's greatest kings were Anjous. One of them was Charles Robert, whom the Magyars called Róbert Károly (1307–1342), and the other one was Louis the Great, whom they called Nagy Lajos (1342–1382). During their reign Hungary not only played a role in world history but she became one of the major powers. Even though partly of alien origin, both rulers were accepted as Hungarians, and indeed their policies were pivoted on Hungary. Both of them attempted to solve a problem which was to bedevil the world—East Central Europe, the valley of the Danube.

An ethnographic map reveals the nature of the problem. It shows this part of the continent as basically different from the rest, lacking even a limited ethnic homogeneity. Eventually, Western Europe was to crystallize fully into such strong national states as France and England. Eastern Europe, on the other hand, could not congeal into homogeneous units because of its ethnic fragmentation, which was due to a variety of causes.

Oceanic Europe was able to settle down to farming pursuits because of its abundance of rain. On the other hand, Eastern Europe, under the influence of the drier continental climate, kept on looking for its livelihood on the scant grass of the semiarid land for a much longer time. The nomads' chronic irruptions into the sown area kept on disrupting the political framework of countries in the process of crystallization.

There was also the disruptive influence of the great East-West conflict between the First and Second Romes, both claiming to be universal. The antagonism between the two Christian centers could not have been more acrid even if they had followed different creeds. The gravitational pull of these centers lost its potency in proportion to distance. Eastern Central Europe was marginal to both of them and that was its bane. Hungary, Poland, and Croatia subscribed to the Roman faith, while their neighbors to east and south looked to the Golden Horn for inspiration. Closer integration of these regions was therefore the problem to be solved. This was all the more imperative because the East kept on disgorging its hungry pagan hordes. This area was the outpost and the rampart of all Christendom.

Another ingredient of this problem was the lack of a

strong group sentiment. Because of the constant devastation of these regions by Mongols and other human plagues, aliens had to be introduced constantly and the atomization continued apace.

Integration was thus the need of the age, and it was integration that Hungary's two great Angevin kings sought to bring about. The natural unit would have been the area extending from the Baltic Sea in the north to the Adriatic in the south, a veritable rampart against the hungry East, strategically defensible, the new *limes*, corresponding to the fortification chain set up by the Romans in the face of the barbarian threat. Such a Baltic-to-Adriatic region would have centered around Hungary and Poland, including also Moldavia and Walachia to the east of the Carpathians, and the lands of Serbia, Croatia, Bosnia, and Dalmatia in the south. Louis the Great, of the Angevin line, did indeed become the ruler not only of Hungary but also of Poland, while Serbia, Walachia, Moldavia, Dalmatia, and even Bulgaria, in the coreland of the Balkan peninsula, became his vassals.

Under the Anjou rule Hungary adopted the medieval pattern of military service which was to prevail for many centuries, into the modern age and even into the nineteenth century. Under this system the magnates led their troops to war under their own banners, *banderia*, while members of the lesser nobility were recruited by county sheriffs. The king as the supreme magnate had his own special troops.

Louis the Great confirmed Hungary's Golden Bull, and in order to strengthen the military defenses of the country he introduced the landholding system of entail. Under this regime the inheritance of land was limited to a special class of descendants for several generations. Thus landholdings were to be prevented from falling apart. At the same time, the future was to show that the system of entail encouraged inefficiency and laid the dead hand of tradition on the land.

Eastern Central Europe in those days must have been

considered a fairly wealthy region. Besides its rich farm lands, it had those precious metals which the preindustrial age treasured. Even in Roman times Transylvania had the reputation of being the most abundant source of gold in the then known world. An important ore of gold, called sylvanite, a gold and silver tellurite, was actually named for Transylvania, where it seems to have been found. In the Angevin times, too, Hungary, which included Transylvania and her eastern marches, produced more gold than any other region. Indeed, she was the Klondike of the Middle Ages. King Charles Robert of Hungary had the first gold coins minted in 1325.

Hungary's neighbor Bohemia had abundant silver supplies. Much of that silver was mined in Joachimsthal—Valley of Joachim—and the coins of that region enjoyed widespread recognition as Joachimsthaler, abbreviated into *thaler*, or *taler*, from which, eventually, the word "dollar" was derived.

Under the revealing title of *The Calm and Peace of Louis the Great*, a contemporary author, John Küküllei, wrote a eulogy of Louis' reign: "He left his country and its peoples in the full possession of their liberties and customs, governing them with their own laws."

CHAPTER **3**   THE AGE OF THE SCORPION

A NEW EPOCH OPENED in Hungary's history, which was also a new phase in the history of the world. Again the dark cavern of Asia opened to disgorge its famished hordes. A certain regularity could be observed in the spilling over of Asia into Europe. It began on a large scale with the invasion of the Huns and their whirlwind campaign into the distant West. This was followed by a succession of invasions of the cultured parts of the continent by the groups involved in the great popular migrations of the *Völkerwanderung*. Danubia's invasion by the Magyars was an epilogue of this historic sequence

Before that event, however, another part of Asia spewed out its hungry horsemen onto the western world. The Arabs were the sons of the dismal deserts of the Great Quadrangle, and with an incredible *élan*, for which few historic parallels are offered, they surged across the entire top of Africa, transforming and engulfing ancient cultures. When they reached the end of the world where the Mediterranean curves into the

Atlantic Ocean, they crossed the straits separating Africa from
Europe at the rock that was to be named after their leader,
Tarik. The lonely rock standing guard at the entrance of the
world thus became known in Arabic as the Mountain of Tarik,
Jebel Tarik—Gibraltar.

The Arabs all but engulfed Western civilization. The momentum which carried them onward was not only their
strength but also the weakness of the world they found.
At the last moment that world rallied to the defense of its
ways. Had those historic battles, fought not too far from the
center of what was to become France, turned out otherwise,
the pattern of life in the western world would have assumed
radically different forms.

Many centuries later it was the Mongols that erupted from
the unknown vastness of Asia, and their seemingly irresistible
strength might have prevailed but for the intrinsic weakness
of their own governmental organization. And now, after the
lapse of many more generations, another great danger was
darkening the horizon, a new invasion of the human locusts
from Asia. The history of Hungary was dominated for centuries by the Turkish danger.

These were all "population explosions," and they all seemed
to reveal a cataclysmic regularity. First, it was invariably the
East that was moving on the West. This westward march
appears to have been motivated by some appalling disaster
affecting the invaders' livelihood. The events were most likely
connected with the creation of dust bowls in borderline areas
where the scant rains were irregular. When the rains failed
to come, the land was turned to dust. Despair drove the
nomads toward the land of life-providing clouds.

These had to be movements of mass migration, as individuals could not have crossed the thirsty land and survived.
Should they have reached their western goal, they would have
found the gates firmly bolted. The hope of success was therefore in large numbers, as people of the continental climate

were moving toward the oceanic climate. The push was effected by hunger.

There was also a pull. These vast movements of migration held the promise of success only if the place of future settlement was afflicted with a debilitating weakness that incapacitated it for effective defense. Usually it was the decline of a culture that exerted that fatal pull. It took centuries before the ailment afflicting the Roman empire became manifest. The onward rush of the Huns, the spasmodic explosions of the *Völkerwanderung*, and the surge of the Mongols were motivated by the decline and fall of Rome.

In turn, the Magyars' ability to establish themselves in Mid-Danubia was due to the existence of a twilight zone between the two embattled branches of Christianity in East and West. Medieval anarchy and the struggle for supremacy between emperor and pope enabled the Mongols to pierce the defenses of Central Europe. And now came the Turks from the depths of Central Asia, pulled westward by the decline and inevitable fall of the Eastern Roman Empire, with its magnificent headquarters at Constantinople on the Golden Horn.

The push and pull were thus due to interconnected causes —the pushing force of hunger threatening the nomads, and the pulling effect of cultures in decline. Every time the nomads effected a successful invasion of Europe there was a power vacuum, a void not filled by people able to offer resistance to aggressors. As soon as the void was filled, aggression was halted. Centuries later, the Western world moved into reverse, having accumulated sufficient surplus energy and the force to raise its living standards to higher levels. In years to come the great colonizing nations, Spain, Portugal, England, France, and the Netherlands, were to fill the Eastern power voids.

None of the incursions of the East into the West affected Hungary's fate as much as the march of the Turks. It gave her history a different twist and for a time provided her with a mission. Who were these Turks who made such a powerful impression upon Hungary?

The Historic Impact of the Turks

The grazing areas of the Turkish tribes had been north and west of China, in today's southern central Siberia and the Soviet Central Asian republics, such as Turkmenistan and Uzbekistan. While one cannot speak about a "Turkish race," one is justified in talking of Turkic-speaking people of varied strains, including Mongol blood. These Turkic nomads lived in tribal units on open ranges, periodically sealing compacts for mutual self-defense.

Two major Turkic groups made history. One of these was the Seljuks who, originating in Central Asia, descended upon tenth-century Iran and embraced Islam, which provided them with an effective warrior ideology. Killing the infidel foe was the greatest virtue, and death in battle was the price of admission to the endless blissful existence of the seven heavens. In their line of march the Seljuk Turks encountered power voids. One of these was the region nominally under the headship of the Arab dynasty of the Abbasids in Baghdad. In an attempt to manage an unwieldy empire that extended deep into the Iberian peninsula, that dynasty had turned weak. Seljuk chieftains now established themselves in Baghdad as omnipotent major-domos of the palace.

They found another power void to the northwest, in the Byzantine Empire, legal heir to Rome and therefore named Eastern Roman Empire. By this time the very name of that realm had become synonymous with sycophancy, corruption, and degradation. The Seljuks crossed swords with the Byzantines, scored a great victory at Manzikert in 1071 over Romanus IV, and pushed their regime deep into Asia Minor. Farther south, it was the Seljuks that gained mastery over the Holy City, Jerusalem, and their reign was the major factor in motivating the Crusades.

The Seljuks, however, spent themselves in vain attempts to stem the Mongols' march and also in domestic squabbles. It was the Mongol plague that dislodged another Turkic tribe from its native habitat. These were the Osmanlis, so named after one of their chiefs. The Seljuk, nominal rulers of much of Asia Minor, assigned the Osmanlis the defense of their eastern marches, and from there these border guards fought their way into the rough Anatolian highlands at the cost of their fellow Turks. These Osmanlis were then still an "insignificant fragment of human wreckage," writes Arnold J. Toynbee,* which had been hurled to the farthest extremities of the land of Islam by the tremendous impact of the Mongol wave that broke upon the eastern marches out of the heart of the Eurasian steppe.

Where other groups had failed, the Osmanlis succeeded in maintaining themselves. Their success was due, in Professor Toynbee's explanation, to their ability to respond creatively to a challenge. As nomads they were used to dealing with cattle. In their new home they had to deal with human subjects, and they applied to their government the technique they had acquired when dealing with animals. This was graphically summarized in the term they applied to their non-Muslim subjects: ra'iyah, the herd. The Osmanlis, also known as Ottomans, succeeded where other nomads failed because they adopted the nomad's skill in training "animal assistants, the dog, the horse and camel, to keep their herd in line." The Ottoman rulers now created a system of human auxiliaries to keep order among the human cattle. Out of their slaves they made generals and prime ministers. "Perhaps no more daring experiment," says Toynbee, "has been tried on a large scale upon the face of the earth."

The Turks set up an incomparable fighting body which the Hungarians, too, encountered. These were the *Janissaries*,

* A *Study of History*, Royal Institute of International Affairs, Vol. II, p. 151.

whose name was derived from *Yeni Cheri*—New Troops. This force was established by Orkhan, the Ottoman ruler, in 1330: a regularly paid army recruited from forced levies of war captives and Christian youth. These youths were torn from their parents, lost all contact with them, and were trained under stern discipline into human fighting machines. There was no contemporary force equal to them in strength.

The logic behind this seemingly illogical policy was clear to the Osmanlis. Since these slaves were young men without family ties, the selection to the posts they held could be made purely on the basis of merit. The task of selection was not complicated by "pull." Once he had the post, the slave was untrammeled by considerations other than the desire to reveal his worth. "Those who hold the highest posts under the Sultan," wrote an observer, Ogier Ghiselin de Busbeq, "are very often the sons of shepherds and herdsmen, and, so far from being ashamed of their forefathers, they make it a subject of boasting, and the less they owe to their ancestors and the accident of birth the greater is the pride they feel."

With these troops the Turks finally broke out of Asia. Bypassing Constantinople, they crossed the straits into Europe in 1345, a fateful year for the Western world. They were pulled into Europe by a power vacuum. Ironically, it was in defense of the Byzantine Emperor John Cantacuzene that they crossed the Dardanelles. The Emperor was waging war on his fellow Christian ruler, Stephen Dushan of Serbia, and he called in the Turks to help.

Once out of the confining influence of Asia Minor and on European soil, the Turks had a large field of operations. They used not only their superior military force, a nation in arms, but they also learned to employ the method of successful colonial powers of playing off one prospective victim against the other, the age-old game of divide and rule.

One of the crucial battles of history was fought on the "Field of Blackbirds"—Kosovo Poli, in 1389, between the

Ottoman Turks under Murad I and the Christian coalition of Serbs, Bosnians, Bulgarians, and Montenegrins. At the beginning of the battle Murad was assassinated, but the Turkish military machine operated with precision and the Osmanlis won the battle. The battlefield is situated in what is southwest Yugoslavia today, and from there the Balkans were open to the Turks. To the north, beyond the Danube, the Hungarians observed the emergence of this new Asian plague.

However, for the time being the Turks were restrained by another Mongol peril in the East. Timur the Lame—Tamerlane—beat the Osmanlis at Angora—today's Ankara—and captured their Sultan Bayazet I. This saved the Hungarians from immediate danger. Eventually the Turks began to move northward, reached the broad Danube, and fortified themselves on its southern bank. Now they were facing the Hungarians on the opposite bank.

Facing the Storm

An attempt had been made to create a vertical bulwark on Europe's eastern marches from the Baltic to the Adriatic—the union of Hungary and Poland, both conscious of their apostolic mission. This time, however, the danger threatened from the south, in the form of the Muslims, abominated by the West as the despoilers of the Holy Places and therefore the most abhorrent of all "pagans." It was obvious now that the Turks were not just an Asian people, as so many others had been, knocking at the gates of Europe in search of bread. They were a conquering race in possession of great reserves of strength. What would happen if the Turks smashed the Hungarian gate and surged northwestward into the heart of Europe?

The Turkish danger lent impetus to attempts to build up the defenses of Christianity in depth, the horizontal solution. Under this scheme, all of Central Europe was to be organized in one large political body, and it was to extend deep down into Eastern Europe. Hungary was to be part of this monumental structure.

The architect of this plan was no longer an Anjou. Princess Mary, daughter of Hungary's Louis the Great, the Angevin monarch, married Sigismund of Luxembourg, who ruled as Hungary's king for a very long time (1378–1437). History remembers him as Emperor Sigismund. He was the son of Emperor Charles IV. Sigismund became the Elector of Brandenburg at the age of ten. It was the coreland of what later was to become Prussia. Besides being the King of Hungary, Sigismund was also King of Bohemia and, eventually, German Emperor. His realm represented a long-hoped-for integration of Central and much of Eastern Europe.

In the accepted spirit of the age, the rule of Sigismund was both personal and dynastic, not national. He was engaged in many wars, not only against Muslims but also against Christians, even his own subjects, the Hungarians and Bohemians. He was a cantankerous person, not at all popular with his peoples. The Bohemians spurned him as a Magyar, while the Hungarians scorned him as a Bohemian.

Sigismund was the Emperor who sought to heal the schism within the Christian Church at a time when not fewer than three Popes claimed St. Peter's throne. In order to restore church unity he called the historic Council of Constance. That council became notable for another reason, too, since it was there that the Bohemian religious reformer, Jan Huss, was burned at the stake in 1415, in spite of the safe-conduct given to him by the Emperor.

It was during Sigismund's rule that the Turks appeared as the greatest danger to Christian Europe's very life. The Osmanli Turks were still camping south of the Danube, but there was real apprehension that they might vault that barrier and resume their onward march. Sigismund, Apostolic King of Hungary, issued a call for the crusade against the "detestable infidels." Among the distinguished participants in the crusade were John the Fearless of Burgundy and Marshal Boucicaut II of France, famed both as a warrior and a ballad writer, who was to play a historic role at the Battle of Agincourt against England. The battle was fought near the town of Nikopol on the Danube, in what is Bulgaria today, and the year was 1369. The haphazard methods of the western type of warfare could not prevail against the disciplined superiority of the Turks' New Troops. They won the battle, and another barrier to the Muslims' northward advance was removed.

The successor of Sigismund ruled for only two years, and yet he was important, because King Albert was the first member of the Habsburg dynasty to occupy the Hungarian throne. A good many years later the House of Austria was to return to the Hungarian throne, never to vacate it to the end of the First World War. Albert became Hungary's king because of the delightful custom of those days; the bridegroom received a country along with the girl. Albert's wife, Elizabeth, was Sigismund's daughter.

The Turks had recovered now from the defeat which Tamerlane had inflicted upon them, and they resumed their westward march. King Albert had time only to make his preparations to meet the challenge when death called him in 1439. He was followed by Uladislaus I (1440–1444)—I Ulászló in Hungarian—first member of the House of Jagiello, which was to give Hungary three kings. He ascended the throne as a result of one of those involved marital transactions for which the age was famous.

The Jagiellos were kings of Poland and Lithuania, sometimes also of Bohemia. As rulers of those countries, they wore variants of their Hungarian names and sometimes also different numerical designations, which makes the record more confusing. Uladislaus I, for instance, was identical with Ladislaus III, King of Poland.

This dynasty took its name from Ladislaus Jagiello, Grand

Duke of Lithuania, who then became King of Poland as
Ladislaus II. He married Queen Jadwiga of Poland, daughter
of Hungary's Louis the Great. At the age of ten Ladislaus III
became King of Poland, and at the age of sixteen he collected
his second crown as King Uladislaus I of Hungary.

Hungary and Poland were again united as Christian Europe's bulwark against pagan Europe—the great East-and-
West conflict of that age. This time the threat to Western
culture was so overwhelming that the crusading spirit was
reinvoked to fight the Turk. Hungary first appeared as the
defender of Western civilization against the Muslims under
this young sovereign's rule. Under his reign, too, the West
learned the name of the man who became the hero of all
Christendom, János Hunyadi (ca. 1385–1456), a name that
was synonymous with the defense of the West. In Hungary
he was known as *törökverő*, conqueror of the Turk.

The Conqueror of the Turks

Hunyadi appears to have been of Slavic or possibly Romanian
origin, and his real name had been Vajk or Wayk—wolf.
A noted historian, Gáspár Heltai, sought to prove that Vajk
was the illegitimate son of Emperor Sigismund with a Romanian peasant girl. The date of Vajk's birth was conjectural,
but he must have been in his middle twenties when Sigismund gave him the castle of Hunyad in Transylvania—hence
the name under which he attained world renown. His wife
was Elizabeth Morsina, a Romanian. Nationality divisions in
those days were not as clear-cut as they were to become in
later years.

Already under Sigismund, Hunyadi had crossed swords
with the Turks and had distinguished himself by his superior
strategy in the face of massive Muslim strength. Young King
Uladislaus appointed him the voivode, or governor, of Transylvania. Hunyadi's reputation grew greatly, and the Turks, too,
realized that he was their most effective foe. In one of the

crucial battles in the many campaigns that now began, they were bent on destroying him. The Turkish designs became known to one of Hunyadi's knightly admirers, who prevailed upon him to exchange garments, mount, and armor. The name of the young man was Simon Kemény, a legendary name in Magyar history. The Turks, mistaking him for the commander, concentrated their fury on the pseudo Hunyadi, whom they killed. The young hero's reward was immortality in Hungarian textbooks.

Hunyadi now took the initiative, not content with merely containing the Turk, but making an attempt to drive him back. This he did in the war of 1443, known as the Bulgarian or Long Campaign. He penetrated this time deep into the Balkans and relieved Sofia, which was the seat of the Turkish governor of Rumelia. This feat shook the very foundations of the Ottoman realm and elicited the admiration of Christian Europe. Was it possible that the Turks would be ousted from Europe? The West took ample notice of the Hungarians, who were described in paeans and fulsome eulogies as Paladins of Faith, Shields of Christianity, Defenders of Christ. The cynical Machiavelli, not addicted to praising other people, was to write about the Hungarians' land: "Being martial, her people serve almost like ramparts." Centuries later Professor Toynbee was to write: "Hungary standing at bay under the leadership of John Hunyadi and his son, Matthias Corvinus (*regnabat* A.D. 1458–90) was the most stubborn opponent whom the Osmanlis had yet encountered; and she was stimulated culturally as well as militarily by the tremendous effort involved in withstanding the Ottoman pressure almost single-handed." *

The Turkish Sultan Murad II sued for truce, which Hunyadi granted. However, international politics intervened. Pope Eugen IV at the Council of Ferrara-Florence had the union of the Eastern and Western Churches proclaimed. It

* Toynbee, *op. cit.*, Vol. II, p. 178.

was vital that the seat of the Eastern Church, Constantinople, should not fall into Turkish hands. He therefore urged
the Hungarian King to continue the fight. The Papal Legate,
Cardinal Julian Cesarini, informed the Magyar sovereign
that a pledge conveyed to the "infidel" was not binding. At
his urging, King Uladislaus actually broke the truce, and the
war against the Turks was resumed. The crucial battle was
fought at Varna on the Black Sea shores, where Hunyadi led
an army of crusaders against Murad's forces. This time fortune turned against the crusaders, and they were beaten. The
twenty-year-old King was slain in battle. Hunyadi had to flee
the field. He was intercepted, however, and captured, not by
the Turks but by a Christian prince. The Western world was
outraged, and eventually he was released.

After the young King's death, the Hungarian magnates
turned again to the House of Anjou and raised to the throne
a four-year-old child whom history knows as Ladislaus Post-
humous, son of the late King Albert and of Elizabeth, grand-
daughter of Louis the Great of Hungary. The King was known
as Ladislaus V of Hungary and Ladislaus I of Bohemia. During the minority of the King, the "Turkbeater" became Regent, a post he held from 1442 to 1452.

The year of 1453 was a turning point in history. The Rome
of the East, Constantinople, fell to the Turks, a pivotal point
of tremendous strategic importance. Again the Western
world needed a defender and found it in the person of
Hunyadi. Another crusade was proclaimed against the Turk,
of which he became the commander, a man of international
fame. The spiritual leader of the crusade was Pope Calixtus
III himself, who called upon Christendom to pray for victory
every day at the midday Angelus. Hunyadi was given stout
assistance by the Franciscan John Capistran, a fanatic adversary of the Turk, who was later to be canonized. Hunyadi
collected a river fleet of some two hundred ships with which
he sailed down the Danube into the Turks' Balkan heartland.

This time the crucial battle was fought at Belgrade on July 21–22, 1456, and the Turkbeater won again. The victory was great. The Pope decreed that August 6, the day on which the news was received, should be celebrated as a holiday—the Feast of Transfiguration—in all Christendom. János Hunyadi himself, however, could not celebrate. He contracted a disease and died in the arms of John Capistran, his faithful friend. The Franciscan monk died soon thereafter.

Historians are inclined to the view that Hunyadi's victories staved off the conquest of Hungary by more than threescore years. Also, it is possible that if Hungary under Hunyadi had failed to stem the Turkish tide, it would have overwhelmed all Europe. The Continent was badly divided in those years.

The Age of the Hunyadis

The Turkbeater had two sons whose lives invited the compliments of saga and the envy of rivals. They were the richest landlords of the country, having inherited a vast estate, estimated at four million acres, from their father. They also inherited fortified castles that had been parts of royal demesnes. Greed was coupled with jealousy as some of the magnates persuaded Ladislaus V that the Hunyadi boys were coveting his crown. The older one, László, persuaded the King that the charge was false, and the younger one, Mátyás, was still a child. The monarch gave his oath to the boys that they were as brothers to him. Armed with this assurance, the Hunyadis left the security of an armed paternal castle and followed the ruler to Buda.

There the enemies of the house of Hunyadi persuaded the King to have the brothers arrested, on the ground that they were making preparations to kill their liege lord. Both László and Mátyás were sentenced to death and to the loss of their properties. The twilight hours of March 14, 1457, the time set for the execution, have been woven into Magyar saga.

On the heights of the Vár, overlooking the Danube, was St.

George Square, and there the execution block was set up. Folklore describes László Hunyadi as beautiful of face, his head covered with long locks, as was the custom of those days. Wearing the shroud of the dead, he placed his head on the execution block. The headsman's hand may have been unsteady when carrying out his distasteful task, or the young scion's hair may have been too long. At any rate, the ax glanced off and the head remained unsevered. The headsman repeated the gruesome performance again, and then again, and each time the ax glanced off the noble neck. According to saga that will never die, the young hero scrambled to his feet and loudly proclaimed to the assembled crowd that pursuant to ancient custom his life was saved. That was not, however, the view of his foes. The headsman was ordered to make another try, and this time the head was severed.

It was now the turn of the other Hunyadi scion, Mátyás, the child. In the last minute, however, the execution was stayed. Whether it was because of the revulsion of popular feeling in St. George Square, the saga does not reveal and the historian does not know.

Matthias the Just

In the absence of clear-cut dynastic succession, the selection of kings in Hungary was a haphazard affair. The choice was mainly in the hands of the *fő urak*, chief lords, as the magnates were called. All went fairly well when the influential ones among them were of one mind, but there was trouble when opinions were divided. For fear of a plot, the faint-hearted Ladislaus V fled the land and took young Mátyás, Matthias, with him. Death overtook the King abroad, and the Hungarian throne became vacant. Several candidates presented themselves, but the chief lords failed to agree. A mighty noble was Mihály Szilágyi, uncle of the Hunyadi boys. He was as strong as he was obstinate, and he advanced the candidacy of his young nephew, Matthias, bearer of the magic Hunyadi name. He convinced the families who had sought László's life that the Hunyadi family bore no grudge against them, and he was lavish with gifts. One of the influential magnates was László Garai, a high court official and determined Hunyadi foe, but Szilágyi persuaded him that if he voted for young Matthias, the young man in due time would marry his daughter Anne.

Matthias was now in Bohemia, which was under the rule of George Podiebrad, a man of great ambition. He was pro-Hunyadi, and would let Matthias depart only on the condition that he would eventually marry his daughter Katherine. Here, then, was a real problem for a boy who at the time probably was not more than fifteen—two brides, and he not even physically mature.

To this day the year of birth of Matthias cannot be determined; it is placed between 1440 and 1443. His education certainly began at a very early age, and it must have been an excellent training indeed. He was well versed in Latin and Greek, able to read the classic originals. He spoke German too, and several Slavic tongues. He was a promising boy in every respect. It was, however, not so much his gifts as the skill of his uncle that determined his fate.

According to a dramatic account of the proceedings, which students in Hungary are told as a fact, Uncle Szilágyi produced a telling argument in his nephew's favor when he drew up an armed force of some fifteen thousand men on the ice of the Danube on a wintry day of 1458, which in that exceptional year was frozen solid. The men-at-arms were facing the windows on the hill where the magnates were deliberating about the identity of the future king. Their arms represented the "voice" of the people. In the face of such overwhelming preponderance of popular sentiment for the Hunyadi boy, the Chief Lords decided to elevate him to the throne.

The Hunyadis' family emblem was the raven—*corvus* in

Latin—and the ruler became known to history as Matthias
Corvinus (1458–1490). Besides being King of Hungary, he
was temporarily also King of Bohemia and Duke of Austria.
The nobility elected his uncle, the "Kingmaker," as his
guardian for five years.

The deeds of no other Hungarian king have been woven
into so many sagas as those of Matthias, a legendary figure,
beloved by his people. Eventually, the common people began
to talk about him as a Danubian Harun al-Rashid, a benign
father of his people who mixed with them in order to learn
how they fared. He turned up now here and now there,
not in royal robes but in simple garments, lending ear to the
common people's complaints and solving their problems with
the magic of absolute might. Occasionally he turned up as
a fair-faced young hunter asking for a night's lodging in the
gamekeeper's hut, where this worthy's young daughter was
dazzled by the young man's countenance. The punch line of
the story was always the same. Calling at the address given
to her by the young man, she found herself in front of the
royal castle, where she learned the youthful hunter's identity—
her own anointed King. King Matthias would have needed at
least ten times man's allotted span to be at all the places
where he was sighted.

Sagas notoriously shun human failings, and it is little
wonder that Matthias always appears as the very embodiment
of ultimate perfection. The radiance of unanimous praise
may have warped even the judgment of the historian. While
he was an unusual man, he was also thoroughly autocratic and
frequently cruel. However, these may be general human traits
which the age of the Renaissance did little to conceal. King
Matthias was proud to be called "The Master of Dissimula-
tion." When he earned his battle spurs, King Matthias was
still a young man. War was in the Hunyadi blood and also
in the veins of the age. Matthias waged war against enemies
at all the points of the compass, and he also waged wars

against the foe at home. The giant shadow of the Turks, conserving their energies for a big effort, fell upon Hungary. The Ottoman hosts were entrenched in the very back yard of the kingdom. The other external foes were Christians, but they hesitated not a moment to draw benefit from the Turkish presence and to fall upon the man who wore the name of the most distinguished warrior in Christendom.

Thus Matthias was threatened by arrogant Venice in the south. In the north he had to contend against the Poles who looked upon Hungarians as weaker "brothers." In the west it was Emperor Frederick III who threatened Hungary's integrity. He regarded the peripheral lands of the Empire as his potential fiefs. Matthias married Katherine, daughter of the Bohemian ruler, and thus laid claim on the throne of that country. However, she died young in childbirth, and Matthias waged war on his father-in-law, whom he accused of being in league with the Emperor.

The Ottomans had been quiet for some time—they had a semiglobal scale on which to operate. Now, however, they began to stir and broke into Transylvania. Matthias resisted them. For a time the war was fluid and even inconclusive. Then the Hungarian King gathered strength, and beginning in 1463 he advanced deep into the Balkans, where Christians again wove the Hunyadi name into their prayers. Matthias defeated the gifted Ali Beg, the Turkish commander, freed some fifteen thousand prisoners, and pushed the Turks all the way into Bosnia.

Certain critics in the West censured Matthias for not concentrating more on the Turkish danger. He was also reproved for having given the impression of aspiring to become the head of the Holy Roman Empire. His apologists claimed, on the other hand, that even if he sought to combine all the forces of Middle Europe against the Turks, his policy was not wrong. He might have had a better chance of enlisting the help of all Central Europe against the Turk if he had gained the prestige of the imperial title. Hungary's independence was threatened by some of the Christian princes no less than by the Turkish overlords. The Hungarian King, being a realist, knew how to face the facts of life.

At the moment, the danger from the West did indeed appear to be greater. The German ruler was Emperor Frederick III and he held the reins until 1493, for the uncommonly long span of fifty-three years. He was the head of the rapidly expanding Habsburg dynasty. The mysterious anagram with which he adorned his books puzzled his contemporaries greatly. What was the meaning of that anagram: AEIOU? It was only after his death that the mystery was solved and the extent of his real ambitions revealed. The clue was provided by a note in his own handwriting, giving two versions of the idea, one in German and the other one in Latin. The latter version read *Austriae est imperare orbi universo*—"It is Austria's fate to rule the entire world." The German version was not less ominous: *Alles Erdreich ist Oesterreich untertan* —"The entire earth is subject to Austria." The time was to come when these ambitions were well-nigh realized. As his most effective tool in diplomacy, Frederick employed love and marriage—perhaps more marriage than love—like a true Habsburg. With the aid of that tool, the House of Austria was to extend its sway, eventually even across the broad Ocean Sea into newly discovered America.

Even in those formative years of Habsburg might, Matthias Corvinus had the statesmanlike insight to realize that the dynamic dynastic policy of the Habsburgs represented a major danger to the independence and integrity of Hungary. Several rebellious magnates made common cause with the Habsburg ruler and went so far as to elect the Emperor as Hungary's king in February 1459. Matthias thereupon seized the sword to beat the nominal head of Christian Middle Europe into submission. He was so successful that he forced the Emperor to retreat all the way into Styria. Pushed into a corner, the Emperor sought the aid of diplomacy to save himself. Once his aim was achieved, he turned around and took the sword against the King of Hungary. Three times Matthias marched to war against the Emperor. He was so successful that in 1485 he besieged and took Vienna. He moved onward and conquered Carinthia and Carniola, besides Styria—Habsburg crown lands. He designated Vienna as the seat of the royal government. Not since the days of the marauding Magyars many centuries earlier did Hungary possess so much alien land.

Matthias Corvinus fought his battles with an exceptionally effective army that bore the unusual name of *Fekete Sereg*, or in Latin *Legio Nigra*—the Black Army, so named because of its uniform. It was the first standing army of foot soldiers in that part of the world, well manned and well officered. It attracted also people from foreign lands and was thus a medieval anticipation of the French Foreign Legion. This Black Army was an effective riposte to the Turks' fighting machine.

The civil wars the famous King waged were not because of any weakness on his part. This was still the age when the feudal principle of decentralization was strong. There were some "little kings" in the land, and not the least aggressive of them was the King's own uncle, the Kingmaker Szilágyi, a man of boundless arrogance. So bad was his reputation that the burghers of the town of Beszterce, which was bestowed upon him as an appanage by the King, wanted to have nothing to do with him. Thereupon Szilágyi laid siege to the town and had many of the burghers put to the sword, while others were maimed. Nephew Matthias was outraged, but Szilágyi entered into league with some of the King's most notorious foes. Not to be trifled with, the sovereign had his uncle jailed and even issued an order to have him beheaded. However, the papal legate took a hand in the matter, and the King countermanded the order. Eventually a reconciliation took place when uncle and monarch marched against the Turks. Szilágyi was captured and transported to Constantinople, and it was there that fate overtook him in 1460. He was beheaded at the order of the Sublime Porte, the Sultan.

Matthias the Renaissance Ruler

In the fields of law and learning Matthias also made his name. The name of this Hungarian king is best known to the outside world because of his unusual collection of beautifully made books, the *Corvina*. It is recorded that the monarch spent annually some 33,000 gold pieces on these books, a vast sum for those days. He had his own workshops at Buda, under the experienced librarian Felix Ragusanus, who superintended the work of about thirty copyists. The *Corvina* are favorably known the world over because of the beauty of their covers—velveteen or black and red goat skin—and the exquisite work of illuminated parchment. Some of the books were printed at the press installed at Buda. This famous book collection may have contained some three thousand specimens in its days of glory. Most of these were destroyed in the many wars that broke upon Hungary, and especially during the long Turkish occupation of the country in years to come.

The books were guarded closely at the palace, but they were available to scholars. Matthias was not merely a collector but also a reader of the books, and it is recorded that he had a convenient place for himself in the library where he could pore over his treasures at leisure. While the world of yesterday was uncritically ardent about the beautiful *Corvina*, the greater sophistication of the contemporary world has been inclined to minimize their intrinsic value. It has been said that the resplendent exteriors of the books were far superior to their contents, and especially that the Biblical texts had been provided with little higher criticism.

The palace of Matthias was much like an Italian Renaissance court. Italian architecture was in great vogue under his

rule; many poets, artists, and scholars enjoyed his royal patron-
age. It is recorded that he collected minstrels and bards at his
table, chanting the great national heroes' deeds. As in other
such courts there may have been some sycophants at Buda
extolling the glories of the man who fed them. These lays
may have percolated down to the common people, where they
were turned into foundations of sagas. Italian influence at
the Buda court was enhanced by Matthias' marriage to
Beatrice, daughter of the Neapolitan king.

King Matthias had many of the laws collected and codified,
so that justice should prevail even among the common people.
He lent a helping hand to the middle classes and granted
special rights to the country towns. His object seemed to have
been to create counterbalancing forces to the arrogance of
the "little kings." In order to finance his wars he sought to
impose taxes on all his subjects. We have seen that under
the Golden Bull the nobles were not supposed to be subject
to taxation. They resented the action of the King, especially
since he failed to ask the magnates for money appropriation.

This remarkable Hunyadi appreciated the importance of
education. He established a university in Pozsony, near the
western boundary of Hungary, and he also set up a theological
seminary at Buda.

While the date of the birth of King Matthias is in question,
the year of his death, 1490, is known. Not known, however,
is the cause of his end. Death came to him in Vienna, and
the official diagnosis was: stroke. The unofficial diagnosis
was whispered: a poison potion administered by his wife.
However, this accusation has never been substantiated. Matthias had no issue from his marriages, but he did have an
illegitimate son.

"Matthias the Just" was the name given to him, and no
other Hungarian monarch has ever been mourned so much.
All over the land the word spread: *Meghalt Mátyás király*,

oda az igazság—Dead is King Matthias and justice went with him.

In retrospect, these appear to have been the late King's aims: to keep the Turks at bay; to co-operate with the West whenever feasible; and, above all, to safeguard Hungarian independence. To use a current phrase, King Matthias was strongly oriented toward the West. His shortcomings were many, and he certainly could not have been the Knight in Shining Armor of the popular saga. But he was an able ruler, and he was not completely blind to the problems of the poor. His reign may have appeared more radiant in retrospect because of the age of darkness that followed.

The Peasant Revolution

The death of Matthias marked the end of strong royal rule. Only strong hands were respected by the feudal lords of the Renaissance, and the successors' hands were weak. The King was again a Jagiello, King Uladislaus II, who was also King of Bohemia as Ladislaus II. Under him, the reforms of Matthias were allowed to lapse; the condition of the peasantry became worse, and finally utterly intolerable. Nor could the King support the Black Army, which fell apart and turned into a rabble—savage bands of roving brigands, which had to be destroyed by the all-powerful Chief Lords.

Irrespective of covenanted royal prerogatives, the magnates kept on carving out sovereign domains for themselves. They had private armies, and the ruling regimes were as numerous as the mighty lords. The privileged status which Matthias had conferred upon the towns fell into neglect. The country was stagnating.

Hungary's enemies noticed their chance, and they were pressing against her frontiers—the Turks from the east and south, the Habsburgs from the west. The House of Austria concluded a pact with the House of the Jagiellos, under which the crown would go to a Habsburg in case the King died childless. Some strong members of the nobility, however, wanted no more foreign monarchs, and in 1505 they entered into compact on the Meadows of Rákos, on the outskirts of Pest, under which the crown was to revert to a Hungarian in case the ruler died without an heir.

Increasingly, Hungary was in line of the Turkish onward march; the danger grew. The time came now to proclaim another crusade against the Turk, and this was done by Pope Leo X, a Medici, best known to posterity as the patron of the painter Raphael. The Hungarian Cardinal Tamás Bakócz was on his way to Buda with the Papal proclamation. By the time he got there, the weak King had concluded an unfavorable peace with the Turks. The prelate thereupon prevailed upon the magnates to run counter to the will of the King and to proceed with the crusade. He summoned a Transylvanian nobleman of great valor, György Dózsa, to lead the crusade. This was 1514, and a terrible year it was to be.

The call went out to the people to rally to the sacred banner of the cross, but few could have foreseen what was to be the result. The oppressed peasantry rushed under the protection of the Cross by the tens of thousands. As serfs they were treated as beasts, while they felt free as the soldiers of Christ. Indeed, on the land of their masters they were pariahs, *bétail humain*. Tillers of the soil were held in disesteem in other countries, too. After all, they had to work, and to work very hard. Respect was due only to those who made other people work. To this very day the English word "boorish"—peasantlike—brands a person, and the French word *paysan* is an insult, as was *Bauer* in Germany. The Hungarian word *paraszt*, peasant, is a grave affront when applied to non-farmers, and many adages reflect this derogatory attitude: *Huncut a paraszt, mihelyt egy araszt*—"crafty is the peasant as soon as he is an ounce long"; and *Büdös paraszt*, "stinking peasant," spoken almost as one word.

The magnates were less concerned with the Turkish peril

than with the danger to their crops. The peasants left their
work in field and barn to rally to the banner of the Cross. The
landlords began to prevent their peasants from leaving work,
waylaid them on their way to the crusaders' camps, laid their
heavy hands on the families of the soldiers of Christ so that
the cries of their women and children should force them to
turn back.

The peasants were outraged, and bitterness welled in them
as a result of the inhuman treatment to which they were
subjected. Were they to be treated as animals even when they
were soldiers of the Holy Cross? Were they to be prevented
from following the call of their religion to prevent the infidel
from desecrating their Christian country? The reaction of the
peasants was spontaneous and terrible. They needed no agi-
tators nor propagandists to tell them what to do. Their landlords were worse than the Turks, un-Christian and even
anti-Christian. They turned against the magnates instead of
the Turks.

The history of peasant revolts, *jacqueries*, is particularly
hideous. People who were normally treated as wild animals
acted like them when their blood began to boil—savage,
ferocious, revelling in violence. By the thousands the crusading peasants slaughtered their Christian masters, setting fire
to their mansions and their harvests, slitting the throats of
their women and even their children. It was a frenzied ex-
plosion of irrepressible hatred. Not even the churchmen
were spared.

György Dózsa, even though a nobleman, was caught up in
this elemental outburst of hatred and made common cause
with his rural crusaders. He drew up a program which, in
terms of that age, was revolutionary in the extreme. The
program called for the elimination of royalty. No longer was
the Hungarian crown to be sacred, to be worn by an anointed
king. Nobility was also to be eliminated. Centuries before the
French revolution, the Hungarian peasants predicated the

success of community life on the equality of all men. An even more revolutionary idea was introduced into the peasants' program. Land was not to be kept by the human drones but was to be distributed among the toilers, the peasants. This was a declaration of war against the established order.

The magnates now had to go to war, not against the Turk looming large on the horizon, but against fellow-Hungarians. The Chief Lords issued an invitation to the one of them who had the strongest and most reliable army, János Zápolya, a magnate from Transylvania, on Hungary's eastern marches. He recruited an army of noblemen which was far superior to Dózsa's frenzied rabble. The noblemen knew how to maintain discipline, and they were fighting in desperation, with their backs against the wall. Eventually they overwhelmed their serfs, their slaves, and the victors' revenge was appalling.

Their fury was concentrated upon the "renegade," Dózsa, whose unspeakable crime it was to side with the downtrodden and the poor. The nobles had spread word that it was Dózsa's aim to become king. In a mock coronation ceremony, they placed him on a throne of scorching iron and made him grasp a red-hot royal scepter, while they thrust a burning crown on his forehead. Then they gave hunting knives to some of his former subjects, ordering them to cut the living flesh from the "royal" body and to eat the flesh. Contemporary accounts report that Dózsa died without an outcry, nobleman that he was. Some seventy thousand people were killed in this savage peasant war. Thus ended the crusade of the fatal year 1514.

The "Savage Diet"

Thus, however, did not end the appalling fate of the Hungarian peasantry. The peasants' revolt represented a dividing line in Hungarian history. The "Savage Diet" of the nobles met, and it sanctified the Triple Code, which dealt with three phases of the law: the rights of the nobility, the civil law, and the criminal law. It tied the peasants to the soil even more than they had been before, as slaves rather than serfs. While in some parts of Western Europe feudalism was relaxed, it became more stringent in Hungary and remained so for centuries. The people who worked, and were therefore ignoble, were thrust out from behind the protection of constitutional ramparts. There were now two nations in Hungary, the ruling master class and millions of near-slaves, as the famous early twentieth-century Hungarian historian, I. Acsády, was to say. With wolfish hatred these two nations, worlds apart, glared at each other, the master regarding his serf as inhuman, the serf crouching like a shackled beast awaiting his chance to pounce again upon his tormentor. The "greatest European" of the early nineteenth century, Goethe, said that until her feudal rule was uprooted it was impossible to introduce social reform in Hungary.

The weak Uladislaus died in 1516, and was followed by his son, a child of ten, Louis II of Jagiello. Foreign legates accredited to the Hungarian court reported that dissension among the magnates was so great that the land was falling apart. On the one hand there were the so-called nationalists, who wanted again a Hungarian on the throne after the expected extinction of the Jagiellos' male line. And then there were the courtiers, who were hoping for the success of the Habsburg court. The strong candidate of the nationalists was János Zápolya, the ruthless magnate who had defeated Dózsa. He had been groomed for an exalted office by his father, a man of strong will. At the death of Matthias the Just, Zápolya the elder swung little János on his shoulders and exclaimed that he would be already king if he were that tall. János was then three years old.

And Then the Plague

Suleiman the Magnificent was the potentate of Turkey, a mighty ruler, who was to launch several campaigns beyond the borders of his vast Ottoman realm. For years he fought his enemies in different parts of the world, subdued them in Egypt, and ejected the Knights Hospitalers for the strategically placed eastern Mediterranean island of Rhodes. Having accomplished his task in the East, he finally turned his face toward the West.

All of Europe dreaded this moment. The Turks had tarried in the Balkans for generations, restrained by the new Mongol irruption and by their desire to base their march against the West upon the firm foundations of a huge realm in the East. The Hungarian nobility was still distracted, each magnate exercising sovereign rights behind the walls of his estate, when word reached the West that the brilliant Sultan, seconded by his able Grand Vizier Ibrahim, had struck camp and was headed for the West. This was the year 1526.

Suleiman crossed the Danube and headed northward, toward the core of Hungary. If ever Christianity faced a mortal peril, it was now; but the chronic state of civil war in Hungary delayed her preparations for defense. Conditions in the land before the crucial battle were described by Monsignor Burgio, the Papal Legate: "If Hungary could be saved from this great danger with three florins, I do not believe that three men could be found to give this money." The Papal Legate also observed that some of the Magyar magnates were plotting with the Turks. He predicted that, short of a miracle, the country was bound to fall.

It was only in the last minute that the imminence of the danger stimulated some nobles to action. Special imposts were quickly voted, and church treasures were offered for the successful prosecution of the war. However, the nobility was slow to rally to the royal banner. The memory of the dreadful peasant war being still vivid, the common people could not be trusted. The youthful King was finally invested with supreme power to save the nation and with it the Christian world.

It was on July 20, 1526, that the King left the royal palace at the head of an inadequate force, in the hope that his army would wax as he moved southward to meet the advancing Osmanli hosts. Particularly, he was expecting the army of Zápolya from the east. The march of the royal army was very slow, and it was late in August that it reached the town of Mohács on the Danube, a few score miles to the south of Buda. It was an army equipped with odds and ends, consisting of some 26,000 noblemen, often following their own whims. The question was now whether to await reinforcements from the east or to accept battle before the noblemen got bored. The real leader of the Hungarian forces was the Archbishop of Kalocsa, Pál Tomori, to whom this war against the Muslims was a crusade. It was he who decided not to await the eastern contingents even though the Turkish forces outnumbered the royal army many times. The crucial engagement took place on August 29. The army of Zápolya was still in the distance.

The dashing Hungarian noblemen rushed at the Turks. Were they not knights of the Cross, Christians, facing the inferior Muslims, not better than worms in the eyes of the Lord? The first attack daunted the Turkish lines. Not only were they more numerous, however, but also they were better organized, a well-oiled fighting machine. Their strong lines were too much for the Hungarians, whose forces began to waver. Once the horses began to rear and to shy away, a panic set in. At this fatal moment there was still no sign of the relieving forces from the east. The brilliant leadership of the Turks asserted itself. The second round was also the final one.

To compound the tragedy, "the sluices of heaven," as Hungarian accounts say, "opened and the battlefield was drenched by a summer shower." It turned into a mire, so that the beaten Hungarians had not the chance to retreat and realign their forces. The majority of the noblemen died there. The

young King tried to ford a brook, the waters of which had
been overflowed by a flash flood. His mount lost its footing
and he was drowned. The battle had taken no more than
two hours. Still there was no sign of Zápolya and his hosts.

The Sultan began to make his preparations to meet what
he believed was the Hungarians' major army. He could not
believe that with one blow he snuffed out Hungary's armed
forces. The Turks had not been prepared for such a quick
victory and they did not immediately follow up their advantage; they even moved back for a while, to advance again
in due time. The mystery of Zápolya's failure to appear has
been interpreted in many ways. It is possible that he did not
want to save the King and his army. He certainly was not
dreaming, but seriously thinking of the crown of Hungary.

In Hungarian chronicles the battle just described is known
as *Mohácsi Vész*, the Mohács Disaster, one of the best-known
happenings in the country's history. It was one of those events
which ended an epoch and began a new one. Never was
Hungary to be the same after this defeat, one of the most
cataclysmic and traumatic in her millennial history. We shall
see how fatal were the results of the battle.

Three Hungaries

The Turks continued their cautious policy in the alien and
hostile world of Christians. First they let the Hungarians
weaken each other, and then they assumed control. Zápolya
was elected king on November 10, 1526, but the following
December Ferdinand I of the Habsburgs was also elected
king. Zápolya—whom history knows as King John I—became
the Sultan's satellite, and even Ferdinand paid tribute to the
Turk. This was an absurd situation, and eventually the two
Kings reached an agreement under which the former was
to follow the latter, an older man, after his death. John was
then without issue. However, unexpectedly, he married and
had a son, John Sigismund Zápolya. John I died in 1540, and

his few-months-old baby was quickly crowned King of Hungary, as John II. This the *aulic*—court—aristocracy, attached to Habsburg interests, disliked. On the pretext of protecting the rights of the royal baby, Sultan Suleiman launched another campaign in Hungary, which could not resist. This time he took Buda, the center of the country, strategically located at the intersection of major routes. The Turks were to stay in that city on the western bank of the Danube until 1686, almost a century and a half. They were now in full glory.

There was now not one Hungary but three countries by that name. The Turkish rule halted short of the westernmost and northernmost part of the country, forming a narrow crescent. This was the Hungary under Habsburg rule, and the one which was to exert the most vital influence in generations to come.

The Turks were undisputed masters in that part of Hungary which was most Magyar and fertile, the coreland. They organized this land on the pattern of the Ottoman regions, dividing it into *vilayets*, governorships, of which there were two, Buda and Temesvár, at the head of each of which there was the governor, *vali*. The Turks also created a throne in Transylvania, the eastern marches, about which we shall hear much more, and gave it to their protégé, John II, the Zápolya King.

The Turkish rule in Hungary's heart was on the model of their reign in other non-Muslim regions. Since the Ottomans were supremely conscious of their superiority as a chosen race and as Muslims, they did not want to contaminate themselves with too much contact with the *giaours*, infidels. Theirs was a rule of theocracy in which religion and oppression were leagued. The Turks were a small minority in the midst of a vast majority of an entirely different type of people. They were armed, the majority was disarmed. They allowed non-Muslims to look after their own interests in self-governing units, *millets*. The word from which it is derived, *millah*,

means both nation and religion. The *millet* in Hungary was
Christian, the nation was organized along religious lines. The
Christian was Hungarian, the Muslim was Turk. The non-
Muslims were expected to pay their taxes. The Turks were
so contemptuous of them that they cared little if they talked
a lot. A *kutya ugat, a karaván halad*—"The dog is barking and
the caravan proceeds."

A Negative Record

What are the memories of the long Turkish rule in Hungary?
The Turks did not mix with their non-Muslim subjects. They
may have made some converts among the Hungarian career-
ists, but their number could not have been large. In Hungary
there are no Muslims, as there are in the Balkans, many
hundreds of thousands of them. The Turks were a proud
race, but so were the Hungarians and they produced few
renegades.

The Turks were a military race and to that they owed their
success. There are a few ramshackle Turkish forts in Hungary,
mementos of the past. The record of the Turks is completely
barren, and nowhere is this more manifest than in Hungary.
The West knows no Turkish scientist, historian, architect,
philosopher, or traveler. There were a few Turkish poets. The
Turks concerned themselves so little with their subjects' cultural lives that their mark on them is nil. There remained a
Turkish bath or two of Buda, perhaps also elsewhere, the ruins
of a few mosques. The new Turkish words in the Magyar
vocabulary dealt mainly with pillage and lawlessness. There
is no golden-age nostalgia about the Turkish period in
Hungary.

In this respect it is informative to compare the record of
the Turks with that of their Arab co-religionists. Wherever
the medieval Arabs moved there was a flowering of the
sciences and arts. The so-called Moorish architecture in Flor-
ida and California is a heritage of Arab rule in Spain. No

Turkish Alhambra or Alcázar has remained in Hungary, not a vestige of architectural magnificence. The Turks remained a nomadic race even when they settled in "urban camps."

The contrast is just as great in the cultural field. The West is under deep obligation to the medieval Arab genius, which sustained the continuity of Western culture. The encyclopedic talent of an Avicenna or Averroes still astounds the world. Our own English language, with its many Arab words, is a testimony to Arab greatness. Arab poetry fructified the West, and Arab travelers crossed and recrossed the continents. The Turks, on the other hand, destroyed alien cultural values.

There was one important result of this negative record. When the Turkish occupation was over, the Hungarian national sentiment was still alive, as were the national sentiments of other countries subjected to Ottoman rule. In the peripheral areas in those days, religion also meant nation. A Hungarian could not have become a Turk without first becoming a Muslim. The rigidity of the Turks in religious matters helped to keep the subject peoples' national sentiments alive.

There was also another important result of the Turkish rule. We have seen that the Ottomans needed Christian slaves. They drove tens of thousands of them toward their Asia Minor homeland, and contemporary accounts record that at one time it was possible to travel all the way across Anatolia, the Turkish heartland, by speaking only Hungarian. Also the mortality rate was exceptionally high under Turkish rule; famine and epidemics were common. Since the mortality rate was much higher than the rate of reproduction, the Hungarian countryside became empty. The case of Somogy County may be cited as a classic illustration. At the end of the fifteenth century it had some 11,000 homesteads. Counting five persons per homestead, its population must have been in the neighborhood of 55,000. By 1543 the figure had slumped to 7,300, and by 1596 to a mere 193. The Turkish rule blighted Hungary.

This blight, in turn, created one of the most serious problems in the land. People from the adjacent countries descended from the mountains and converged on the Hungarian plains, to fill the void. The Slavs moved down from the northern Carpathians, while the Romanians came from the east, and the Southern Slavs, Croats, Serbs, and others came from the south. To fill the population gap left by the Turks, the Hungarian monarchs later carried out a planned policy of settlement. It was thus that Hungary became a nationality state, one of her biggest problems, and in due time the ethnic Magyars were swamped by alien peoples.

The Decline of the Turks

The Turkish decline led to their expulsion from Hungary at the end of the seventeenth century, and it was due to several causes. The Ottoman army had turned from conquest to loot. As they were marching across the province of Rumelia in the eastern Balkans on one occasion of which there is record the peasants burned their huts and took to the hills rather than face the merciless Ottoman soldiers. At the walls of Vienna in 1683 the Turks were beaten, the high-water mark of their westward expansion in Europe and the beginning of their global ebb. The morale of the reputedly invincible Turk suffered greatly. Also, the bureaucracy of the Turks was no better than any other bureaucracy, and it entangled itself in endless red tape. The place of merit was now taken by the prerogatives of birth. But, above all, the Turks never knew how to develop a constructive program of helping others to help themselves.

The decline of the Turks was also the consequence of changing conditions in the West. The Habsburgs became the most powerful dynasty of Europe, staring at the Turks across Hungary. Obviously, the House of Austria was to play a leading role in the liberation of the Magyars from the Turks. As the Ottoman empire weakened, the Habsburg dynasty obtained additional fields for its military and diplomatic operations. Vienna developed a strong gravitational pull, ready to create satellites in Mid-Danubia, while the gravitational force of Constantinople was being reduced to zero.

In the confused game of politics the Magyar aristocracy lost much blood. However, it continued to remain on the top. When compared with what happened with the elites of other people under Turkish rule, this appears to be an unusual situation. In the Balkans, for instance, the Turks exterminated the native aristocracies of the Serbs and the Bulgarians, and all but rooted out the ruling classes of the Danubian principalities, Walachia and Moldavia, that were eventually to be united into the Kingdom of Romania. When those countries were freed from the Turkish yoke centuries later, their native ruling classes were extinct.

Not so, however, in Hungary. There the magnates retained some power even at the height of Turkish rule, rusticating on their estates, protected by their overweening self-confidence. Many of them co-operated with the ruling Turks just enough to be able to survive. When their chance came they turned against the Turks. In the confused period of civil wars, they changed sides often with surprising agility or remained steadfast to their conditions and interests. The number of casualties among the magnates was large, but the institution itself remained intact. After the Turks had left, the power of the Little Kings was not completely smashed.

The Land Beyond the Woods

The "third Hungary" was Transylvania, the land of the eastern marches, which the Turks allowed to have a certain measure of self-government, either because it was a difficult terrain or else because its status enabled them to use it, in case of need, as a staging area against the Habsburgs, whom they recognized as their chief foes.

Its very name indicates the region's sylvan nature, a lovely, hilly, forested country spreading westward from the Transylvanian Alps. Its Hungarian name, Erdély, is derived from erdő, forest, and its German name, Siebenbuergen, seven burghs, reveals its strategic role. Even before the Turks came, this 24,000-square-mile land led a hectic life. It was both a curse and a blessing that it was rich in precious metals, including gold, since it invited greed and invasions.

The heart of Transylvania is occupied by an enigmatic people. They are known as Székelys, and they speak Hungarian, although they are surrounded by alien people, mostly Romanians and also Germans. The Székelys' folklore speaks about their descent from Attila's Huns. Sometimes they were also called Black Ugrians. Scholars are in disagreement as to the Székelys' arrival in their present habitat. Some maintain that they had moved into Transylvania before the Magyars' arrival, while others hold that they were settled in the mountains as frontiers guards by Hungary's King St. Ladislaus. They acquired a reputation for nonconformism, and this manifested itself in the numbers of religions they chose in the days of the great religious conflicts. Unitarianism had its origin in Transylvania and in Poland. Many Székelys embraced this creed.

Transylvania attracted nomadic invasion long after the Magyars had settled in Mid-Danubia. To protect this important region and also to fill the gap left by many wars, Hungary's twelfth-century kings sent there German settlers from the Rhineland and the Palatinate. They were invited guests. These Germans became known as Saxons, and they were the ones who built those enchanting towns which still enthrall the visitor. (According to a popular legend, the Germans of Transylvania are the descendants of the children

of the town of Hamelin, lured there by the blandishments
of the Pied Piper.)

When Protestantism swept across Europe, Transylvania
became an enclave of that faith in the midst of Roman and
Greek Catholics. Many Hungarians of the area embraced
the Calvinist creed, while many Germans became Lutherans.
A goodly number of the Székelys, as we have seen, were
Unitarians. As we shall see, Transylvania played a role in the
religious wars of the age entirely out of proportion with her
size.

The Religious Wars in Hungary

A new era was being born in Europe as strong forces arose
against the Catholic religion. Hungary was far removed from
the centers of Protestantism, and the Hungarians were considered crusaders of the Roman Church. The king of the land
was called Apostolic. How did the Hungarians respond to
the new creeds?

Their response was remarkable. It is estimated that at the
height of the Reformation some three-quarters of the population belonged to one or the other of the reformed churches.
Particularly strong was the appeal of the Reformation to the
purely Magyar regions. The teachings of Calvin were even
more popular than those of Luther. So great was the impact
of the Geneva creed on Hungary's plains that Calvinism
became known in Mid-Danubia as the "Hungarian religion."
One of the most Hungarian of all cities, Debrecen, on the
outskirts of the typically Magyar landscape of the Hortobágy
puszta, semiarid steppes, became a stout rallying point of the
Calvinists. There an important college of the creed was
founded in 1588, and it became a university in the twentieth
century. To this day the Hungarians call Debrecen the "Calvinist Rome."

What were the main reasons of the success of the Reformation? The Turkish masters manifested the tolerance of

contempt and indolence, because these theological arguments made no sense to them. All Christians were "infidel dogs" and the spectacle of dog eat dog was pleasing to their eyes. The Hungarian clergy of the time was ignorant and ineffective; it lacked the strength to stem the tide. In the eyes of the peasantry itself, the Church represented the authority it hated. As to the nobility, many of its members hoped to benefit from the distribution of farm land.

Since the Habsburgs had a toehold in Hungary, they were in a position to launch a massive movement of counterreformation not only on the territory occupied by them and in Transylvania, but also in the region occupied by the Turks. The House of Austria was the strongest pivot of the Roman Church at the time. Leader of the Hungarian Counter Reformation was the Prince Primate himself, Cardinal Péter Pázmány (1570–1637). He was the scion of an old noble family, was born a Calvinist, and was converted to the Catholic faith. He had the unbounded fanaticism of the convert, and it was coupled with a remarkable eloquence that earned him the sobriquet of the Hungarian Cicero. Having joined the spearhead of the Counter Reformation, the Society of Jesus, he set himself the task of regaining the realm of the apostolic king for the Church.

Prince Primate Pázmány had to concede that it might have been because of an inferior priesthood that the Protestant inroads had been made possible. His first task was therefore to improve the quality of the clergy. He established a seminary in northern Hungary, at Nagyszombat, a town that was under Habsburg rule. That school became a lighthouse of Catholic education. In the eighteenth century it was transferred to Pest, where it became the nucleus of the Péter Pázmány University, of Budapest, the largest and most important one in the country.

The Cardinal's next task was to provide the clergy with an arsenal of arguments, and this he did in his famous book,

Igazságra Vezérlő Kalauz—Guide to Truth. The book was important for more than one reason. Until Pázmány wrote it, the Hungarian language was considered too uncouth to express lofty ideas in religion. Pázmány helped to ennoble the language, and he also brought the Church closer to the people.

The wars of religion overlapped with the age of feudalism, where possession of the land meant also possession of the human soul. The watchword of the age was expressed in the Latin adage: *Cuius regio eius religio*—"Religion belongs to the owner of the land." Pázmány therefore had to concentrate his main effort on the conversion of the large land-holding families. He succeeded in many cases with his fabulous eloquence and irresistible conviction. Tens of thousands of souls were converted with the conversion of a key person.

It was thus that the Prince Primate regained the bulk of the population for the Roman Catholic Church. About one-fourth of Hungarians are Protestants—Calvinists and Lutherans—to this very day. Even though Pázmány converted many magnates, many others clung to their new faith. Protestants have played a part out of all proportion to their number in Hungary's history. Several prime ministers were Protestants, including the Counts Tisza, father and son, who guided Hungarian destiny for a generation, and Count Bethlen, who did the same for a crucial decade between the two twentieth-century wars. The regent governor of Hungary in that inter-bellum period, Nicholas Horthy de Nagybánya, was also a member of the Protestant nobility.

Transylvania to the Fore

In the first half of the seventeenth century the Thirty Years' War saw the emergence of modern nationalism. Beginning as a religious conflict, it was transformed into a nationalist one. The various Christian creeds fought one another at first, but later the nations were at war, irrespective of creed. The real battle was no longer between Catholics and Protestants but between Austria and France, Spain, Prussia, and England. At one time the chief antagonists were all defenders of the Christian faith: *le roi très chrétien* of France facing the king of Hungary *très apostolique,* who was also the emperor, and between them the sovereign of *Espagne très catholique.* As their nationalist interests demanded, these rulers concluded pacts with the Turks or paid tribute to them. After their defeat at the walls of Vienna, the Turks were no longer considered formidable foes.

In the history of Transylvania and Hungary, too, the "most Christian kings of France" fought the Apostolic Habsburgs with the help of the "infidel" Turks. The different parts of historic Hungary were exposed to different pressures, and alliances were changed on brief notice. The Hungarian warrior made common cause with the Turk today, and tomorrow he switched over to the Habsburg side. The reader of this book may feel inclined to sympathize with its writer when he studied Hungarian history in Budapest schools. Since national heroes could never do wrong, they were right when fighting by the side of the Turk today and when joining the Habsburgs tomorrow. That meant that today it was the turn of the Turks to be right, while tomorrow it was the Austrian's turn. The issues were, of course, identical on both days. Complications arose only when one of the heroes was confronted by the other one as his prisoner. There was such a hero in this confused age of plots and counterplots, Brigadier László Ocskay, who was caught red-handed when performing a particularly daring *volte face.* However, we were taught to respect him, since he was a thoroughbred Magyar; and besides, how was he to know which side was right at that particular moment?

In Transylvania the Báthory family sought to foster an Eastern European integration through the union of Hungary and Poland, to create what today we would call a "third force" between Constantinople and Vienna. Such a force was to fill the Eastern European vacuum, placing it out of bounds for both Habsburg and Turk. The failure to fill the void may have brought civilization to the brink of the abyss.

The most outstanding member of the Báthory family was Stephen, Prince of Transylvania (1571–1581), who was also to become elected king of Poland in 1575. No other Polish king ever aimed as high as he. His object was to turn Russia into a Polish satellite. He was successful in defeating Ivan the Terrible of Russia and extended his domains along the Baltic Sea. Among the Polish kings his name became greatly revered.

Genius and insanity were fused in the Báthory family. Sigismund Báthory (1572–1613) first served the Habsburgs as Prince of Translyvania, then turned against them with Turkish aid. In order to promote the Christian cause, he withdrew into a monastery; then he changed his mind, and traded the cleric's garb with the warrior's armor. Now he sought to recover his throne with Turkish help. He was a fanatic who believed that blood was the most effective cleansing fluid. His streaks of cruelty, restlessness, and abnormal fears point to a split personality. Another Báthory, Elizabeth, achieved the questionable fame of being a human werewolf. She is said to have ordered the slaughter of six hundred virgins so that by bathing in their blood she could reinvigorate her youth. She found a dismal end in jail.

A member of one of the ancient Magyar families, Stephen Bocskay, was faithful adherent of the Habsburgs. He was born with a deep hatred toward the Turks, and he prevailed upon his nephew, Prince Báthory, to turn to Vienna against the Sublime Porte. He was persecuted and accused of treason, and his lands were confiscated. He now led a campaign against the emperor and was elected Prince of Transylvania in 1605. He considered Transylvania a bulwark of Hungary. He also believed that it was desirable to have an independent

Protestant principality so as to hold the balance between East and West.

The Habsburgs oppressed their part of Hungary, and they did the same with Transylvania whenever they had a chance. That principality played an important role in the decades to come, in its own right, because of the strong personalities of some of its princes, and also as a sanctuary to prominent refugees from Habsburg oppression.

Protestant Transylvania entered world history through Gabriel Bethlen, who is considered one of the strongest pillars of the Reformation, not only in Eastern Europe but on the entire continent. Through Bethlen the principality of Transylvania acquired international recognition.

Gabriel Bethlen is one of Protestantism's greatest heroes, whose monument in Geneva, birthplace of Calvinism, proclaims his fame to this very day. He too was a member of an ancient family, and he too was forced to make common cause with the Turks against the Habsburgs. It was in the year 1613 that Gabriel Bethlen was proclaimed prince of Transylvania, but his historic moment came with the outbreak of the Thirty Years' War, five years later. He marched his troops against the Catholic imperial troops in Central Europe as the most representative spokesman of Protestantism in the East. He waged war on the Habsburg domains in northern Hungary and scored so dramatically that some nobles offered him the royal crown. He also hoped to gain the Polish crown and thus create a strong group of powers between the Habsburg and the Turk. Chroniclers spoke of him as a just and wise ruler.

Hungary in World Politics

The people of Europe began to dream of a new Age of Gold while they were immersed in the most cruel of wars, a religious conflict. The more learned among them recalled the glories of *Pax Romana*. The Holy Roman Emperors of the

German Nation had made their bid. As the sharp-tongued M. Voltaire was to quip about them, they were neither holy, nor Roman, nor emperors. He might have added, however, that they were more than all these, they were a fondly cherished dream. The German world itself consisted of some three hundred sovereignties, an utterly absurd situation. The Habsburgs had come closest to creating a world commonwealth, but it must have become obvious by now that they too had failed. What was the cause of their failure? Did they lack ability, or was it because of the Turks? Or was it because the force of nationalism began to stir, a new force not centered around a creed but around a mystical idea of common background and mutual aims? Had the Habsburgs failed because they ruled over a hodgepodge of people lacking a strong national foundation?

A new force arose in Europe to combat the Habsburgs, a new sun, Louis XIV of France, *le Roi Soleil*. He was a self-confident "sun" and ruthless too, but very able. Was he the framer of the new future, of *Pax Gallica*? The Bourbons represented comparatively fresh forces, and they occupied Europe's most strategical location, flanking the new overseas trade routes of the Atlantic Ocean and the older routes of the Mediterranean. This was Europe's pattern for generations, Bourbons and Habsburgs crossing swords.

The statesmen of Hungary and Transylvania, too, now had their choice—Bourbon or Habsburg; and most of them chose the French. In the history of his country and of a part of the rest of Europe, Imre Thököly played a role. He too was a prominent Protestant in constant jeopardy in northern Hungary. He too, like so many other Protestants, sought sanctuary on that Protestant island surrounded by the non-Protestant sea, Transylvania.

The Habsburgs' hands were turned against the Protestants, and Emperor Leopold I particularly considered the reformed religions "festering sores." He shut down one after another of the Protestant churches and consigned ministers of the Gospel to the galleys as outlaws and slaves. His hand was heavy in northern Hungary too, where the cry went up, and it was answered by the scion of the noble Thököly clan.

The age of the little wars was over by now, and it was mighty monarchs that faced each other. Attempting to take advantage of the titanic conflict between Habsburg and Bourbon, Thököly turned directly to the Sun King for help. The French monarch was not only Catholic but aggressively so. In his own country he placed the Huguenots, French Protestants beyond the pale of law by revoking the Edict of Nantes, which had granted them widespread rights. But being a Bourbon, he was by now far more anti-Habsburg than anti-Protestant where foreign countries were concerned. He promised help to the Protestant Hungarian magnate Thököly, who also received help from the sultan, and thus was able to inflict a beating upon the imperial forces in northern Hungary. Gone were the days when Christian and Muslim were mortal foes. Christian Thököly now prevailed upon the Muslim sultan to make war on the "apostolic" Habsburgs by making the supreme effort of marching against Vienna. Did Thököly know what the result of the Turkish victory might have been? Did he know that after cracking open the defenses of the imperial capital, the Turks would have been able to penetrate deeper into the West? If he knew the answer, did he care?

The Turks suffered their greatest defeats at the walls of Vienna. Thököly was helping Grand Vizier Kara Mustapha to storm the bastions of Vienna. Relief came to the imperial forces from the Polish King John III, and from Charles V of Lorraine. Who was to blame for the Turkish defeat? Kara Mustapha blamed Thököly, but the sultan blamed Kara Mustapha and sent him the dreaded silken cord with which he had to take his life. Thököly was rehabilitated and played a role briefly in Transylvania.

The imperial forces under Prince Eugene of Savoy followed up their victory against the Turks and inflicted the final defeat on them at the battle of Zenta, in southern Hungary, in 1697. The Treaty of Karlovic was concluded with the Turks, who relinquished all Hungarian territory with the exception of a border region. The road was now open to the Habsburgs.

CHAPTER **4**   THE AGE OF THE HABSBURGS

THE HABSBURGS were of German-Swiss background, originally lords of Habichtsburg—Hawk's Castle—hence the name Habsburg. That castle was on the River Aar, near its junction with the Rhine, in today's Switzerland. No ruling dynasty was ever to come near the Habsburgs in the possession of so vast a realm. It extended at one time from the lower Danube to the Atlantic Ocean and spanned the Ocean Sea to newly discovered America. Not all of these continental regions were theirs, of course, but they had enough land to outstrip all their contemporaries. Until Napoleon I extinguished the title, they had been Holy Roman Emperors for centuries. They ruled over the western and northern crescent of Hungary after 1526, and over nearly the entire country after the expulsion of the Turks. The grand imperial title of the Habsburgs conveys some idea of the vastness of their holdings:

"By the Grace of God, Emperor of Austria; Apostolic King of Hungary, King of Bohemia, of Dalmatia, Croatia, Slavonia, Galicia, Lodomeria and Illyria; King of Jerusalem, etc.;

Archduke of Austria; Grand Duke of Tuscany, of Cracow;
Duke of Lotharingia, of Salzburg, Styria, Carinthia, Carniola
and Bukovina; Grand Duke of Transylvania, Margrave of
Moravia; Duke of Upper and Lower Silesia, of Modena,
Parma, Piacenza and Guastalla, of Auschwitz and Sator, of
Teschen, Friaul, Ragusa and Zara; Princely Count of Habs-
burg and Tyrol, of Kyburg, Görz and Gradiska; Duke of
Trient and Brixen; Margrave of Upper and Lower Lausitz
and Istria; Count of Hohenembs, Feldkirch, Bregenz, Son-
nenberg, etc.: Lord of Trieste, of Cattaro and above the
Windisch Mark; Great Voyvod of the Voyvodina, Servia,
etc. etc."

The "etc. etc." included at one time Spain and her overseas territories, Sardinia, Naples, Sicily, Milan, the Netherlands, the Franche Comté, Artois, and some more "etc."

What was the cause of the Habsburgs' success? Is it possible to judge the quality of their rule by the epithets conferred upon them by their contemporaries? These epithets
show considerable variety. To mention only a few of them,
there were Albert the Rich and Albert the Wise, then Rudolph the Old and Rudolph the Younger; furthermore there
were Frederick III the Fair and Ernest the Lion. There was
also John the Parricide. Not one member of this vast family
ever was called "great," and the record reveals few outstanding personalities among them. "Several members of the
family," writes Professor C. A. Macartney,* "displayed
marked traces of insanity and during the last century of their
rule they were proverbial for their scandals and eccentricities."

The Habsburgs' success is usually attributed to luck and,
above all, to their marital policies. *Bella gerant alii, tu felix
Austria nube!*—"Others wage war; thou, happy Austria,
marry!" As illustrations again, a few skillful maneuvers may
be mentioned. There was, for instance Maximilian I, Emperor and German King (1459–1519), whose sobriquet was

* *Encyclopaedia Britannica*, 1947, Vol. XI, p. 60.

"The Last Knight"—and the term was not meant as a pun. He obtained the valuable possessions of the Netherlands and Burgundy through marriage. Even more profitable were the marriage vows of his son, Philip the Handsome (1478–1506), who acquired Spain and the Indies through his marriage with Joanna the Mad. With the aid of such successful marital operations, Emperor Charles V (1500–1558) anticipated the British by holding sway over an empire so vast that the "sun never set on its frontiers." In this case, too, the remark may be pat that this must have been so because God could not trust the Habsburgs in the dark.

Growth fed upon growth, and small countries on the peripheries of the Habsburg realm were sucked into its vastness. The creation of defensive positions was determined by needs of security and these in turn became launching sites for new offensives. The Habsburg empire began to grow vastly as the Ottoman empire began to shrink. However, the seeds of destruction were carried in the dynasty's living body as nationalism made rapid headway. The Habsburgs represented so many nationalities that they could not afford to have a national allegiance of their own.

At the time we are considering, the Ottoman Empire had been pushed beyond the Danube, which remained the dividing line between East and West. It was an impenetrable "Iron Curtain." North of it lay the Occident, and south of it was the inscrutable Orient. Crossing the Danube, one crossed the chasm between two entirely different worlds. The other side of the river was the land of darkness and the breeding place of all the plagues, in the Western view. It was a capital offense in the Austria-Hungary of the early part of the nineteenth century to traverse the cosmic abyss.

What did liberation from the Turks mean to the Hungarians? They were now in the land of light instead of the land of darkness, as Christian Europe conceived their plight. The reality, alas, was different. Austria treated the Hungarians not at all as fellow Christians released from heathen bondage but as the vanquished foe. The oppression continued in different form. The House of Austria wanted to have nothing to do with "stiff-necked" Magyars. The provision of the ancient Constitution, the Golden Bull, which authorized the nobility to take arms against its sovereign in case its prerogatives were violated, was repealed. The Habsburg technique convinced many patriotic Hungarians that they could depend only upon their own strength. Nowhere in the wide world had they friends. The presumed friendship of the Bourbons was purely political.

Thus, no sooner were the Turks out when a "creative minority" of Magyars had to turn against the "liberators," the nation's Habsburg oppressors. Leader in this war was the scion of another famous family, Ferenc Rákóczi II (1676–1735), who was to become a world figure.*

Rákóczi's March

Two members of the family, George Rákóczi I and George Rákóczi II, had occupied the throne of Transylvania for thirty years prior to 1660. The Habsburgs must have suspected that if Hungary were to rise against their tyranny, young Ferenc would make the perfect leader. They left little undone to alienate him from his own people. He was brought up as a member of the Austrian ruling class, and he married a German princess. The young prince was romantically good-looking, very wealthy, and endowed with an ingratiating human personality—qualities around which legends could be woven.

The official Austrian policy aimed at the denationalization of the Magyar ruling classes. It placed unbearable burdens on the Hungarians, and the little they received in return was not even the rule of law. The more oppressive the Habsburg officials became, the greater grew the momentum of the Hungarian resistance. In the political climate of those days

* The family name was Rákóczy but this Prince wrote it with an "i."

the opponents of the Habsburgs sought the Bourbons' aid. The Sun King was still the sovereign of France, and he was still interested in gaining allies to harass the Habsburgs' flanks. The Habsburg ruler of Spain, Charles II, had no issue, and this seemed to be Louis XIV's great chance to create a vast Bourbon bloc of powers on both sides of the Pyrenees. The War of the Spanish Succession thus began in 1701. This time, however, Louis faced not merely the Austrians, trying to defend their Spanish throne. He also faced the English, who now appeared in history as a world power. They had now set themselves the task of maintaining the European balance of power, under which no continental country was to amass overwhelming weight. Such a preponderance in Europe would threaten the position of Britain and might work havoc with the position she was building up in the world as the leading maritime power. The British, therefore, could tolerate no Western Europe dominated by France; they wanted to have no *Pax Gallica*.

Rákóczi had been sought out by Hungarian patriots to lead a national uprising against the Habsburgs. Preparatory to his organizing a revolt, he established contact with the French court. Unfortunately for him, the messenger who carried dispatches from France to him betrayed him to the Austrian court. He was arrested and jailed. He had committed high treason, the penalty for which was death. This was the Habsburg point of view, with which his Princess was well acquainted. The wife of young Rákóczi was a high-spirited lady of quick reactions. She prevailed upon her husband's jailer to make good the Prince's escape. Rákóczi obtained the uniform of a soldier of the dragoons, and in that he fled the jail. There was now no going back for Ferenc Rákóczi. The war between the Hungarians and the Habsburgs was on.

Where was Rákóczi to get his soldiers? Many members of the nobility sympathized with his cause, but they were apprehensive about calling the people to arms. Should this be done, would the common people not turn against their own masters, as their ancestors had done at the time of Dózsa's Peasant Revolt? At first, most nobles themselves kept away from this patriotic enterprise.

Rákóczi's first soldiers consisted of a nondescript group, half freedom fighters and half bandits. Many of these were known as *hajdúk*. The word is derived from *hajtók*—drivers. They were really cowboys, drivers of cattle to foreign markets. This was a hazardous occupation in those days, because the cattle had to be driven cross-country in the absence of adequate roads, and this meant trampling on tilled soil. It was the locusts when the *hajdúk* came with their cattle, and the peasantry met them with muskets. This never-ending enmity finally demoralized the drivers, many of whom turned to banditry and went completely wild. Others were hired by the magnates to keep their recalcitrant peasants in line. The *hajdúk* were experienced men of arms, and they turned out to be good soldiers. It was with only some three thousand men of arms that Rákóczi launched his war against the House of Habsburg.

To encourage the people to a national uprising, Rákóczi issued a famous manifesto: "The wounds of the famed Hungarian people reopen"; and he enumerated the *gravamina*, grievances, of his land under the Habsburgs' heels and demanded human freedom rights. Seeing no ominous signs of another peasant revolt, many members of the nobility began to join the Rákóczi forces. Hungarian fighters in those days were still more used to facing the "pagan" Turk, and the word "crusade" had not lost its appeal. This was also a crusade, a strange one indeed, directed against Christians, and more than that, against the anointed "apostolic" king of Hungary, a Habsburg, entitled to wear the Holy Crown. The Magyar freedom fighters designated themselves as *kurucok*, derived from the Hungarian word *kereszt*, cross, and with that designation they marched into war. They dubbed their imperial opponents *labancok*, a derogatory term derived either from *laffanc*, rag, or a distortion of the German expression: *Lauf, Hans!*—"Run, Hans!"

The élan of the revolutionary uprising was such that by the autumn of 1703 Rákóczi's troops reoccupied Hungary all the way to the Danube. Riding high on the elation of success, Rákóczi was elected ruling Prince of Hungary, and he began to exercise sovereign rights, such as the issuing of his own currency, named *libertas*, freedom.

The Hungarian uprising was a side show of the War of the Spanish Succession. The main theater of war was in the West, and there the bulk of the imperial Habsburg troops was engaged. The Hungarian Prince now had a large army under his command, about a hundred thousand men. His ultimate success, obviously, would depend on what happened in the principal theater, the West. There the French faced the overwhelming force of the coalition against them, and they lost a crucial battle against the English at Blenheim. Rákóczi's star too began to sink. As an extreme measure, he assembled the nobility siding with him at Onod on June 13, 1707, and there he declared the Habsburg dynasty dethroned in Hungary.

Everything seemed to go wrong thenceforth. In an important battle the following summer Rákóczi tumbled from his horse. His men thought him dead, and in a panic they fled the battlefield in utter confusion. It turned out that he had only fainted, but this engagement was lost. Some of his good lieutenants deserted him, and he lost large slices of land in a number of battles. The Habsburgs were now in a position to transfer large contingents of their fighting men from the Western theater of war to the East, bearing hard down upon the *kurucz* forces. Then the Rákóczi camp was visited by the worst scourge, the plague. Soon the Prince had only a couple of towns of northern Hungary in his hands.

Austria herself had been exhausted by the War of the Spanish Succession and wanted peace. The Habsburgs offered highly favorable terms to Rákóczi, practically all he could want. The terms included religious freedom, full amnesty, wiping off the slate. Rákóczi was to retain his own large estates. There was only one condition he had to fulfill. He had to take the oath of allegiance to the Habsburgs. High-principled as he was, this he refused to do. The war was over in 1711, but Rákóczi's role was not yet over.

He left the country and made his way to France, where Louis XIV gave him a royal welcome and also an annuity. Rákóczi was an exile now, and he had the exile's mentality. He thought that his absence from his native land was only temporary and that his great good friend, the King of France, would help him oust the Austrians and gain not only the throne of Transylvania which had been his for six years but also the throne of Hungary. He did not know that, autocratic though Louis was, such decisions were in hands much stronger than his own—the hands of history. Rákóczi was very popular at the French court because of his pleasant personal qualities and his romantic fame. He awoke to the facts of life only when the Sun King died in 1715. Rákóczi retired to the quiet of a French monastery.

He became involved in international intrigue again briefly. The Spanish Bourbons sought to prevail upon him to rekindle the Hungarian uprising against the Habsburgs, hoping to grab the Italian possessions of the House of Austria. This scheme came to naught. Then the Ottoman Empire crossed swords again with the Habsburgs. Now the anomalous situation arose that Rákóczi offered his "crusaders" to the Muslims in their fight against one of the most Christian of kings. The Turks had little use for him, however, looking at his plans as the dreams of a professional exile. They remained friendly to him, though, and made it possible for him and and his friends to spend their last years in the quiet of a

Turkish town on the shores of the Marmora Sea. The town was Rodosto, a romantic name in Hungarian history. Today it is called Tekirdag.

The memory of this romantic Hungarian Prince never died in the Western world. That world knows about him mainly through the stirring strains of the "Rákóczi March," composed by John Bihari early in the nineteenth century. In due time it became a kind of Hungarian "Marseillaise," a revolutionary march. It was incorporated in the famous *Damnation of Faust* by Hector Berlioz and also in Ferenc Liszt's Rhapsody Number 15.

Rákóczi remained an ever romantic prince of handsome countenance, pining away in his Turkish exile while listening to the mournful murmur of the waves. His own nostalgic autobiography and a number of books about him kept his fame constantly green. Hungarians felt that the remains of their great fighter for freedom should rest in Hungarian soil. At the time when this desire surged to the surface with great force, early in this century, the Habsburgs were Hungary's rulers—the same dynasty he had dethroned. However, the House of Austria bore no grudge against the man who was now merely a historic memory. It was under the auspices of that House that Rákóczi's remains were taken home in 1906, to a nation that gratefully remembered its great son.

As had happened so many times in Hungary's history, the endless series of wars left the country depopulated. It seemed that the Magyar land was in the fulcrum of whatever international conflicts broke out in Europe. Again the rulers of Hungary fostered immigration from the adjacent regions— Romanians, Slavs, and Germans. Again the great problem of Hungary was aggravated. Here was a high-spirited, proud nation, manning the eastern ramparts of the West, whose people were gradually displaced by newcomers. What aggravated the problem further was the fact that most of the newcomers occupied the peripheries of the country, backed by their own kin under different loyalties. They were separated from the dominant Hungarians not only by language and historic tradition but also by religion. It made a vast difference whether one was a Roman Catholic, a Greek Orthodox, or a Uniate—these latter under Roman authority but with rituals of their own. It was possible in such nationality areas of Hungary to have little self-contained worlds occupying the same small town or even village. The neighbor spoke not the language of the neighbor and worshiped in a different church; intermarriage among them was scant. There was no melting pot in Hungary. Whatever schools there were belonged to religious denominations that sought to perpetuate their own distinct ways. There were no state schools to operate as meeting points. Also the policy of the Habsburgs perpetuated diversity. Because the Hungarians were an anomaly in the midst of a hostile Europe, they came to be known as a difficult race to handle—full of complaints, recalcitrant, cantankerous. It was easier for the authorities of Vienna to keep them under control by strengthening their non-Magyar neighbors. The device of divide and rule never fails under such conditions. This was to become Hungary's greatest problem and also the nation's tragedy.

Nobles and Peasants

In fact, the House of Habsburg ruled mainly over the nobility, while the peasants were subject to the Magyar magnates' rule. Hungary was a blind alley, issuing nowhere, abutting against the Ottoman Empire, the vast Iron Curtain, the impenetrable Chinese Wall. We have seen that there was practically no communication between these two totally alien worlds. The transportation system in Hungary was primitive, medieval. During the summer the crude roads were wrapped in dust, and during much of the inclement season they were fathomless streams of mire. If there was to be some kind of order it had to be decentralized. Authority in the country

centered around the county, and in the counties it was the
magnates, not the Habsburgs, that ruled.

Nominally there were two main classes in Hungary at
this time and for many more generations to come. There were
the people of quality and the people of quantity. The former
were the nobles and the latter were the peasants. Within the
ranks of the nobles there was supposed to be equality—democracy within autocracy. Irrespective of the nobleman's status,
he was exempt from the payment of direct taxes; his only obligation was military service in case of war.

There were some 700,000 members of the nobility at the
beginning of the nineteenth century, and this was a comparatively large number. Sometimes the peasants of entire
villages had been ennobled because of a royal whim or some
service they had performed. In reality, the equality of the
nobles was only on paper.

Real power in the land was in the hands of the *főnemesség*
—chief nobility—the magnates. These were holders of large
estates, members of old families. It was never work by which
they had gained these estates. In many cases they inherited
them from ancestors, who had been medieval gangsters,
robber barons. In other cases they acquired them through
marriage. They gained them in feudal wars against their less
fortunate neighbors. They were invested with title deeds by
their sovereign because of the helping hand they gave to the
kings. Frequently they received them as a reward for some
service, which from the national point of view may have
been unpatriotic. The more land the magnate had, the easier
it became for him to acquire additional land. Their holdings
became the centers of a kind of solar system which exerted a
strong gravitational pull on the surrounding satellites.

Many of the magnates continued to live in isolated country
mansions, Little Kings, *kiskirályok*, as their ancestors had
been. They remained feudal lords even after the feudal period
had passed its prime. Others, on the other hand, were at-

tracted by the dazzling life of the Vienna court and became
the so-called *aulic*—court—aristocracy. They built their magnificent buildings in the very shadow of the imperial residence
in Vienna, and many of them are there to this day. They
added color to that court with their lavish spending, resplendent national garb, exotic Hungarian dances, excellence in
sports. Others sought to become adjusted to aulic ways, spoke
German, and began to look down upon their own countrymen.

In Hungary there was a National Assembly, and there the
magnates had the right to appear in person. Then there was
the lower nobility, *közmemesség*, which was represented at
the Assembly by delegates. Some members of this lower
nobility were known as *bocskoros nemes*, sandaled nobility,
too poor to have boots. They lived like the peasants, except
for the enjoyment of the constitutionally granted prerogatives.

Finally there were the peasants, the bulk of the people.
The attitude toward them was that they were inferior creatures, half animal and half man, certainly not created in
Gods' own image. They were the working people, treated con-
temptuously because they were not smart enough to live by
their wits. The best treatment they could hope for was
paternalism. There were probably nine million of these at
the beginning of the nineteenth century, and they were
mainly serfs.

Originally there had been two types of serfs, those who
could move freely, *homo liberae conditionis*, and those who
were tied to the soil, *glebae adstrictus*. After the great Peasant Revolt of 1514, however, the half-free peasants lost their
freedom and were attached to their masters' soil.

The serfs were subject to the civil and criminal jurisdiction
of their lords, and this was known, quaintly, as the "master's
chair"—*uri szék*. It included, in some cases, the right to pass
sentence of death upon the accused, and this was known as
the "right of the sword"—*jus gladii*. This right had to be

specifically conferred upon the magnate by a royal act. The serf had the nominal right to appeal the lord's decision to the county court. However, that court was under the control of his master and the master's confrères.

The serfs owed their landlords both compulsory labor and a part of the produce, a tax. They had to perform both private and public work, known in Hungarian by the Slavic term of *robot*, work, which was the equivalent of the French *corvée*. The taxes were numerous, and included dézsma, which is a corruption of the Latin word *decima*, a tenth part, the tithe. The serfs also owed their masters census money and often had to buy their supplies in the lord's stores—company stores—at high prices.

Some of the serfs had merely the usufruct of the land, while others owned their own huts. Still others had neither the one nor the other and were thus completely dependent upon the magnates' whims.

A Notable "King"—Maria Theresa

It was Voltaire who said that the history of Europe was changed by a pot of mushrooms. This happened when Charles VI, Archduke of Austria, and head of the Holy Roman Empire of the German Nation, who was Charles III, Apostolic King of Hungary, died of mushroom poisoning on October 2, 1740.

The royal succession in Hungary had been a haphazard affair in the past. The throne was elective but the election was limited to one dynasty. Under the Habsburgs the succession was limited to first-born sons of the rulers. Now, however, for the first time the Habsburgs had left no male heir. Emperor Charles had taken his cap in his hand and made the rounds of the courts of Europe, begging them to permit a change in the rule of succession, known as the Pragmatic Sanction, so that he might be followed by his daughter, Archduchess Maria Theresa. As a bribe for their acceptance

of her as his heir, the Emperor had turned over a slice of
Lombardy to the King of Sardinia, had promised the Grand
Duchy of Lorraine to the King of France, and had been
forced to cede parts of Serbia and Walachia to the Turkish
Sultan. The Pragmatic Sanction was promulgated in 1724.
Yet on his deathbed Emperor Charles VI had feared that
his passing would be a signal for the rulers of Europe to rise
and snatch away his daughter's crown.

Four months after Maria Theresa (1717–1780) had as-
cended the throne, the armies of Frederick II, who was to be
known to history as "Great," had invaded Silesia, part of the
Habsburg legacy. Shortly after the outbreak of hostilities the
Prussian King wrote the following letter to the Hungarian
Queen and Archduchess of Austria:

MADAME, MY SISTER:

Nothing could grieve me more than the knowledge that
you have misunderstood the motives that have actuated the
occupation of the Silesian provinces by my armies. The danger
to which the menacing attitude of two of your neighbors exposed your crown lands impelled me to occupy a strategic
position from which their movements can be controlled and
their offensive purposes frustrated. My heart is for you, even
though my arms must be against you, but believe me, Madame, my sister, that the stability and future of your successful reign could be best vouchsafed by the move which I had
to undertake and which, history will show, was solely motivated by the desire to be of service to you and of the
illustrious house of which you are a member. Madame,
my sister's affectionate brother

FREDERICUS REX

("Sister" and "brother" were metaphorical terms, used in
the correspondence of sovereign rulers.)

Maria Theresa was familiar with national traits, and she
knew that Hungarian noblemen could not resist the entreaty

of an attractive young woman. On June 25, 1741, she had herself crowned with the Holy Crown in Pozsony on the Danube, and on September 11 she appeared before the Hungarian magnates in the same coronation town with her newborn baby, the future Emperor Joseph II, in her arms, pleading for help. The magnates broke into a spontaneous cry: *Damus vitam et sanguinem*—"We give our life and blood!" Another version makes them cry out even more dramatically: *Moriamur pro rege nostro Maria Theresia!* "We will die for our King, Maria Theresa!" They used the word "king," not "queen," considering her exalted position.

Some historians have pointed out that the Magyar magnates offered "blood" but no money to help out their beautiful "King." Others have cast doubt on the authenticity of the scene. However, there can be no doubt that she did appeal to the Hungarians and that they did respond.

"He is a bad man," Maria Theresa wrote to a confidant about Frederick. "He has stolen Silesia from me and I shall never forgive him. He took unfair advantage of me when I was hopelessly forsaken and when I had to fight the entire world. Nothing will ever make me see him in any role except that of a wicked man. His motives are far from being those by which he pretends to be actuated. In his dealings he is unscrupulous and stoops to any practice, no matter how objectionable."

The Prussian King obtained Silesia, but Maria Theresa continued the struggle to regain it. The Seven Years' War followed, her greatest war effort, which brought to a head the struggle between the Habsburgs and the Prussian Hohenzollern family for supremacy in the German-speaking world. In a bold attempt to down the Prussian, Maria Theresa headed a league of royal women. Their front was held in the East by Czarina Elizabeth, Autocrat of All the Russias, the most attractive-looking member of the league. She was as brilliant in many ways as her legendary father, Peter the

Great, but she was even less reliable. Madame la Marquise de Pompadour, *maitresse en titre* of King Louis XV of France and real power behind the bedroom curtain, was the representative of the royal Amazons in the West. France had been Austria's traditional enemy, and through generations Europe's history had been little more than the feud of Habsburgs and Bourbons. With a stroke of genius that gave Austria's diplomacy a new direction, Maria Theresa came to terms with the French, assisted in her negotiations by Prince Wenzel von Kaunitz, her chancellor. It was he who drew Madame de Pompadour into the plot which resulted in the dynasties on the Danube and on the Seine fighting as allies. When the war came to an end seven years later, when the dead, the maimed and the widows were counted, Europe found that between Austria and Prussia not one village had changed hands. It also found a new world power—Prussia.

The rule of Maria Theresa coincided with the period of development of European political institutions when the authority of the central government was gaining strength at the expense of the surviving centrifugal forces. She did much to nationalize the public administration in Vienna. In her Austrian domains she improved the serfs' condition by specifying the amounts they owed to their masters and the compulsory work they had to perform. Mining was stimulated and industrialization had a modest start. She opened new markets for the products of her Danubian lands, discarded some export and import restrictions. She forestalled some of the most disastrous floods of the Danube by having its lower reaches regulated and extending its navigable area. She took the initial steps toward making Trieste Austria's main outlet to the sea and improving the highways leading to that Adriatic port. Maria Theresa did more for higher education than any of her predecessors, and she established the Theresianum in Vienna for Hungarian youth. She cut down the number of religious holidays, which had taken up nearly one-fifth of the year. Although a devout Catholic, she ordered the Jesuits expelled because she considered them a state within the state. The modern nation could tolerate no such competition.

In Hungary, Maria Theresa did her best to resettle the depopulated plains, *Alföld*, a perennial problem in view of the fact that the land of the Magyars was an almost perennial battlefield. She satisfied a deep Hungarian craving by giving them their own seaport at Fiume, on the Bay of Quarnero, near the head of the Adriatic Sea. She would have liked to help the Hungarian serfs too, and to introduce improvements in the government, but she was thwarted by the magnates, who stood on their constitutional rights. She attracted members of the Magyar nobility to her court and thus enhanced its cosmopolitan traits. She seems to have had real fondness for the Hungarians and said as much in her frank way: "I am a good Hungarian and my heart is full of gratitude toward the nation."

While Hungarian history views Maria Theresa with gallant affection, it has never been wholly uncritical of her actions. In spite of her affection for the Magyars, Maria Theresa helped the Austrians far more. She held that the policy of the Hungarian nobility made it impossible for that land to make its proper contribution to the economic development of all her realms. Since the nobility refused to pay taxes, some means had to be found to pay for the costs of the government. This was done largely through an internal tariff wall between Austria and Hungary. Austria and Bohemia were the industrialized regions of the crown lands, where textiles, paper, glass, ceramics, and processing industries flourished. Hungary had no such industries and had to buy her products from Austria, paying duty on the imports. Hungarian customs duties against foreign industries were so much higher that they could not compete with those of Austria. On the other hand, the export duties on agricultural products to foreign countries were high. The Hungarians, therefore, were forced to sell their grain cheaply to Austria. This looked to Hungarians very much like a colonial policy. Hungary was Austria's colony, forced to sell her raw materials to Austria cheaply and to buy back the finished products dearly.

History has an autobiographical record of Maria Theresa's self-appraisal. She was in the habit of writing down her thoughts—bad grammar, spelling mistakes, and all. "In matters of the church, religion and the law, in bringing up my children and maintaining my dignity," she wrote, "I am not aware of sins. But I do accuse myself for many covert flaws. I am guilty before God for the wars I waged because of excessive ambition. I am also guilty of envy, wrath, flabbiness and sloth. I am guilty of having neglected the holy confession, offending my neighbors with words and of the lack of loving-kindness."

The Revolutionary Emperor

Maria Theresa bore sixteen children. She was followed by her eldest son, Joseph II, a unique Habsburg, and one who came closest to greatness. He was called a Jacobin by his worst opponents. Joseph was probably the most human Habsburg, a sovereign honestly striving to help his people with all the means at his command. He was one of the most hated rulers and one of the greatest failures in his dynasty's long history.

He ruled for a decade (1780–1790), during which he issued some 6000 decrees and signed 1100 new laws. "The distinctions between nations and religions must disappear," he had written to his mother, "and all citizens must consider each other brothers." To Maria Theresa, a deeply religious woman, such remarks made no sense. She was concerned with prayer and confession. She answered him: "You are an intellectual coquet."

Joseph was in the habit of traveling incognito in his lands.

On one of his travels in Hungary he encountered the bodies of eight children in one single field, dead of starvation. Twelve more children were on the point of death; he collected them and sent them to Vienna to be fed and instructed. On the same trip he noticed an old man in the chain gang of a mine and inquired about the cause of this cruel punishment.

"I found a dead hare," was the answer, "and took it home. I was seen, and now here I am."

"Are you charged with nothing else?"

"Nothing else, sir."

"Who is the man in charge? I want to speak to him."

"Oh, no, please, don't do it, sir. Another kind sir did it and I was given fifty lashes when he was gone."

Joseph was stung into action by what he had seen. "Hasten everything," he wrote to a chief assistant, "that brings me closer to the accomplishment of my plans for the happiness of my people."

He freed the serfs in the first year of his reign. He was in such a hurry that he had no time to work out the countless details of this revolutionary change. This order was completely ignored in Hungary. Joseph ordered that the Hungarian nobility should be taxed, contrary to the land's ancient constitution which provided that only the peasants and the aliens should pay for the public expenditures. This decree too was flouted. Joseph founded hospitals, orphanages, asylums for the insane; ordered free food and medicine to be given to poor people; opened parks and public gardens. He gave the Protestants freedom of worship and emancipated the Jews. He subjected the administration of his realm to the most thoroughgoing change. It was to be even more highly centralized than under his mother—this time including also Hungary. The center of this government was to be Vienna and its official language was to be German. In Hungary the official language had been Latin. By imposing German on Hungary too, Joseph believed that he merely replaced one

alien tongue by another one for greater efficiency. But that
was not the view of the magnates of Hungary. To them he
was the incarnation of the Devil, the Antichrist himself. They
applied the most derogatory epithet to him: "Peasant God."

His death was celebrated in Hungary not only by the
magnates but also by the peasants whom he had wanted
so desperately to help. Scarcely one of his countless reforms
survived. The sharp-tongued Frederick the Great of Prussia
said of Joseph II that the trouble with him was that he took
the second step before taking the first. An American biog-
rapher, however, had this to say about the Revolutionary
Emperor: "Joseph was the first great ruler in Christendom to
establish compulsory education; the first to grant freedom of
speech and conscience—and this voluntarily, in the face of
fierce opposition." *

Hungarian Jacobins

Joseph's successor was his brother Leopold II, whose undis-
tinguished regime lasted only two years, 1790–1792. He restored the privileges of the Magyar nobles.

In Hungary the French Revolution was seen as the darkest
work of the Evil One. Its philosophy received scarcely any
attention, but the Terror was well known. The very idea that
all men were created equal appeared to be the sheerest blas-
phemy to the ruling circles, not only in Hungary but also in
Austria. Rulers were invested with their power through the
dispensation of Providence, and to question it was a Godless
act. It was the will of God, too, that people should remain
in the station to which they were born.

Even in the midst of the great changes which converged
upon France, Hungary remained isolated from those historic
events. She continued to be a farm country, selling most of
her produce to Austria. In spite of Fiume, she was largely

* *The Revolutionary Emperor,* by S. K. Padover. New York: Robert O.
Ballou, 1933, p. 11.

landlocked. The strongest spiritual influence in the country was exercised by the clergy, whose main function in the social system was to exhort the faithful to carry the burden of human life with patience. The number of people who followed world events was small.

However, no country is ever completely isolated from the rest of the world, and that was true of Hungary, too. The road to Rome was never closed. On the way there the curious-minded stopped off at other Italian towns, staying at noted fountainheads of learning. Others ranged farther afield, trying to quench their intellectual thirst in France and England. Even though their search was mainly for theological knowledge, the by-products of such learning grew apace. The travelers could not help observing how much more advanced the Western nations were in learning and technical skills. Comparing their backward country with the nations of the West, they felt a pang of shame.

It is notable, of course, that the Hungarians were so strongly Western-oriented even in these years of stagnation. They felt they could learn nothing from the Turk, their neighbor. Also, they could learn nothing from Russia, much closer than France and England. Then, too, the land of the czars was always suspicious of aliens.

Thus it was that even in the face of the deeply rooted conservative traditions of the people, the historic heritage of taking things for granted and leaving to Providence whatever change it saw fit to impose, also in the teeth of the massive resistance of the established authorities, there were some people—although few in number—who sought to propagate the ideas of the French Revolution in Mid-Danubia. Paradoxically it was a man of the church, a Franciscan monk, who was Hungary's most noted Jacobin. He was Ignac Martinovics.

He was a brilliant man, this Franciscan monk who, in the year of the outbreak of the Revolution in Paris, 1789, was

appointed professor of mathematics and philosophy in the
Monastic College of Buda. He left this teaching post after
a while and became an army chaplain in one of the more
outlying parts of the Habsburg realm, in Bukovina. His knowledge must have impressed a noted Polish aristocrat, who
engaged him to accompany him on a grand tour of Europe;
and it was then that the young scholar fell under the spell
of revolutionary ideas.

His interest in such appalling things was not suspected, as
he wrote learned books on mathematics and natural sciences
which aroused such attention that he was appointed *ordin-
arius*, full professor, at the Academy of Lemberg, in the
Galician or northeastern portion of the Habsburg realm. He
reached the pinnacle of the academic career at the age of
thirty-five.

He did not tarry in Lemberg for long, however. He became
a court chemist and imperial councillor, and eventually he
was appointed to a high position in the Foreign Affairs Department of the Imperial Cabinet in Vienna. Unbeknown to
the world, Martinovics wrote several political treatises in the
spirit of the Jacobins, which were published anonymously
while all these scholarly honors were showered upon him.
In these writings he attacked the Habsburg policy of oppression and especially the restraints on freedom of speech.

Martinovics seems to have established contact with a group
of the so-called Illuminati, progressive-minded people bent
on reform, related to the Freemasons of some European
countries. He must have been also in contact with some
French Jacobins. Back in Hungary, he started working more
openly for the realization of revolutionary ideals. One of the
bodies he helped to establish was the Society of Liberty and
Equality. It propagated such daring ideas as that the rulers'
oppression should be shaken off and power be placed in the
peoples' own hands. Another organization in which he allegedly had a hand was the Reformers' Association, which

came out openly in favor of a republic and the confiscation of Church property. Martinovics had some adherents among the impoverished nobility, and his aim later was said to have been to gain the backing of at least a quarter of a million people before sounding the tocsin of the revolution, the call for human freedoms.

The Habsburg empire was a police state, and he was easily found out. At his trial it turned out that he had no more than a few score followers. Since his trial took place behind closed doors, we know of his conduct there only through the report provided by the authorities. The picture they gave of him at the trial was dark indeed. He was a cringing coward, they said, who quickly revealed his associates' names in the vain hope of saving his own life. In another publicized view, he was a neurotic and an exhibitionist. It was in 1795 that this "Hungarian Jacobin" and his associates were decapitated in Buda, at a place appropriately called Vérmező, Bloody Meadows.

The Age of Metternich

The short reign of Leopold II was followed by the long rule of his son, known to history as Francis II, Holy Roman Emperor, and Francis I, Emperor of Austria. His rule (1792–1835) spanned one of the most revolutionary and turbulent epochs in man's recent history. It covered those days of the French Revolution during which it was devouring its own children, the rise of Napoleon the Great, his dazzling march across the pages of history, the spreading of the revolutionary ideas in the wake of the great change, the collapse of the Napoleonic dream and the integration of Europe under the aegis of France, the victory of legitimacy, and the Congress of Vienna, one of the most important parleys in history. The rule of Francis further spanned the emergence of the Holy Alliance, which was an attempt to solve the European problem through integration by way of the absolute monarchy, and the beginnings of modern nationalism.

Francis was the nephew of the "Revolutionary Emperor," who did not think highly of his intellectual gifts. But even though Francis was not a man of abundant intellect, he was a strong man because of his unshakable trust in himself and his belief that his actions were guided by an inscrutable divine will. The rule of his dynasty was preordained to endure to the very end of time, in his view. The assumption of the Revolution about human equality was worse than arrant nonsense—it was criminal, and so was the insane policy of nationalism which considered the nation, not the dynasty, the depository of the divine will.

However, this epoch is not known as the "Age of Emperor Franz" but as the "Age of Metternich," after Prince Clemens Wenzel Lothar Metternich (1773–1859), for fully forty years the Habsburgs' Minister of Foreign Affairs. He was a brilliant man with a deep knowledge of diplomacy, enterprising and bold in the execution of his plans. Intelligent though he was, did he see that he was fighting for a lost cause, legitimacy, against the ascendant cause of nationalism? At the end of his long life Metternich asserted that while he held Europe in the palm of his hand sometimes, he never ruled Austria while Francis was alive. This was indeed the triumph of mediocrity over brilliance.

The Metternich system appraised Hungary from the dynastic point of view. The source of all authority remained the House of Habsburg, while the Magyar magnates continued to rule their small royal realms. Their country was removed from the great international currents. At the Congress of Vienna, dubbed the "Dancing Congress," there must have been several dashing magnates performing the Magyars' fiery *csárdás*, but Hungary was one of the very few countries whose name was not even mentioned in the important diplomatic documents.

Under the Metternich system Hungary settled back into

her comfortable stagnation. Most of the Magyar magnates and the Vienna authorities agreed to leave the basic conditions unchanged. However, should some misguided person toy with such subversive ideas as freedom of expression, the retribution was prompt and harsh. As the French *ancien régime* was associated with the Bastille, so the Age of Metternich became associated with a dreaded Central European prison, Spielberg, on a hill overlooking the Moravian city of Bruenn of the Habsburg empire .It was immortalized in its day by a famous book, *Le Mie Prigioni*—My Prisons—by the Italian dramatic poet, Silvio Pellico, a prisoner himself. Some of the most famous men of the Danubian monarchy were inmates of this jail, including the Hungarian patriot Lajos Kossuth.

The Writers' Role

In spite of Spielberg and the secret police, ideas of the great change were incubating in Hungary. The revolutionary ideal of nationalism could not be halted at the country's sleepy frontiers. Those people who kept on thinking about their country and its needs, members of the "creative minority," were drawing up plans. It is often a quiet philosopher who starts a revolution, and it was not otherwise in Hungary. It was Magyar authors who popularized the ideal of nationalism as opposed to dynasticism. Writers it was again that gave impetus to the midcentury Hungarian revolution. Again it was authors who launched the revolt against the Russians in 1956.

Early in the nineteenth century writing in Hungarian was not merely a literary but also a political achievement. Using the native tongue was contrary to the policies of the magnates, addicted to Latin, and the dynasty, which spoke German.

Hungarian in those days was crude, good enough for peasants but inadequate for the expression of modern notions.

Hungarian authors who tried to improve the native tongue promoted the cause of nationalism—a revolutionary deed.

Among these Ferenc Kazinczy deserves special attention, because he found the language incapable of expressing modern thought and he modernized it. His handiwork was arbitrary sometimes, but he did create a workable tool. To acquaint Hungarians with the thought currents of the world he translated classics from Latin, Greek, English, German, and French.

Ferenc Kölcsey was the author of the Hungarian national anthem, "Isten Áldd meg a Magyart"—"God Bless the Hungarian"—and was cofounder of the influential journal *Life and Literature*. Mihály Vörösmarty helped to arouse stout national sentiment by writing epic poems about Hungary's past, and he was also the author of "Szózat," another national hymn. The brothers Károly and Sándor Kisfaludy were founders of the Magyars' stage. This was a particularly important phase of the literary national awakening. Lovers of the theater had to go to Vienna, as Hungary could offer them nothing. After the creation of the native theater these pilgrimages to foreign dramatic shrines became superfluous. For generations stage players were to call themselves "workers of the nation," indicating that they were performing a patriotic act. Many years later the Hungarian theater was to achieve world-wide fame.

Travelers to Distant Countries

Hungarian nationalism drew inspiration also from the writings of travelers to far-off countries. Many Hungarians visited the Western European nations, and they expressed their admiration for the greater freedom enjoyed by the nationals of those countries. Typical of this admiration of the West was the attitude of Joseph Irinyi, a young attorney, who held up the institutions of England and France as worthy of emulation. He added, and these were bold words in those days: "Parliamentary government would be fine also in the rest of the world and not only in England and France."

The Hungarian poet, Daniel Berzsenyi, expressed another popular idea, addressed to the forward-looking younger generation, when he eulogized George Washington and America's institutions: "Our democracy must not be that of reckless lawlessness but of wisdom and human understanding, like that of George Washington. Such a democracy proclaims the victory of civilization, and it is the writers who should lay its foundations."

Several Hungarian writers went all the way to the United States. One of them was Sándor Bölöni Farkas, who covered 2450 miles in America and wrote an enlightening volume about his experiences: *Utazás Éjszak-Amerikában—Journey in North America*—which was published in 1835 and appears to have been so successful that it had two editions within one year. The Hungarian author was impressed by the fact that in every town he visited, no matter how small, he found a library. For the book-minded Magyar this was indeed Utopia. He inquired about wages and was told that even unskilled labor was paid as much as a dollar a day, sometimes even two dollars. In comparison with the pittance passing for wages in Hungary, this was nothing short of fabulous. The keynote of his book was that while America was progressive, Hungary backward; America was happy, Hungary unhappy, America was young, Hungary old; and yet in this instance the young could teach the old. As this traveler's five-hundred-ton boat, *Albania*, set sail for Europe, he exclaimed: "Farewell, glorious country. Keep on being the eternal defender of man's rights and keep on being the inspiration of the oppressed."

Not many years later another Hungarian found inspiration in America. He was Ágoston Mokcsai Haraszthy, author of a two-volume work *Utazás Éjszakamerikában—Journey in North America*—which was published in Pest in 1844.

"The attempt to do justice to the greatness of the North American States," he wrote, "is doomed to failure in advance. . . . The European never stops marveling at America, the enchanted land. The Hungarian is even more amazed since he has been entertaining the illusion that his is the perfect country beyond whose borders life is hardly worth living. . . . The boundless energy and self-assurance characterizing the American above all other nationals is truly breathtaking. He seems to live twice the life span of the others and to accomplish a hundred times more."

Those who could not travel sought to become acquainted with the intellectual treasures of the Western world, particularly French and English authors. One of the men who was to play a leading role in Hungarian history, Ferenc Deák, noted that young Hungarian intellectuals were reading the famous book of Alphonse de Lamartine, *Histoire des Girondins*, as their bible. The book was a glorification of the Girondists of the French Revolution. "We derived our political philosophy from the history of the French Revolution," wrote a general of the Hungarian 1848–1849 War of Independence, Moritz Perczel, in his recollections. Another widely read book in Hungary was the classic of Alexis de Tocqueville, *De la Démocratie en Amérique*, in which he justified democracy and predicted its ultimate success. We are even told that *The Writings of George Washington*, edited by Jared Sparks, the American educator and historian, also found eager Hungarian readers.

IT WAS MEMBERS of the Hungarian upper classes who fought for the rights of the lower classes. There was no middle class to speak of in the first part of the nineteenth century, not many white-collar workers, tradesmen, free artisans, professionals. The lower classes lacked the articulateness and the spirit of enterprise to stand up for themselves.

The struggle which now ensued was fought on two fronts. It was directed against the Habsburgs' oppressive policies, in favor of national liberation and a free Hungary. At the same time, it was directed against the domestic spirit of feudal oppression, and for the new spirit of seeing man as a sovereign being and not a mere object which could be traded on the market. Some of the fighters for Hungary's freedom were members of the highest nobility.

The Greatest Hungarian

It was a political opponent who called Count István Szé-chenyi (1791–1860) "the greatest Hungarian." The Hungarian

113

War of Independence was launched by him and men like him. The Count was "an aristocrat of the aristocrats," descendant of an old and distinguished family, a rich landowner. He was not one of the stick-in-the-mud noblemen who never ventured to go beyond Vienna. He traveled much in the West, and like many other well-traveled Hungarians was amazed to "discover" Britain. The England young Count Széchenyi found had standards that could not even be compared with those of his own native land. He felt "humiliated," he said, when he returned to his native Hungary.

On the British Isles he imbibed much of the spirit of Western nationalism. It was not as democratic a world as it is today, but the spirit of democracy was already abroad and there was a substantial middle class that was coming to the fore. Széchenyi was greatly impressed by English economic conditions, which he linked to the prevailing spirit of freedom.

Travel was one factor that acted upon the young Count. He was sensitive to an intangible force, the spirit of the times, the close link between politics and economics. Man was at his best in the economic field, said Adam Smith, founder of what we know as classical economics, if he pursued his interests and did not leave it to the authorities to tell him what to do. He was kept in check by the "invisible hand" of the market mechanism, which gave him a reward if he produced what was wanted and withheld that reward from him if he produced what was not needed.

It was in this spirit that Count Széchenyi saw economics as a dominant factor in the nations' lives. He gave a program to his country, and it was revealing that the title of the first book in which he did so was *Credit—Hitel—*published in 1828, a half-century after the publication of *The Wealth of Nations.* He chided the Magyar aristocracy for their distrust in their country's future, for their reluctance to invest their funds at home. The lifeblood of modern civilization was credit, and progress was linked to its expansion. Hungary was backward, stagnant, suffering from financial anemia. "It is our own fault and not that of the King if we are wasting our estates as poor farmers." The Hungarian landlords, he cried, were not bold enough to take their rightful places in a competitive world. The Magyar vine growers, whom he used as one of his illustrations, were not interested even in listening to other people's experiences because they were convinced that their work could not be improved upon. Hungarian wine, he pointed out, had great possibilities in Britain, but the producers would have to study this market in order to make the best of their opportunity. The Hungarians in general, the Count continued, were quick to censure others while admiring themselves, but that had never been the way to national improvement.

This was a meek way to start things stirring, but this was just the beginning. Count Széchenyi had to feel his way. In another book, entitled *Stadium*, he presented a bold and explosive program, which many of his fellow aristocrats must have considered subversive, revolutionary. The great polarization of wealth, he pointed out in his harsh prose, was not conducive to sound economic conditions. The rich had so much money that they had no interest in applying themselves to work. Also they failed to see the invisible links that connected them with society as a whole. The poor, on the other hand, were so wretched that they constituted no market for the purchase even of staple goods. Nothing could be accomplished—and this was a revolutionary thought—as long as the poor people were taxed and the rich remained untaxed. The first requirement for Hungary's modernization was, therefore, universal taxation. By getting tax money from the rich, the nation could develop its constructive resources. By leaving money with the poor, they would be enabled to enter the market as consumers.

He also pointed to the importance of transportation, which he correctly compared with the blood circulation of the human body. Unless the roads and waterways were improved, Hungary would be unable to advance. He also attacked the supremacy of guild and monopolistic practices.

Stadium was noticed by the imperial censors, and its publication was forbidden. Its contents became known, however, while it was still in manuscript form, and it may be illustrative of the penetrating power of seminal books that it had a widespread effect by reaching numerous influential people.

Széchenyi was denounced as a "nationalist," as opposed to a "dynasticist," and that he certainly was. He was even more than a nationalist, and in that respect he was far in advance of his time. He looked at the nation, his own Hungary, not as the ultimate aim but as an instrument for the promotion of the greater happiness of man. "The Hungarian will keep quiet in me," he wrote in one of his works, "if his desires enter into conflict with those of the just man." He was also denounced as a pessimist, and that he was not. He painted the picture of the contemporary scene as he saw it, and his conclusions were optimistic: "The past is out of your hands, but the future may still be ours. Let us then discard useless memories and work for the great awakening of our homeland through consistent patriotism and loyal unity. Many people believe that Hungary belongs to the past, but I believe firmly that Hungary was not but will be."

The Count was not mainly a writer but a man of action. The terms with which we are familiar were, naturally, unknown to him, such as "creative minority," "power élite," or, to use a popular German expression of the past, "*Tonangeber*," "pacemaker." But he was familiar with the concept and knew that Hungary could not become a modern country as long as the influential people were flocking to Vienna.

He wanted above all to have an intellectual center in Hungary. With this end in view, he pledged his income for a year, which was a large amount, for the building of the

Hungarian Scientific Academy. It has been a decorative land-mark on the Danube Embankment of Budapest for many generations.

He exerted a missionary zeal in ways and for purposes that seem incomprehensible to us. He was intensely interested in introducing horse racing into Hungary. This interest can be understood only against the setting of his time. Hungarian aristocrats were passionately interested in such races, and they flocked to Vienna because of them. By having races in Buda-pest * he hoped to keep more of the Hungarian aristocrats at home. He also founded the National Casino in Pest, a club for the high-bred gentlemen, where they could indulge in social amenities, especially card-playing. Strange indeed were some of the ways by which Hungary was to be democratized. However, Count Széchenyi knew his fellow aristocrats.

Much more serious were the connotations of the bridge which he proposed should span the Danube at Buda-Pest. As we have seen, one of the main constitutional privileges of the Magyar nobility was its immunity from paying taxes. At the insistence of Széchenyi it was decided to build the bridge, and it was also decided that a toll should be exacted of those who crossed, irrespective of status. This was a prece-dent-shattering innovation. For the first time, the Hun-garian nobleman was to pay a toll—a tax.

Széchenyi saw that one of the reasons for Hungary's con-servatism and backwardness was the absence of roads and other means of transportation. The country had a magnificent natural highway which lay neglected. Széchenyi conceived the idea and launched the project of the Danubian Steam Navi-gation Company. Near the point where the river leaves Hun-gary, between the towns of Orsova and Turnu-Severin, the Danube is squeezed into the frothing narrows, the Iron Gate, where it breaks through the outposts of the Carpathians and

* In those days Buda on the right bank of the Danube and Pest on the left bank were two different cities, and they were united only in 1873.

the Balkans. Széchenyi took the initiative in having that part of the river regulated.

Hungary was then and is now part of the eastern Central European breadbasket. Southwestern Russia, the Ukraine, grew good grain on its famed black soil, *chernozem*. Széchenyi saw that wheat from Russia and the two Danubian principalities which were later to be united into Romania could be shipped up the river to Budapest. He backed the building of the first large flour mill at Budapest. Eventually, the Hungarian capital became the world's largest milling center, next to Minneapolis.

Széchenyi made articulate the enlightened aspirations of his age, and he found an audience. Other members of the privileged classes rallied to him, and one of the best known among them was Baron Miklós Wesselényi. With special emphasis he called attention to the fact that unless the Hungarians themselves put their house in order, it would be done by the House of Habsburg, ready to turn the performance of this task to its own advantage. "Putting a deceitful mask on its horrid face," he wrote, "the Austrian government extracts the fat of nine million people * and is now awaiting the uprising of these nine million and would like to undertake the role of the liberator. . . . If this should happen, woe to us, because we shall be debased men instead of free men."

Count Széchenyi was a man of moderation. He wanted change but not revolution, believer in gradualism that he was. Even though he was a great man, he did not realize that the temperature of a revolutionary age could not be regulated and that it followed its own course, its own intrinsic laws. Leadership thus began to slip out of Széchenyi's hands. It was grasped by Lajos Kossuth (1802–1894), and it is with his name that Hungary's midcentury revolution and War of Independence are associated.

* The figures for Hungary's population at that time are conjectural and therefore often contradictory.

While Széchenyi kept counseling moderation, Kossuth became the peoples' idol. The Count assailed Kossuth in a bitter publication, *Kelet Népe—People of the East—*(1841) in which he forewarned that the new policies would inevitably lead to revolution. He accused Kossuth of unleashing forces no human hand could restrain and called him a publicity seeker.

Kossuth's defense was as dignified as it was eloquent. He thoroughly disagreed with Széchenyi's cautious policy, which the rush of events had rendered antiquated. It was this chivalrous adversary, Kossuth, who bestowed upon Count Széchenyi the epithet under which he became best known in Hungarian history: "the greatest Hungarian."

An Age of Revolutions

Revolutions erupted all over Europe; "the revolt of the masses" was on. A major Polish revolt broke out in 1830, but it was crushed. Many Polish revolutionaries trekked across the Carpathian Mountains into Hungary and found cordial welcome there. In those days no magnate's household was complete without its *lengyel*, its Pole. In Hungary's impending fateful hours, Polish refugees, such as Joseph Bem and Henrik Dembinszky, were to play important roles.

Still, it was Paris that continued to be the Hungarian progressives' lodestar. Events on the banks of the Seine were followed with the closest attention on the Danube's banks. The tattered inhabitants of the Faubourg Saint-Antoine of Paris appeared to Prince Metternich to be just "rabble," which was to be taught a lesson by a whiff of the grapeshot. Great man though he was in some ways, his ears were not attuned to the new times of the common man. He was not familiar with the malaise that had gripped the people. The Austrian Chancellor was too much wrapped up in the idea of legitimacy to realize that the change was basic, that power was shifting from one class to another, that the landed aristocracy was being dislodged from its dominant position by the urban aristocracy of the industrial, banking, and commercial magnates, and that the barricades erected by the rabble represented the beginnings of a new age.

From Paris the restlessness spread to Portugal, where Dom Miguel was expelled by the Constitutionalists; into Spain, where the rhapsodic Queen María Cristina was forced to grant a constitution. Trouble was endemic in Italy—not a geographic expression, as Metternich thought, but a nation in everything except its legal shape.

A series of revolutions erupted in Italy, under alien rule except for the native state of Savoy, also known as the Kingdom of Sardinia and Piedmont. The Sicilians were particularly restless under their Bourbon despots, and it was on that island that the chain reaction of 1848 began on January 12. A few weeks later the King of the Two Sicilies had to grant a constitution. On February 17 the Grand Duke of Tuscany was forced to follow suit. But *The Revolution* was on again when Paris rose. This time it erected its barricades against the hero of the 1830 revolution—the Bourgeois King, Louis Philippe. When the people spoke, who was to contradict them? The Second Republic of France was proclaimed.

Somnolent little Luxembourg erupted a few days later. In another week the King of Sardinia himself had to grant his people a constitutional charter. Pius IX, famed as the Progressive Pope, kept in step with his fellow monarchs by granting reforms to the Papal States.

Now Hungary took the initiative in Central Europe—the Hungary that mostly followed. Lajos Kossuth delivered a speech on March 3 in the Hungarian Diet, and strangely it was Vienna that responded to it first. Kossuth's address was rightly called the "inaugural speech of the Austrian revolution," which was staged mainly by students and industrial workers, the best-organized and most articulate segment of the populace.

Revolutions broke out in different parts of the empire: in Prague, where František Palacký, the Czech political leader and historian, presided over the first Pan-Slav Congress, that was to unite all the Slavs; in Galicia, where the Poles of the cities of Cracow and Lemberg rose against the Habsburgs. Then came the dramatic event. In the evening of March 13, Metternich resigned—the end of his era. Soon he was on his way to England.

The Hungarian revolution broke out on what romantic Magyars called "the Ides of March," the fifteenth of the month. To Hungarians it was to become the greatest national holiday, what the Fourth of July is to the United States. It began auspiciously in Budapest, the heart of the country. Writers and poets took a leading part in the formulation of revolutionary ideals.* Most prominent among them was Sándor Petőfi (1823–1849), Hungary's greatest poet. Two days earlier he wrote the poem *Talpra Magyar, hiv a haza/ Itt az idő most vagy soha . . .*"—"Arise, Hungarian, the Fatherland is calling/ The time is here, now or never"—which became to the Hungarian revolution what the "Marseillaise" had been to its French predecessor.

On March 15 this poem was recited to the people of the twin cities, who responded to it ecstatically. The demands of the nation were formulated in twelve points, which, in substance, asked for human rights, the various freedoms, emancipation of the serfs, and a parliamentary regime based on universal suffrage, but did not ask for a basic change of regime—a republic. The revolution accepted the House of Austria, the Habsburgs.

This too was a city revolution, as all the revolutions of that year were: Paris, Berlin, Vienna . . . and now Budapest. The countryside was hard to move, the peasant was under the magnate's thumb. The leaders of the March 15 revolution

* Writers and poets took a prominent part also in the uprising of the late autumn of 1956—thus following the 1848 tradition.

were not even always members of the lower nobility, the "gentry." The leadership of a Count Széchenyi was over. Petőfi himself was a child of poor people, but a nobleman.

Lajos Kossuth

The most prominent leader of the revolution was Lajos Kossuth (1802–1894).* He became what the French would call *Kossuth la Révolution*—the embodiment of the revolutionary idea, eloquent spokesman of his nation, inspired war leader, Hungary's conscience for generations.

This most Magyar of all Magyars was not of native stock. He read Slovak-language prayer books in church when young. Yet he became fanatically dedicated to the Magyar cause. While he was of noble origin, he was not a magnate.

Kossuth was only in his twenties when he entered politics in a roundabout way. He accepted employment as the aide of a magnate who had a seat in the National Diet. The magnate was frequently absent, but he was anxious to be informed of the proceedings of the legislature, and newspapers did not print such news in detail. The Habsburgs did not want to publicize opposition statements, which were becoming bold. It was Kossuth's task to report the Diet's proceedings, and this he seems to have done with unusual brilliance. Following his own inclinations, however, he lent special emphasis to points scored by members of the opposition, while glossing over the remarks of the adherents of the court camarilla. Soon others heard about his letters, and Kossuth was persuaded to make them public, which he did under the title of *Országgyűlési Tudositások—Parliamentary Reports*. It was these reports that made him known nationally.

Speakers in the Diet were immune to prosecution, as the debates were considered privileged. However, reporting them was another matter. Under the system of lawless law then prevailing, Kossuth was arrested and placed on trial, and the

---

* His family name is pronounced "Koshoot."

charge against him was high treason. It was a monstrous
charge, of course, but guilt or innocence in such matters were
not affected by the rules of evidence. The accused were judged
on the basis of reasons of state, which required that opposition speeches should not be published. The trial was of the
star-chamber type, where the accused was assumed to be guilty
and was afforded no chance to prove his innocence. Kossuth
was convicted and sentenced to three, and later—under court
pressure—to four, years in jail.

The Austrian Bastille

His prison was Spielberg in Bruenn, the Austrian Bastille.
The jail helped to make Kossuth Hungary's greatest national
hero. Soon the country knew, even without newspaper edito-
rials, what had happened to the young reporter. There could
not have been too many more romantic figures than Kossuth
was in jail. He was an attractive-looking man, possessed of
that "hypnotic" influence that made him one of the historic
figures of the world.

Spielberg enabled Kossuth to perfect himself in two different fields. He had ample leisure to analyze Hungary's condition in her European setting and to develop a plan of
liberation. The Habsburgs could not have provided their
victim with a better school to learn revolutionary ways.

Also, the jail provided Kossuth with time to combine his
uncommon linguistic gifts with his unusual oratorical talents.
There were at his disposal only the collected works of Shake-
speare and the King James version of the Bible. With these
two books he perfected himself in English. More than that,
with their aid he became the most eloquent English-speaking
orator of his age, as both Great Britain and the United States
were to testify a few years later. That fabulous eloquence
which welled out of him spontaneously was seasoned with
the condiment of a slightly archaic language he had acquired
from the Bard and the Bible.

Indeed, Kossuth in jail was not forgotten—it was not that type of age. On the contrary, he became ever more alive in his admirers' minds. Popular pressure grew in his favor to such an extent that he had to be amnestied. He was freed in 1840.

Progressive ideas, meanwhile, had made headway even in the refractory monarchy. A group of admirers made it possible for Kossuth to speak to his entire nation on important issues. He became editor of *Pesti Hirlap*—*Gazette of Pest*—and it was soon revealed that his writing ability was not inferior to his oratorical gifts. Kossuth now exhibited the influence of his studies in the "jail university" and presented a bold revolutionary program that left the cautious Count Széchenyi far behind. Under this program, not only were the nobles to be taxed, feudal charges abolished, and the serfs freed promptly, but also modern social reforms anticipating the twentieth-century "welfare state" were to be introduced. In the hands of this remarkable man the newspaper was a great success, and contemporaries spoke in ecstatic words about this "intoxicating" journal written in a "style of thousand hues."

Admiration, however, was only one of Kossuth's companions. There was also jealousy. He was too successful and too much in the public eye. In the guise of ideological differences, mediocrity was plotting against him. Eventually he was forced to relinquish his editorial post. He turned to a different field, where his great rival, Count Széchenyi, seems to have provided him with a model.

It will be recalled that the Count saw the absence of credit as an important cause of Hungary's backwardness. Kossuth too turned to economics and launched a campaign in favor of the country's industrialization. With this end in view he founded *Védegylet*—Protective Association. It was his view that as long as Hungary remained a mere raw-material-producing agrarian land, she was to remain dependent on

Austria, the more highly industrialized nation. His nation's dependence on Austria would lessen when Hungary entered the path of industrialization herself. With that aim in view he started a campaign the object of which was to make his more affluent countrymen invest in industries, first small and then larger.

Kossuth was not an economist, and not only did his venture fail but also he lost personal funds. Still, his popularity remained unimpaired to such an extent that the Austrian government decided to lure him to its side by offering a lucrative government post—which, however, he rejected.

He was elected to the National Diet in 1847, and that provided him with a forum from which to address the entire country. He outlined his program in his speeches, a western plan that would line up Hungary with countries like Britain. It was often that he quoted notable English statesmen, and he also spoke about the sagacity of Benjamin Franklin, the noble character of George Washington, and the exalted principles of Thomas Jefferson. He gave his whole-hearted endorsement to the revolutionary twelve points: 1) Freedom of the press; 2) ministerial responsibility; 3) universal suffrage and annual parliamentary sessions; 4) equality before the law as well as personal and religious freedom; 5) a national guard irrespective of the guardsmen's birth; 6) equal taxation; 7) suppression of feudal privileges; 8) a jury system; 9) a national bank; 10) a national army not subject to service abroad; 11) amnesty for all political prisoners; and 12) the union of Hungary with Transylvania.

Facing the Storm

When the revolution of 1848 spread to all parts of the realm, the Vienna court got panicky. At its head stood the son of Emperor Francis I—Emperor Ferdinand I, a feeble-minded Habsburg, who had left the business of government to Metternich. Now that the great Chancellor was gone, he was help-less.

On March 17, two days after the "Ides of March," the court granted all of Hungary's demands. She had a constitu-tional government headed by Count Lajos Batthyány, a pro-Kossuth leader, member of an old princely Hungarian family. He was the country's first Prime Minister. Hungary's tradi-tions were so deeply rooted that a magnate was placed at the head of a very liberal, democratic cabinet.*

Kossuth became Minister of Finances, and Count Szé-chenyi was Minister of Transportation. Within three weeks the reform work of centuries was accomplished. Independent Hungary was turned from a feudal country into a parlia-mentary, democratic state, with a responsible ministry through which the king exercised his prerogatives as a constitutional monarch. His decrees were valid only if countersigned by the responsible minister. The peasants were liberated, and taxa-tion became general. The press was declared free. Transyl-vania and Hungary were joined. Ferdinand I sanctioned the bills on April 11, which became the country's official national holiday.

At this point the revolutionary movement should have halted. That it continued and was soon to lead to war between Hungary and Austria was due to the Vienna court cabal. Although Metternich was gone, his spirit was alive. As soon as the immediate pressure was relaxed, the die-hard camarilla wanted to undo all the reforms.

Hungary had a weak spot—her nationality policy. The Vienna reactionaries therefore turned to the minorities, which actually formed the majority. They encouraged the Croats, in the southwestern part of the country, to fight the Hun-

* It was another magnate who became the head of a radical republican regime in 1918—Count Mihály Károlyi. The only two Hungarian governments of the Left that had no counts at their heads were the two Communist regimes, after each of the World Wars.

garians, and the Croats declared their independence from Hungary. The court camarilla placed means at their disposal to march against the heart of the country, and this they did under Count Joseph Jelačić de Bužim, their governor. The Magyars reacted by organizing the Fatherland Defense— *Honvéd*—and the Croat units were quickly dispersed. But other nationalities rose now against independent Hungary. The Serbs in the south demanded an autonomous territory for themselves, to be governed by one of their own chiefs or voivodes, and Vienna supported this demand too. In Transylvania the court camarilla stirred up the Romanians and the Saxons against the Magyars, and there too warfare broke out. In the north the Slovaks were divided among themselves, some of them turning to the Bohemians, their western neighbors, while others went along with the Hungarians. Only the Ruthenians, primitive mountain people in the northeast, remained quiet.

While the Hungarian government was busy with all these conflicts, Austria took a direct hand in the hostilities and dispatched an army to undo the work of the revolutionary laws of reform and to regain Hungary. The troops pressed on to Budapest, which they took. The Hungarian War of Independence with the Habsburgs was on.

At this point cleavages appeared within the Hungarian cabinet. Now that the Habsburgs had broken their oath, was not the time opportune to depose them? The Prime Minister, however, was a monarchist, a member of the old historic class, a man of moderation in favor of a compromise. Count Széchenyi, too, now began to see his worst fears justified. Gradually his actions became so eccentric that his colleagues exempted him from participation in the meetings of the government. It turned out eventually that he was afflicted with a grave mental illness. At one time he attempted to take his life by jumping into the Danube and had to be placed in a strait jacket. There took place now the tragedy of the "Greatest Hungarian," parallel with the Hungarian tragedy which the world was to witness. Count Széchenyi had to be confined to a lunatic asylum, where he continued to draw up programs for Hungary's salvation—his nation's illustrious "living dead."

The prime minister's post was now vacated by Count Batthyány, and on September 21, 1848, a Committee of Home Defense was established, and its chairman was Kossuth, virtually a dictator. His official title was Governor of Hungary. He was more than that—he was the national hero to millions of Hungarians, who had never had any close relation with any of their leaders in the past. Countless sagas and folk songs were in circulation about the man whom the common people called *Kossuth Apánk*—Our Father Kossuth—and he was only forty-six. The songs were primitive, poor poetry but wonderful human sentiment. "The rain is falling on Kossuth's hat," said one of the songs, "and there should be as many blessings on him as there are raindrops on his hat."

The country had to be aroused to the danger, and 200,000 new recruits had to be obtained for home defense. "The nation is in danger," Kossuth exclaimed, traversing the country from end to end on his recruiting mission. The cadres were quickly filled. In the fullness of his heart Kossuth uttered the sonorous words that generations of young Hungarians were to learn, in the same way young Americans have memorized the Gettysburg Address: "I bow to the greatness of the nation and declare that if we can display as much energy in the implementation as we have shown in our offerings, Hungary will not be shaken by the furies of hell itself."

From all directions the imperial forces converged. During the war Hungary had two principal commanders-in-chief. One of them was the Pole, Count Henrik Dembinszky, who had been discovered in his Parisian exile by a Kossuth envoy. The Polish Count had led his countrymen's 1830 insurrection and displayed sterling qualities. We have seen that there was much sympathy for the Poles in Hungary. They were brother nations guarding Europe's eastern ramparts against Asia, and both of them were oppressed by alien tyrants. The type of warfare Hungary now had to wage was familiar to the Polish army leaders. Dembinszky may have been a good soldier, but unfortunately he was not the type of man to kindle zeal in Hungarian breasts. He was quarrelsome and grouchy. Besides, his strategy was not successful.

Another Polish army leader, however, created an entirely different impression. He was a short little man, Joseph Bem, whom his Hungarian soldiers affectionately called *Bem Apó*— Father Bem—because of his age. He was fifty-six at the time, but still a dashing Pole with an unquenchable hatred for tyranny wherever he could find it. In 1830 he fought on the Paris barricades, and in March, 1848, he fought the Habsburgs in the Vienna streets. When the war in Hungary broke out he offered his services to the government. Bem Apó operated mainly in the east, in Transylvania. Apart from his valor he became immortal in Hungarian history because of the young aide he had, Hungary's greatest poet, Sándor Petőfi. It was while fighting in Bem's army that Petőfi vanished without a trace. He was probably buried in one of the mass graves with hundreds of soldiers.*

The most famous general of the Hungarian War of Independence was Arthur Görgey. He was of Hungarian-Saxon origin, had his education abroad, at the Military Academy of Ulm, in Germany, and served as a hussar in the Habsburgs' imperial army. For a time he left the services in order to study chemistry. It was a paradoxical fact that this man, who

* Bem's career was far from being over when the war in Hungary ended. He made his way to Turkey where he embraced the Muslim religion and under the name of Murad Tevfik became the governor of Aleppo in Syria. The Turks were hereditary foes of the Muscovites, and Bem, the Pole, was a fanatic enemy of his country's despoilers, the Russians. The Hungarians erected a monument in Budapest to his memory, and it was there that the revolution of 1956 erupted.

threw himself wholeheartedly into this war, and who at one time sought death at the head of his troops in desperation, disliked the Hungarians. It was still stranger that he detested Kossuth, whom he considered a national catastrophe. He held the view that the Governor's military ideas were childish. In return, Kossuth did not think highly of Görgey's personal qualities, while he admired the General's military gifts.

While Dembinszky lost crucial battles, Görgey kept on winning them in the teeth of the greatest odds. He was aided for a time by the chaos that reigned in Vienna. The people of the capital rose against their rulers again, and the Habsburg court fled. On December 2 Ferdinand I was replaced by his eighteen-year-old nephew, Franz Joseph I (1830–1916), who was to occupy his throne for sixty-eight years, until the middle of the First World War. This change represented the final victory of the "hard policy" of the Habsburgs. On March 4, 1849, the court discarded the Acts of 1848 and re-established the *status quo* in Hungary. She was reduced to the position of a mere province, from which both Transylvania and the Serb-inhabited southern regions were detached.

Hungary responded to this challenge with a revolutionary act. The government had withdrawn from Budapest to Debrecen, and in the great Calvinist church of that city the nation's deputies met on April 14 to listen to one of Kossuth's most historic addresses.

"The House of Habsburg," he declared, "has forfeited its right to the Hungarian throne. We feel in duty bound to make known the motives and reasons that have impelled us to this decision, so that the civilized world may know that we have not taken this step out of unbounded confidence in our wisdom nor out of revolutionary fervor, but that it is an act of extreme necessity which we have had to adopt in order to save from utter destruction a nation that has been driven to the limits of a most enduring patience."

The House of Habsburg was dethroned in the Calvinist

church of Debrecen. The language of Kossuth's address is a clear indication of his source of inspiration—the American Declaration of Independence. Kossuth was named Governing President, and Hungary was now a constitutional republic.

Neither Görgey, now Commander-in-Chief, nor many other leading Hungarians viewed this turn of events with pleasure. Western public opinion, while sympathizing with the Magyars' struggle for independence, inclined to the belief that the nation had gone too far. Both Britain and France favored a constitutional Habsburg monarchy. Britain's Foreign Secretary, Lord Palmerston, did not think that it was possible or even desirable to replace Austria by a group of smaller states. He held that "Austria was a European necessity and England's natural ally in the East."

The Twilight Hour

In the face of all the adversities, Görgey scored a series of notable victories against Austria's imperial forces. They culminated in his recapture of Budapest on May 21. That victory, however, marked the end of his triumphs. It might have been a mistake to spend so much energy on the "prestige victory" of Budapest. It might have been a better plan to try to break the backbone of the Austrian army.

Nevertheless, Hungary, the midget, appeared to be on the point of vanquishing Austria, the giant. At that point the Vienna court asked for foreign aid. The request was addressed to Czar Nicholas I, and it was promptly granted. Nicholas acted in the spirit of the Holy Alliance of unholy memory, under which common people asking for their God-given rights were considered to be engaged in an ungodly act.

There were also other reasons why the Czar hastened to his fellow monarch's aid. Several prominent Poles had a hand in the Hungarian war, and Nicholas was apprehensive that if the Magyars scored against their masters, the Poles of his country might be encouraged to try again. Then, too, he realized that his vast empire needed a tiny addition. Huge as it was, it had no convenient sea routes to the rest of the world. It had to smash its way to southern warm waters by way of the Balkans or the Straits—in line with Russia's historic warm-water thirst. The greatest obstacle to the Russians' march to the south was not the moribund Ottoman Empire, holding all the possessions the Russians craved, but the Austrian Empire. Czar Nicholas I entertained the unwarranted belief that by aiding the Habsburgs he was also helping himself and the Russian cause.

The Russian army crossed the Carpathians and descended upon the Hungarian plains. Its 200,000 men were under the command of Ivan Feodorovich Paskevich, Count of Erivan and Prince of Warsaw. As his princely title indicated, it was he who had captured Warsaw from the insurgent Poles. Again he faced Poles, Dembinszky and Bem—also Görgey. The Russian forces swelled the strength of the antirevolutionary army to 370,000 men, against whom the Hungarians had only 152,000. Even greater was the disproportion in heavy fire power.

Kossuth resigned on August 11, as it became evident that the army must have a free hand, and Görgey became Hungary's dictator. On the battlefield of Világos, near the city of Arad, the Hungarians were overwhelmed on August 13. Marshal Paskevich sent this dispatch to his sovereign at St. Petersburg: "Hungary lies prostrate at Your Majesty's feet." It was to the Russians that the Hungarians surrendered—not to the Austrians.

The Hungarian defense impressed even the Russians. Paskevich recommended to the Habsburgs to grant amnesty to the vanquished, and Czar Nicholas sent his son to Vienna to plead with the court to apply "rightly interpreted mercy." However, the Austrian regime was in no mood to apply any kind of mercy. Kossuth fled, taking St. Stephen's Holy Crown with him, which was buried in Hungarian soil, near the frontier town of Orsova. Without the crown, there was supposed to be no governmental authority in Hungary.

On October 6 thirteen high officers of the Hungarian army were executed at Arad. At the same time independent Hungary's first Premier, Count Batthyány, was also executed. A man of moderation, he had been opposed to the Habsburgs' dethronement and many of Kossuth's actions. However, justice played no part in meting out punishment to "rebels." Hungary now became an Austrian province.

The *Affaire Kossuth* almost precipitated a world conflict. The Russians were spoiling for a showdown with the Turks, so as to smash the bottleneck of the Straits that kept them from warm waters and in landlocked isolation. Czar Nicholas I called upon the Sultan to extradite Kossuth on criminal charges, but Constantinople rejected the demand. The Czar made some threatening gestures in the belief that the Sultan would not be backed by other powers. But France and Britain did back the Porte and the Sultan went so far as to admit French and British warships into the Straits. Nicholas backed down but did not heed the warning. Four years later, in 1853, the Crimean War exploded; Allied ships were steaming through the Straits in an attack upon Russia which found herself completely isolated.

"Austria will astound the world with her ingratitude," a statesman said in connection with Russia's help to the Habsburgs to crush the Hungarians. The Czar had not known that by defeating Hungary, he unconsciously inflicted a deep wound on the House of Habsburg, too. His victory revealed the Austrians' weakness, hitherto hidden to the world. It was Austria's stand that helped the Allies to defeat Nicholas in the Crimean War.

An Epilogue to the War

The Hungarian War of Independence was still undecided when United States Senator Henry Stuart Foote presented a motion to sever relations with Austria. President Zachary Taylor commissioned Ambrose Dudley Mann, the American diplomat, to observe the War of Independence. The Hon. Abraham Lincoln, representative from Springfield, Ill., presented a resolution of sympathy with the cause of Magyar freedom to a mass meeting on September 12, 1849: "Resolved, that in their present glorious struggle for liberty, the Hungarians command our highest admiration and have our warmest sympathy." Daniel Webster declared: "We have had our sympathies much enlisted in the Hungarian effort for liberty. We have all wept at its failure."

Kossuth and some of his friends were interned at first at Viddin, then at Sumla, in Turkey. Rumor spread that the Austrians wanted to kidnap them and the Ottoman government had them transferred to central Turkey.

The stand of the Hungarians against the Austrians was compared with the stand of the Spartans under Leonidas at Thermopylae against the Persian world power. Hungary had been defeated physically, but she was victorious as the emblem of an immortal aspiration. Kossuth and his people appeared to the "free world" as the children of God, while the Habsburgs and the Russians appeared as the powers of darkness.

Seldom, if ever, had so much attention been focused on a small country's leader as on Kossuth. The western world wanted to see this phenomenal man, and in September, 1851, the American war vessel *Mississippi* was en route to the eastern Mediterranean to take him from Turkey to the United States. On his way there he stopped off in Britain, and the stolid English were moved to exuberance in the presence of this human phenomenon. "He is most certainly a phenomenon," said Richard Cobden, the English statesman and economist. "Not only is he the first orator of the age, but he combines the rare attributes of a first-rate administrator, high moral qualities and unswerving courage."

In America he was given a welcome which was probably unprecedented. The decade of 1850 (Kossuth was in the United States in 1851 and 1852) was called "The Age of Kossuth" by the Pulitzer Prize winning American historian, James Ford Rhodes, author of the seven-volume *History of the United States from the Compromise of 1850*. Ralph Waldo Emerson was thus to greet Kossuth: "We only see in you the angel of freedom, crossing the sea and land, crossing parties and nationalities, private interests and self-esteem, dividing populations where you go and drawing to your heart only the good."

"I remember," said the antislavery champion, Charles Sumner, "the landing of Kossuth. The admiration, the enthusiasm and the love of the people which had been gathering force and momentum during the voyage across the Atlantic, gave him an ovation which only two men had ever received—Washington and Lafayette."

"There are few scattered moments in life," said Chauncey M. Depew, famous railway attorney and United States Senator, "when the heights and depths of the significance of the occasion become too great for utterance, when the thrill of electric sympathy touches the whole country at once and brings its inhabitants to their feet with a spiritual shock. Three of these have happened in my time—the surrender at Appomattox, the assassination of Abraham Lincoln and the landing of Kossuth."

So great was the impression made by Kossuth that some 110 English-language books were written about him, more than 100 poems sang his praises. He was written up in thousands of articles, and his name has been mentioned prominently in thousands of books.

The Aftermath

Kossuth received invitations to stay in the United States and work for the independence of his country from there. However he returned to Europe and eventually settled in Turin, cradle of Italian nationalism, to which he felt very close. Like so many other exiles, he thought that he could make history from abroad. During the Crimean War he entertained the idea of organizing a Hungarian Legion, so that "Free Hungary" should have a say in world affairs at the ensuing peace conference table. This romantic idea came to grief.

During the Sardinian-Austrian War of 1859 he organized a small Hungarian Legion in Italy. He was negotiating with the French, under Napoleon III, who were then opposed to the Habsburgs. Under this plan Hungary was to become independent but to remain a monarchy. Napoleon III did not want to paint the devil on the wall by encouraging a republic in Hungary. However, peace was concluded between the antagonists, and Hungary's case was dropped.

Kossuth revised his attitude toward Hungary's nationalities during his exile. He saw his country's future not as a centralized nation under a Magyar "super-race" but as part of a Danubian confederation. This confederation was to consist of Hungary, Croatia, Serbia, and Romania—a viable economic unit of varied ethnic gifts and natural resources. Kossuth held that the Danube was a connecting link among all these countries, a natural waterway for the exchange of their products and for the export and import of their goods in relation with extraregional nations.

When Hungary made peace with Austria in 1867, an amnesty was decreed in Hungary, under which even Kossuth could have returned home. However, he refused to draw benefit from the act and return to his native land while his foes were at the helm.

Yet living in exile was not to his taste. "The Hungarian whom his loyalty to his ideals compels to live outside of his fatherland," he wrote, "is in duty bound to carry his cross but its burden is great and the road to Golgotha is a barren path. Unless he is compelled to do so no Hungarian should bestride this path."

Kossuth was ninety-two when he died in Italian exile in 1894. All Hungary wanted his body to rest in Magyar soil. The Habsburgs were still Hungary's rulers, but both they and Emperor Franz Joseph I were much mellower. The Emperor-King readily assented to the transfer of Kossuth's body to Hungary.

Budapest was hushed on the day the body arrived in the Hungarian capital. All theaters canceled their performances in sign of mourning. There was only one exception, the Royal Opera House, which, as its name indicated, was a royal institution. Few lovers of music were looking for their seats in the Opera. Before they could find them, however, they were accosted by courteous young men in dark suits. "Is the gentleman perchance a stranger, to be unaware of the fact that this is a day of national mourning?" Because of the absence of an audience, the Opera performance too had to be canceled.

Most Hungarians continued to call themselves Kossuth partisans. When the Communists took over Hungary after World War II, they too wrapped themselves in Kossuth's magic mantle.

IN THE VIEW of the imperial court, the Hungarians had forfeited their claim to be treated as a nation. This was the *Verwirkungstheorie*, the theory of forfeiture; the Magyars were treated as the people of a defeated country.

The Bach System

The postrevolutionary regime in Austria—and Hungary was now a part of it—was named the "Bach System," after Alexander Bach (1813–1893). He had been nicknamed the "Jacobin" before 1848 when he swam with the revolutionary tide, paying homage to Kossuth, idol of revolutionary youth. Bach was nicknamed "the man on the barricades" too, and that he was truly, true to the barricades before and after the revolution. He fought on one side while reform appeared to be in the ascendant and switched promptly to the other side when reaction triumphed.

Postrevolutionary Bach knew of only two types of people. The good were those who hated Jacobinism and were con-

138

vinced that the House of Habsburg was to endure forever, that young Emperor Franz Joseph I was ruler by the special grace of God. The bad were those who put their trust in the subversive idea of nationalism, the belief that a nation's subjects possessed rights separate from those conferred upon them by the sovereign's paternalistic benevolence. The sovereign was absolutely supreme, and his authority could not be restrained by any rival source.

Bach became Minister of Justice in 1848, but he wielded the greatest authority as Minister of Interior in the period 1849–1859. As head of that department, he was also in charge of the police.

What was the Bach system? Its pivotal point was centralization around the Vienna imperial court. The traditional units of Hungarian administration since the days of King St. Stephen, the counties, were subordinated to the imperial provinces created by Minister Bach. The counties were regarded as centers of particularism, and therefore their influence had to be weakened.

Germanization was another pivotal point of the Bach system. Throughout the realm the language of the administration was German, irrespective of the population's native tongue. This arrangement was also to serve standardization and regimentation. The administration in the Magyar provinces was turned over to "carpetbaggers," who in many cases had no knowledge of Hungarian. The only concession Baron Bach was willing to grant was to put them in Magyar national garb. Because of this incongruity the Hungarians nicknamed the alien officials "Bach Hussars," so named after the most typically national soldiers. "A swarm of locusts covers the country," a contemporary commented.

An all-pervasive system of espionage infiltrated the empire, cocking censorious eyes not only on prominent people but also on individuals of little prominence. Detailed dossiers were kept of all suspicious persons—those who were believed capable of thinking for themselves. Political thought was considered particularly dangerous unless it followed the official line of complete conformity and unquestioning submission to authority. The "new morality" expected the neighbor to inform upon his neighbor. The informer became a hero under Baron Bach's system. It must be said to the credit of the people, however, that not too many Hungarians accepted this "new morality." Paradoxically, the secret police developed such power that it overshadowed the all-powerful Minister himself. It was learned later that it had collected an impressive dossier about Bach himself.

Another feature of this system was its extreme clericalism. In 1855 Bach negotiated a concordat with the Pope, under which public education and the empire's spiritual care were turned over to the clergy. As a contemporary put it, Bach cast the Church in the role of a super-police, seeing to it that the subjects of the Emperor considered their status on earth as having been ordained in heaven. Not even death released the person from eternal vigilance under this system. After death there was to be an even more vigilant police from which absolutely nothing could be hidden, keeping its own dossier and consigning the sinner against earthly authority to the lowest depths of the Inferno.

The Jesuits, who had been evicted by Maria Theresa, were back again, and much of public education was entrusted to them. Naturally, the clergy was placed in supreme authority in regard to the subjects' marital affairs. It was because of this that the Austrian concordat was dubbed a "printed Canossa," in memory of the famous eleventh-century occasion when Holy Roman Emperor Henry IV humbled himself before Pope Gregory VII.

Being law unto itself, the imperial government developed the customary traits of absolute power. Lord Acton's famous dictum held true even then: "Power corrupts; absolute power corrupts absolutely." The Bach regime became increasingly corrupt. The noted German historian Heinrich von Treitschke referred to the proverbial Viennese trait of joviality when he described the Bach regime as an "imperial-royal mixture of joviality and bestiality." A former revolutionary friend of Bach, Adolf Fischhof, characterized the system as "a standing army of soldiers; a sitting army of officials; a kneeling army of priests and a creeping army of informers."

To pay for the higher costs of administration and police, taxes were increased greatly. Yet not even this regime could turn the clock back, and some of the most important revolutionary achievements remained untouched. The serfs remained emancipated, and some measures were taken to promote economic prosperity. Internal tariffs were abolished, so that Austria and Hungary now belonged to the same customs unit. Many new roads and railways were built. Vienna became the empire's great transportation hub, in line with the general policy of centralization. Both the criminal and civil laws were modernized.

In Hungary Bach became so unpopular that even the helpful economic features of his regime were denounced. The critics said that Bach had acquainted them with the idea of crushing the Hungarians completely. The aid he extended to the peasants and the urban middle classes was part of a plot, according to these critics—part of a policy of divide and rule. Bach's ultimate aim was said to be the weakening of the influence of the nobility, the "nation-building" historic class.

It must be said that it was not only the Hungarians who hated Bach. He was also heartily disliked by the conservative old families of Vienna, who had no stomach for Bach's acrobatics on both sides of the barricades and considered him an undependable opportunist.

Yet he remained on top for a remarkably long time. The imperial court considered him indispensable, on the ground that it took an ex-Jacobin to catch a Jacobin. He was considered an unexcelled expert in the field of subversion. He was dependable because he never wavered from the line of serving his own interests. As long as his interests coincided with those of the court camarilla, Bach was the quintessence of morality.

In all of Europe this was the age of rapid economic expansion in industrialization and transportation. Bach received much credit for the long-range trends. At any rate, the empire was not doing too badly under the regime of Baron Bach. Having received credit for many things he had not done, he also received the blame for Austria's humiliating defeat in 1859 in northern Italy. He toppled from the perch of the mighty and became Austria's ambassador to the Holy See, a post he held for eight years. He lived a long life thereafter, but it was a sad one, because he had neither influence nor much respect.

The Hungarian Exiles

When the revolution was defeated, a dynamic section of Hungary's creative minority was destroyed. Some of the most courageous and idealistic men were executed. Their number has never been ascertained; it may have run into hundreds or even thousands. Others fled in all directions, and some of the most important fighters for freedom found sanctuary in Turkey.

A few of the ex-revolutionaries made their way to America, which appeared to them the New Jerusalem, the country of the future. Some years after the revolution there were about three thousand Hungarians in the United States. One of the former insurgents, László Ujházy, led a group of his countrymen deep into the yet untamed heart of the Middle West. They moved all the way to Iowa and finally selected a spot for settlement on the Thompson River, in Decatur County, not far from Davis City.

"We reached the banks of the chosen stream," Ujházy

exulted, "and the bewitching view made us forget the hard-
ships of the trip. Deeply moved, my head uncovered, I
prostrated myself on the blessed soil, thanking Heaven that
it permitted us to reach our goal. Here we were at last, our
hearts at rest, in silent solitude, away from vanity and guile."

Ujházy was a man of rhapsodic temper, and America was
to him indeed the New Promised Land. The exiles founded
New Buda, which they planned to transform into the capital
of New Hungary in the United States. When Kossuth visited
America, Ujházy sought to persuade him to move to Iowa's
New Hungary and help erect there a Magyar community of
American citizens, which could exert effective influence on
the government in Washington to back Kossuth's solution
of the Hungarian problem. Kossuth did not think, however,
that the project was feasible. He wanted to be closer to his
homeland, hoping to be on hand when the call came through,
but it never did come.

Diplomas and Patents

Bach was gone, but the era of absolutism continued. Lost
wars have usually been the best training schools of governments. The loss of the war in northern Italy in 1859 began
to enlighten even the darkest minds in Vienna. While it was
true that the House of Habsburg was the oldest major
dynasty which at one time or another ruled over large portions
of the globe, it was also true that the mighty House had been
badly beaten. Was this not the proper time to conciliate the
"stiff-necked" Hungarians, who, after all, had a country of
their own for well-nigh a millennium.

In October, 1860, the Vienna government abandoned its
rigid stand and issued the "October Diploma," which Emperor Franz Joseph I described as a "permanent and irrevocably fundamental law." Under this Diploma the "provinces"
of the empire—and this included Hungary too—were to have
a voice in their own government, which they were to share

with the Emperor. Matters of common interest, however, such as foreign affairs, defense, and finances, were to be handled by imperial ministries.

In February, 1861, the "permanent and irrevocably fundamental law" was revoked. Evidently it had not worked. It was replaced by the "February Patent." Under it there was to be established an imperial legislature, *Reichsrat*, in Vienna. Hungary and the other "provinces" were to be endowed with local legislatures, *Landtaege*. Each *Landtag* was to send its representatives to the central legislature in Vienna. Hungary was to have 85 delegates, against Austria's 169 representatives. The Hungarians, Czechs, and Poles partly rejected this brain child of Ritter Anton von Schmerling, head of the imperial cabinet. A publicist of the period characterized the proposed *Landtag* as "a provincial diet leavened with a few lawyers and manufacturers."

Times had changed, however, since the end of the revolution. For years Hungary had been silent, a political graveyard. But now there were Hungarians who began to speak up in public and who published critical articles. Hungarian writers were the spokesmen of the national protest at this time too, as they had been in 1848 and were to be again a century later.

"The Sage of the Fatherland"

Three men of politics towered above all others in Hungary's nineteenth-century history. There was the Mirabeau of the Magyar awakening, Count Széchenyi. There was the revolution incarnate, Lajos Kossuth. And now there was Ferenc Deák (Deyak) (1803–1876), whose name became closely associated with the next epoch in Hungary's history. He has been revered in his country as "The Sage of the Fatherland," and historians have described him as "one of the greatest figures in world history."

No three persons could have been more dissimilar than these three leaders of men: the brooding yet impulsive Széchenyi, who ended his life in a lunatic asylum; the "human tornado," Kossuth; and finally the "Magyar Fabius Cunctator," who won battles by biding his time. In spite of the dissimilarities of their temperaments, Deák was a great admirer of Kossuth.

Deák was an eloquent man too, but not in the great tribune's torrential way. His speeches were factual, well-constructed, designed to appeal to the mind. Even today they read well. Generations of Hungarians learned to revere him as the statesman who knew how to illuminate an obscure situation with a sentence, sometimes with a word. He was best behind the scenes, in private talks, inseparable from his pipe, speaking quietly, while spicing his words with pat anecdotes. The Hungarians were also impressed by the fact that Deák had qualities which were even more important than his eloquence and store of knowledge—the statesman's gift of timing, intuition, high moral standards, and the uncommon capacity to make people heed his words.

"Hotel to the English Queen"

What was the professional background of this unusual man? He first made his mark in the prerevolutionary National Diet, where fellow legislators took note of a young man who did not speak often but who compelled attention when he did so. When the Diet debated the question of the death penalty, for instance, Deák provided the most telling arguments against it. He was also one of the most effective speakers in that body to talk in favor of granting sanctuary to the Polish refugees forthwith.

In the revolutionary cabinet Deák held the portfolio of Minister of Justice. He was not in favor of breaking with Austria. The war cut him off from his government, and that was his good fortune—and also that of his country. Because of it he was not "compromised," so that not even the conservatives considered him an "incorrigible" rebel.

After the revolution Deák became his nation's political leader. There was nothing much he could do in the frenzied early period of the Bach regime. He emerged from his enforced retirement as early as 1854 and became the center of a process of political crystallization. He lived in the *Angol Királynő Szálloda* (Hotel to the English Queen) of Budapest, which became a political Parnassus.

There was much discussion as to how to solve the Magyar problem among the political leaders meeting there. Several of them held that it was impossible to do business with Habsburgs and that Hungary must proceed without it. Others maintained, on the other hand, that a Habsburgless Hungary could not be created without a war. Concerning Hungary's internal policies, there were those who stood on the full implementation of the 1848 revolutionary program, and there were others who would have been content with the less radical program of 1847.

A Diet was in session in 1861 when the question was broached of what method to use in approaching the Emperor with a program of reconcilation. There were those who insisted that Vienna heard only the stoutest voices and that therefore the legislators should frame a "resolution" for the imperial eyes. Deák held that a process of reconcilation should not be attempted by affronting the other side, and he was therefore in favor of submitting a "petition" to the sovereign. Public opinion favored the resolution.

In support of his petition, Deák delivered an address on May 13, 1861, which illustrates his ways:

"I respect the strength of public opinion, but I also know that in parlous times it is hard to determine it because all of us are inclined to regard our views as those of the public. On several occasions I have noticed that public opinion is not the noisiest word. However, I have a faithful friend whose admonitions I heed even more than public opinion, with whom I never haggle, as I consider his command sacred and his

reproof the greatest calamity. This faithful friend is my conscience, whose summons I obey when I now unconditionally
and openly express my firm conviction."

The Diet voted in favor of Deák's petition. The Emperor
rejected it with an insulting rescript. Deák reacted with a
protest. His words have echoed in Hungary's schoolrooms
through many generations:

"It is possible that hard times will overwhelm our country,
but we cannot escape them by ignoring our civic duties. The
nation will endure suffering with forbearance, as its ancestors
did, in order to safeguard its right, because what superior
force takes away the changes of fortune may restore at any
time, but the restoration of what the nation voluntarily re-
linquishes because of its fear of pain is always difficult and
questionable."

Deák was now Hungary's voice, and when he spoke even
Vienna listened. He spoke on Easter day, 1865, in an editorial
in *Pesti Napló*—the *Pest Gazette*—and what he wrote made
Hungarian history. He wrote in the editorial that the dead-
lock, which had lasted seventeen years, had to be broken.
The Magyars were ready to consider imperial security and to
harmonize their policies with it. Withal, they were ready to
concede that Austria and Hungary were faced with matters
of common interest, which were their foreign affairs, defense,
and problems of finance relating to these two. This appeared
to be a serious invitation to the resumption of negotiations
between the Hungarians and Habsburgs. Deák's "Easter Article" became the frame of reference.

There were other reasons, too, why the times appeared to
be auspicious for a change. The Hungarians now had a
friend at the imperial court, and they called her their "Beautiful Providence." Young Empress Elizabeth was not only
beautiful but also very intelligent and always a friend of the
weak. She liked the high-spirited Hungarians, their chivalry
and pluck, as they stood up against the people she herself

loathed, the camarilla at court. The Emperor was very much in love with his fetching wife, and the Hungarians could have had no more effective spokesman near the throne.

In that decade, the sixties, the Danube valley was being visited by cholera epidemics. It was a devastating period, in the course of which Hungary's population failed to grow. As nature's destructive forces had to be tamed, the thoughts of the Hungarians turned to solutions of their political problems which would enable them to focus their attention on ways to exorcize the scourge.

The Compromise

Again it was a lost war that taught Austria her lesson. It took Prussia less than seven weeks to defeat Austria in the summer of 1866 and thus seize leadership in the German Confederation. When Deák heard the news about the outcome of the crucial battle of Königgrätz, he exclaimed: "We have lost the war . . . we have won."

Austria was now isolated from the world, beaten in Italy, defeated by Prussia, hated by Russia. The dominant German-speaking population formed only one-quarter of the total population of the realm. What would happen to the empire if the Magyars were stung into a revolt? In order to prevent the collapse of their regime, Habsburgs and Hungarians had to come to terms. There had been negotiations between them even before the war, but what would the Magyars' terms be now that Austria was beaten? Deák's answer was simple and to the point: "Nothing more after Königgrätz than before."

Deák and his friends set to work on drawing up a proposed agreement and a Hungarian basic law. This draft formed the basis of the negotiations between Deák and the Austrian Minister of Foreign Affairs, Count Friedrich Ferdinand von Beust, a statesman of vision himself. The outcome was the historic Compromise—*Ausgleich*—between Austria and Hungary. On February 18, 1867, the restoration of the Hungarian Constitution was proclaimed.

Thus came into being the Dual Monarchy of Austria-Hungary, two independent nations under one head. Austria's Emperor was simultaneously Hungary's King. Vienna ceased to be the capital of the entire realm, and became capital of Austria. Budapest was the capital of Hungary. Both parts of the monarchy had self-government in their domestic affairs. As envisaged by Deák's "Easter Article," matters of common interest were to be settled jointly: foreign affairs, defense, and finances relating to these two. These three fields were identified as *k.u.k.—kaiserlich und königlich—*imperial and royal.

Was the Dual Monarchy really dual, or did the Austrian part predominate? The Emperor-King had two residences, but the Habsburgs held their court mainly in Vienna. The magnificent royal palace the Hungarians were to build on the crest of the hill, *Vár*, on the right bank of the Danube, remained largely untenanted. Whenever the ruler appeared in public, in Austria or Hungary, it was the Austrian *Kaiserlied*, "*Gott erhalte unser'n Kaiser*"—"God Save our Emperor," that rang out.

There were a few notable ministers of foreign affairs with a Hungarian background in the famous old Ballhausplatz Palace in Vienna, but the Austro-Hungarian foreign service remained basically Austrian. The Hungarian subjects' special interest in the Monarchy received scant attention. The hundreds of thousands of Hungarian prisoners of war in World War I, for instance, had to write their communications home in German if they wanted to communicate at all.

Also, the bulk of the army was *k.u.k.* in such a way that the emphasis was on the first *k—kaiserlich,* imperial. The joint army's official language was German. There were some Magyar units, *Honvéd,* whose language of command was Hungarian, but their number was limited, and the highest command for all units was in Vienna.

The Austro-Hungarian Bank also had its headquarters in Vienna. The money which it issued reflected nationality conditions in the realm. One side of it was printed in Hungarian. The other side was German—with, however, this difference. Small letters indicated the bills' denominations in the main nationality languages of Austria, such as Czech and Polish. Hungary also had many nationalities, but their languages were given no space on the Austro-Hungarian banknotes.

Financial center of the Dual Monarchy was Vienna. It was financial center also of Danubian Europe and much of the Balkans. Its magnificent banking palaces had numerous links with Western European financial institutions. Those palaces were expressive of the economic supremacy of the imperial capital. Budapest also came to have large banks, but they were placed in the shadow by their Viennese counterparts. The Monarchy's credit policy was determined in the Austrian capital.

The Monarchy formed a single customs union. It represented the large internal market of a realm that was well balanced in the possession of raw materials—one of the richest wheat lands of Europe; a magnificent natural transportation line, the Danube; important industrial raw materials, such as coal and iron, many ferroalloys, and even petroleum. The Monarchy also had large industries.

The Hungarians were to complain in years to come that they obtained fewer benefits from the customs union than Austria did. Austria's industrial products had a good market in Hungary, where they paid no customs duties, as did the foreign products. In return, Hungary had a surplus of farm products she sold Austria in a free market. This was fine as long as Hungarian farm prices were competitive with those of overseas products. The time came soon, however, when the Hungarian scythe lost the battle of production against the American harvester. Now American wheat could be sold more cheaply in Austria than Hungarian wheat, in spite of the fact that the former was subject to customs duties. Thus the tariff union was far more of a boon to Austria than to Hungary.

It was believed in the circle of Deák that time would improve upon the handiwork of man, and that the two parts of the Monarchy would eventually reach a better-balanced stage of the Compromise. That these hopes did not materialize was not entirely the fault of the Hungarians.

What was Hungary's relation to Austria? Did she have dominion status, as some historians have said? Was this a "personal union," based on the identity of the ruler, or a "real union," organically joined, inseparable, basic? The history of Hungary revolved around the answer to this question during the entire period up to the end of the First World War.

Hungary was not entitled under the Compromise to give notice and leave the Monarchy. Matters of the greatest importance, such has diplomacy and war, were out of the competence of the individual parts. Austria carried greater weight because she was richer, larger, more populous.

These were, however, problems for the future. For the moment Hungary felt elated by the *Ausgleich*, and the Sage of the Fatherland, Deák, stood on the pinnacle of his fame. To him the country looked for guidance, and he was to recommend Hungary's first Prime Minister-designate to the King. It was hoped that he would take the post himself. He did not do it. As head of the "Deák Party" he nominated his close collaborator, Count Julius Andrássy.

Seldom was Hungary so united in wanting to honor a great son. What honor should be conferred upon the man to whom the nation and the dynasty were so deeply indebted? Deák could have obtained any title or other honor, no matter how great. He wanted to have none of them, however, and remained a commoner. "It was beyond the King's power to grant him anything, except the clasp of his hand."

Deák retired to his country place, where he continued to be

consulted on important occasions. He lived there almost for a decade, and he died in 1876. One of the few notables who had not hailed the *Ausgleich* was the "hermit of Turin," as Lajos Kossuth was known at that time. He had chided Deák for having made peace with the Habsburgs and thus relinquishing Hungary's rights. Now that Deák was dead, the bitterness of the battle was forgotten. Kossuth sent a cypress branch to be placed on Deák's coffin.

The Sage of the Fatherland received in his death the highest honor his nation could bestow upon him. All the Hungarian counties sent lumps of their earth to be placed in Deák's grave, so that he could rest on the soil of the entire nation which he helped to re-create.

Resurrected Hungary

In high society the first Prime Minister of independent Hungary, Count Julius Andrássy (Andrássy Gyula) was known as *le beau pendu*, the handsome hanged man. During the Hungarian revolution he was one of the collaborators of Kossuth, who sent him on a diplomatic mission. It was Andrássy's task to persuade the government of Turkey, the Sublime Porte, to declare war on Austria and Russia. Such a war declaration was expected to relieve the pressure on Hungary. Nothing came of the plan, as the Ottoman Empire was in no position to scare anybody in those days. Just the same, Andrássy's mission was high treason from the Habsburg point of view. He was placed on trial, tried, sentenced to death, and hanged. Luckily for him, he was abroad at the time, so that his trial took place in his absence and he was hanged only in effigy.

The same hand, that of Emperor Franz Joseph I, which had signed Andrássy's death warrant at that time, now signed his appointment to the country's highest office. For four critical years Andrássy remained at the head of the government. After he had vacated that place, he served as the Foreign Minister of the Dual Monarchy for eight years, until

1879. The Monarchy had few diplomats to match Andrássy in ability. In the name of the Austro-Hungarian dual realm he concluded an alliance with Germany and represented the Monarchy at the Berlin Congress in 1878 with great distinction. He helped the Monarchy and the Habsburg dynasty to overcome many a crisis. Emperor Franz Joseph had to admit that his dynasty would have been so much worse off if Count Andrássy had been hanged.

Hungary's Many Nationalities

For the moment, Hungary's problems of reconstruction were Andrássy's main concerns. None of these problems was greater than that of the national minorities.

At the time of the Compromise Hungary's population was about thirteen and a half million, of whom six million were Magyars and seven and a half million were non-Magyars. Thus the "minorities" actually formed a majority.

Deák and his brilliant crew had realized that there was no more urgent problem for Hungary than the solution of the nationality problem. The task of working out a program fell to Baron Joseph Eötvös, one of Hungary's most famous writers.

Baron Eötvös was one of the liberal-minded, thoroughly Western-oriented aristocrats. In his younger days he traveled much in the West, where he was imbued with Occidental ideas. He was still in his twenties, before the revolution, when he became one of the most effective spokesmen for the emancipation of the Jews. He was the author of many books, eventually collected in seventeen volumes, several of which were translated into foreign languages. Best known of them is *The Village Notary*, a Hungarian classic, in which he exposed the corrupt practices of the Hungarian county governments. He also wrote *Hungary in 1514*, the story of the terrible peasant revolution. Baron Eötvös attributed the Hun-

garian tragedy of those years to the blind selfishness of the
nobility.

Eötvös had been Minister of Education in the revolutionary government of 1848, and now he occupied the same position in the cabinet of reconstruction. The basic Nationality
Act of 1868 was largely his work.

The Act set forth that all citizens of Hungary were entitled
to equal rights, irrespective of their nationalities. It provided
that they had the right to have their own elementary and
middle schools, with the free use of their own tongues. The
nationalities were also to have a share in the organization of
higher education.

The local governments, the Act further provided, should
transact their affairs in the languages of their people. In no
way were the minorities to be obstructed in any attempt at
the full development of their cultural and political lives. The
nationalities were also free to develop their religious institutions. A particularly important point of the Act was the
assurance that the nationalities were to have a fair share of
the government jobs. The aim of the law was to advance the
freedom and cultural potentialities of all citizens.

There were no strings attached to this law. Eötvös was a
man of high ethical standards. In framing the law he went as
far as he could without destroying the foundations of the
resurrected state. Hungary could not have survived an internal
dismemberment. The nationalities did not live in compact
units, and regions cut out of the country would not have been
viable.

The nationalities decided to reject the Act. They wanted
to have full territorial autonomy, dominion status within
the kingdom. The nationalities' leaders could not see that the
law was merely a starting point and that it could have been
further liberalized in the course of time. Also, they do not
seem to have been able to comprehend the fact that there
were genuinely ethical people in the Hungarian upper classes,

people of vision, who realized that the destinies of all the people of the country were linked.

This attitude of the nationality leaders turned out to be a tragedy. It was a disaster for the nationalities themselves and not merely for Hungary, which was to be dismembered in the wake of the First World War. After that war the minorities had their own little countries or joined their kinsfolk beyond the mountains. What did they gain? Divided into small units, they could not stand up to the superpowers, the Third German Reich at first, and later the Soviet Union. Had they formed a third force with Hungary after 1867, they would have acquired a fighting chance.

Not all Hungarian statesmen were like Eötvös, Deák, or Andrássy. A great national need created great national leaders. Once the national emergency seemed to have gone, the statesmen were also gone and the politicians appeared. The post-Andrássy governments reverted to the previous attitude of the ruling classes toward the nationalities. Besides, conditions underlying the nationality arrangement underwent a change.

Following the Compromise, Hungary's economic life changed. Basically still an agricultural country, the nation turned toward industrialization and related activities, the expansion of credit facilities, improved transportation and communication. The Magyar ruling classes, however, were not used to this type of work. The leading positions in these occupations were taken therefore by other strata of society, especially Jews. Now members of the Magyar ruling classes found themselves thrown back on their government jobs, and they could no longer allow the nationalities to take the places assigned to them in the 1868 Nationality Act. To justify their intransigence the Magyar bureaucrats had to create the illusion that the non-Magyars were not dependable and were even dangerous in government.

Thus there came into existence the "Magyar Monroe Doctrine," as Professor Oscar Jászi, a lifelong student of the nationality problem, was to call it. This Danubian Monroe Doctrine was an admonition to the nationalities: "Keep out and stay out of government!"

Government jobs, even in the nationality areas, were reserved to the Magyar "gentry," imbued with the belief that it was exercising its bureaucratic authority by the grace of a mystical superiority Providence bestowed upon the ruling class. Members of this class would have thought it utterly absurd if someone had suggested that its attitude was a factor in bringing about the downfall of the nation from its higher estate.

The Forty-Eighters and Sixty-Seveners

Up to the First World War the political battle in Hungary raged largely about the country's attitude toward Austria. Hungary had home rule now, but it was far from full independence. On this issue the country was divided into two groups of unequal strength, the forty-eighters and sixty-seveners.

The forty-eighters stood on the platform of the revolution and were discontented with the Compromise. They favored complete separation from Austria and full freedom of action in defense as well as foreign affairs. They considered the status created by the Compromise not merely pseudo-independence but worse than outright dependence, because it lulled people into an erroneous belief about the country's real condition. The parties to the Compromise were of such unequal strength that all power went to the stronger and merely the shadow of power to the weaker.

The sixty-seveners, on the other hand, favored the *Ausgleich*. A small country in the midst of the giants was bound to be ground by them, unless it obtained protection from one of them, these partisans said. Hungary was caught in the squeeze play of Austria and Russia, and if there had been no

Austria, these people said, it would have been in Hungary's interest to create her. In the absence of the Compromise, Hungary was bound to be absorbed by the Slavs' monumental strength. Proponents of this view pointed to the tragic example of Poland, which had not been able to adjust herself in the midst of the great-power pressures.

Within this larger conflict, Hungary was constantly preoccupied with the problem of the imperial and royal army. The Hungarian peasant boys drafted for the three-year military service did not understand a word of German—the army's language of command. One of the larger nationalities of Hungary was that of the Germans, colloquially known as Swabians. German was their native language, and many of them made it their career. "Thus it came about that the overwhelming majority of the 'Hungarian' officers who achieved any success in *k.u.k.* army . . . were men of Swabian origin. The majority of the remainder were either Serbs or Croats from the Military Frontier or Szekelys from Transylvania." *

The officers entering the *k.u.k.* army were saturated with its traditions, which taught them to consider themselves an elite republic, the lowliest member of which stood immeasurably above any civilian. Their exclusive loyalty was not to any country or to the entire Dual Monarchy, but to the ruler himself. Only a very few Magyars passed through the Staff College, whose certificate could qualify them for higher command.

To make the army less of an alien body, the Hungarians wanted to have the language of command in the Magyar units to be changed to Hungarian. This sounded a sensible enough demand, but was it really? The majority of the "Hungarians" were not really Magyars. Were the country's millions of Slavs and Latins to obey the Hungarian language of command, which they did not understand? The Hungarians had no in-

* *October Fifteenth* by C. A. Macartney, Edinburgh University Press, 1957, Part I, p. 16.

tention of sharing the language of command with their nationalities. German was at least a "world language," whereas
Hungarian was not.

As the Vienna government saw this problem, an army became a real fighting force only if it was standardized, regi-
mented. The subjects of the Emperor-King spoke a dozen
languages and numerous dialects. Where was the line to be
drawn? How many languages of command should be official?
German was a lingua franca, a common denominator, the
agency that helped the armed men to become a fighting force,
an army.

Still, the problem of the language of command remained a
live issue throughout the existence of the Dual Monarchy
of Austria-Hungary.

Politics to the Fore

After 1867 Hungary had a Parliament of her own. After 1883
Budapest also had a magnificent parliament building that
had taken nearly a decade to finish. It was a Gothic structure,
inspired by the "mother of parliaments" on the Thames, a
massive building on the Danube Embankment, facing the
incomparable panorama of the hills of Buda. The grandiose
edifice reflected the nation's pride in its ancient Constitution.
Hungarians never tired of reminding the world that their
Golden Bull, which covenanted the nobility's basic rights,
was only seven years junior to the Magna Charta.

The Deák party was the first of the post-Compromise
political groups. In 1875 it had to yield to the *Szabadelvü
Párt*—Liberal Party of 1867. The party's very name thus indicated its adherence to the ideals of the year of the Compromise and not to those of the revolution. In spite of its name,
this was a conservative party according to Western European
standards, although it had occasional outbursts of liberalism.
In England it would have enjoyed the confidence of the right-
wing Tories.

Hungary's Liberal prime ministers were frequently men of high caliber. Ablest among them, politically, were Kálmán Tisza and his son, Count Stephen Tisza, both of whom played leading roles in Hungarian history. Stephen Tisza played a part also in the history of the world at large.

Kálmán Tisza (1830–1902) was a member of an old Calvinist family. At the age of eighteen, he entered revolutionary politics in 1848. He remained an iconoclast under Hungary's Dark Ages, and he opposed the Compromise with all his heart. He changed his mind, however, and became a stout supporter of the *Ausgleich*. In connection with such dramatic changes Hungarians were fond of quoting the adage: "He who is not a Socialist at the age of twenty has no heart, and he who is still a Socialist at forty has no brains."

It is said that Tisza had been offered the post of minister of foreign affairs in Vienna, one of the "joint institutions" of the Monarchy, and his answer was: "I am as wholly and solely Hungarian as the river [the Tisza] whose name I bear." *

Tisza became Prime Minister in 1875. He strengthened economic ties with Austria; Hungarian finances were rehabilitated; the railway system was built up, fares reduced, traffic increased. Rivers were regulated and canals built. However, much needed irrigation in the semiarid central plains was not undertaken for financial reasons. Compulsory education was introduced.

Buda and Pest had become Budapest in 1873, one of the world's most beautiful cities. Its growth was phenomenal, surpassed in Europe only by that of Berlin. The rate of its growth was two and a half times that of London in the first ninety years of last century. The people of Budapest called a part of their city "Chicago," because of its remarkable growth. On the outskirts of the capital large industries sprang up,

* The Tisza was known as the "all-Hungarian river" because it had its beginning and end in that country.

sizable even according to Western European standards. Many of them were of the processing type—flour milling, brewing, sugar refining, leather tanning. Large steel mills, electric plants, machine and locomotive-building industries came into being.

Under the premiership of Alexander Wekerle a law was adopted in 1894 which aroused much sentiment. The law made civil marriage obligatory and made possible the intermarriage of Christians and Jews. The law was adopted in the face of the initial opposition of the Upper House. The passage of the law was an important event in Hungary's history for two reasons. This measure was taken in the face of the opposition of the Catholic Church—the official church of the country. Also, the passage of the law demonstrated that it was possible to overcome the opposition of the Upper House with a determined government policy.

The most famous Hungarian premier of the pre-World War I era was Count Stephen Tisza (1861–1918), son of Kálmán. Count Tisza headed the Liberal Party, but in the eyes of Hungary's real liberals he was the very embodiment of reaction. Later he reorganized the party and gave it a less ideologically charged name—*Nemzeti Munkapárt*, National Party of Work. Tisza was Prime Minister for two periods, 1903–1905 and 1913–1917. His influence, however, transcended these periods. The fifteen years up to the end of World War I can justly be called the Age of Tisza.

It was an age when the majority of the people in Hungary had very little to say about public affairs. It was also an age when the nationalities had even less to say about their own fates than before. Tisza set his face with determination against all attempts to introduce universal manhood suffrage into Hungary. Even the Vienna court was more liberal than he; it was urging the Budapest government to liberalize the election laws. Tisza believed that only the "historical classes" knew how to govern Hungary, and those classes were the aristocracy. He was apprehensive that any relaxation of the strong hand would bring about appalling social unrest. Under his system Hungary appeared to be an extension of the feudal age into the twentieth century. He was not an evil person, but events were to show that he was a very unimaginative one. Had he followed the Western example Hungary would not have gone through her time of troubles, a succession of revolutions. Under the Tisza regime neither the middle nor the lower classes were introduced into the art of government. When the Hungarian feudal system collapsed, Hungary collapsed too. The way was open to amateurs, adventurers, and dreamers.

By the beginning of the twentieth century, the Liberal Party had outlived its usefulness. The country seemed to favor the opposition, which in turn favored the program of 1848. The elections of 1906 made a clean sweep of the old order, completely buried under the impact of its own uselessness. The elections introduced a new element into Hungarian politics—the national opposition. Several political parties formed a coalition under the shrewd and effective Alexander Wekerle, whom we have already encountered as a Liberal premier.

The opposition had been against everything the government was trying to do. Now that the opposition became the government, it started doing the very things which it had opposed. Almost overnight black turned into white and the forty-eighter became a sixty-sevener. The old order continued unabated and the anti-Compromise politicians accepted the Compromise. Surveying the scene, the more critical press of the capital stated with resignation: *Plus ça change, plus c'est la même chose.* It had been assumed that Hungary had a multiparty system. It turned out that all the parties represented one single fear—the fear of any change. Occasionally the party in power yielded to the inevitable, but even then it was seldom done with good grace. The government represented the monolithic power of the large estates, which iden-

tified themselves with the national interests. Anyone attacking
them was denounced as the enemy of the nation. Destroy
the entailed estates and you destroy Hungary!

Yet Hungary was making economic progress. It was part of
the inevitable progress of Europe, where industries were rising, living standards were improving. The Old Continent became the powerhouse of the "backward areas," which
contained the overwhelming majority of mankind living on
the great bulk of the earth. The Austro-Hungarian Monarchy
was the only major European power with no colonies of its
own. It lacked the strength to have a hand in the global
grabbing contest. Yet it derived some benefits from the colo-
nialism and imperialism of the more "enlightened" Western
countries. Its trade with them was profitable. Thus Hungary,
together with the rest of the Monarchy, was basking in the
Indian summer before the onset of the winter.

Town and Country in Politics

How did the Hungarian parliamentary system operate? How
were the members of the legislative chosen? In 1874 the right
of ballot was limited to 6 per cent of the population, and
there was a slight increase to 6.5 per cent by 1914. The industrial workers were considered "dangerous," so they were all
but totally excluded from the elections. In 1914 fully 98 per
cent of them had no right to vote. When the Socialists called
out their followers in a suffrage demonstration before World
War I, the government summoned the army and blood flowed
on the streets of Budapest.

The rotten borough system flourished. In 1877 the electoral
districts were distributed in such a way that it took about
ten times as many voters of the Independence Party to return
a deputy to Parliament as it took of the government group.
Sometimes one to two hundred voters elected a deputy in
the rural districts, where the voters were "reliable," against
ten thousand in the capital, where they were "unreliable." The

eighty thousand voters of Budapest elected nine representatives; the ninety thousand voters of "safe" Transylvania
elected seventy-four.

Often the voting was rigged; the opposition candidate was
kept from speaking, the opposition voters kept from the polls;
government voters were transported at public cost. Undesirable voters' names were omitted from election registers. The
voting was open, and the gendarmes surrounded the polling
booths. Sometimes the armed forces were summoned to
intimidate the voters. Promises of money payments were
made, and voters were made drunk. If all these measures
failed, the polling booths were destroyed by "irresponsible elements," and these were never found.

"Tammany Hall at its nadir could have taken lessons from
the very gentlemanly Hungarian ruling classes," commented
Oscar Jászi, the noted social scientist. A leading magnate,
Count Albert Apponyi, observed in his memoirs that there
was no serious interest in social problems during the Liberal
Party's ascendance because "not a single member's election
depended on the ballots of the workers."

Yet the Hungarian was not politically illiterate. *Politizálni*,
talking politics, was a national pastime and even passion.
The metropolitan press was also strongly politics-minded.
Debates in Parliament often filled the front pages, and ver-
batim reports of important parliamentary debates were common.

At the beginning of the current century, the imperial court
increased pressure on the Hungarian historic classes to en-
large the number of voters, but to no avail. They resisted all
such pressure with monolithic determination. This stand of
the Hungarian leaders contrasted strongly with those of Austria, where a much larger precentage of the population had
voting rights and where the nationalities had self-government
in domestic matters.

It is a common occurrence in history that the oppressed

of yesterday become the worst oppressors of today. What happened to the Hungarian dream, the millennial parliamentarianism, to the ideals of Széchenyi, Kossuth, and Deák? Why was Hungary characterized by impartial foreign observers as Europe's last toehold of feudalism? What went wrong?

Hungary's Social Strata

Hungary's social structure was greatly stratified. Each group had its historically allotted location and was supposed to keep that place. Yet it was possible in Hungary to batter down the dividing walls, given strong will, unusual gifts, and lots of luck, so that a comparison with the Indian caste system is not exact.

At the top of the social pyramid stood the House of Austria. The Habsburgs stood above nations in a world ruled by national sentiments, while in the social scale they stood between man and tribal deity. When approaching them, magic rites had to be performed. They were addressed in the third person, as if the second one were irreverent. Petitions addressed to the throne had to be drawn up in an awe-struck tone—*alleruntertänigst*, most submissively. The rulers employed the *pluralis majestatis*.

The ruling house was the sun around which the great *aulic*, court, dynasties revolved. The closed circle of the magnates looked like a unit to the outsider, but in reality the stratification within was extreme. Members' places were prescribed by rigid custom which they were not permitted to disregard. The true aristocrat would never besmirch his hand with work. It was proper for the aristocrat to serve at court, in the higher echelons of diplomacy, and in certain armed services, especially the cavalry. Many of the aristocrats were gentlemen farmers, holders of large estates, often entailed—to be inherited according to strict rules so that the land remained even when mismanaged. The aristocrat could, of course, accept top government positions. Playing at gambling casinos was considered a noble occupation, and sagas were sung about bluebloods who lost fortunes in minutes without batting an eye.

Many aristocrats owed their titles to a great betrayal, making common cause with the Habsburgs against their own nation. When the Hungarian people rose against their masters, the House of Austria, some magnates joined their ranks but most of them stood apart. Members of the aristocracy showed the invading Russian forces during the War of Independence into the plains, across the mountains. They became known as "Russian guides."

There were, of course, admirably public-spirited people among the magnates. The names of a few of them we have encountered in these pages. Not a few were lavish Maecenases, who subsidized the arts, especially music. The history of music would be different without the Esterházy family.

The aristocracy was followed on the social scale by the "gentry," an English word that became acclimatized in Hungary. These were mostly members of the lower nobility and similar social classes, who filled the higher offices of state and county, as *főispán* and *alispán*—chief county steward and assistant county steward, and *szolgabiró*—servants' judge—the powerful district official. In many cases they could be recognized by the "y" at the end of their names, corresponding to the German *von*. Győry Janos, for instance, meant John from the town of Győr.

The power of the local officials was particularly great in Hungary, mainly because the system of transportation was poor. As members of the local bureaucracy, the gentry wielded very great power. Nominally they were public servants, but in reality they were public masters in whose presence the peasants trembled. This was what an investigator, Gyula Rubinek, said about the rural social system of Hungary at the turn of the century: "The population of the great plains consists of government employees, rich peasants, and agrarian proletariat. These three groups live in isolation, hating one another. The government employees consider the rural districts as colonies and their jobs as colonial service."

Not all officials were enemies of the people. Some were public-spirited, hard-working, intelligent people, with broad horizons and a deep interest in the welfare of the people under their rule. This was all the more admirable because the bureaucratic "climate" was so different. Sometimes they succeeded in their constructive work.

The professions, especially in more recent times, ranked fairly high. There was one democratic feature of the undemocratic social system. One could acquire a minor status by obtaining a doctor's degree from a university. That was why many people who wanted nothing to do with philosophy or law obtained the academic degrees of Ph.D. or *Doctor Juris.* Then one became—in the inverted way of the Hungarian language—*Doktor úr,* Doctor Mr. If one had a title one had a status too. If one went into banking and had more money than a dozen aristocrats, one still lacked status, and so rich bankers and industrialists were in the habit of buying such titles as "Government Councilor" or "Court Councilor," which entitled one to be called *Méltóságos úr,* High Honor Mr., or even *Kegyelmes úr,* Excellency Mr. The secondary school teacher became a Professor Mr.; the bank clerk, Director Mr.; the genuine director, General Director Mr.; and the reporter, Editor Mr.

A disproportionately large number of industrialists, bankers, and tradesmen were Jews—a fact which calls for some attention. Within two centuries, says Kosáry, the proportion of the Jews to the rest of the population rose from 0.5 per cent to 5 per cent. In 1785 there were only 75,000 Jews in Hungary. In fifty years their number had trebled to 241,000. They numbered 550,000 in 1870 and 835,000 in 1900. Before the First World War there were nearly a million Jews in Hungary. "This enormous increase was the outcome of a steady flow of immigration from the East, partly from Galicia and Russia and partly from Romania."

Hungary was situated on the western marches of the great pale of Jewish settlement, where the majority of the Jews lived like paupers. That great area was also the anti-Semitic belt of the world, where anti-Semitism was endemic and occasionally violent. Pogroms became quite common in the area. The pressure against the Jews was therefore great. Many of them moved to the United States, but a large number of them moved across the mountains, into Hungary. The Hungarians did not have the reputation at the time of being particularly anti-Semitic. Certainly the Jews' condition there was better than in the regions farther east and north.

The Hungarian official policy in matters of immigration was liberal. Also Jews were needed to fill a gap. As a result of the Europewide trend, Hungary was becoming industrialized, trade and banking flourished. The Hungarian aristocracy and gentry had very strong prejudices against such occupations. They were people of the land and wanted to remain that. They were also bureaucrats and to a far less extent soldiers. The Hungarian gentry was not interested in such unglamorous occupations as industry, trade, and banking. These new-fangled occupations did not fit into the languid countryside with its leisurely rhythm and good times, its endless card-playing bouts.

The Jews came very conveniently to open their little shops, to build up Hungary's banking and industries. They did this extremely well, as was attested by the magnificent banking palaces that began to mushroom in Budapest. The Jews also founded great industrial dynasties, sugar refining, flour milling, textiles, and metallurgy. Some of them became very rich and acquired high government ranks, even titles. They belonged to the most highly educated classes, possessing great refinement of taste, patrons of arts, lovers of music. It is

strange to report that the highly exclusive Hungarian aristocracy forgot about its exclusiveness in the presence of super-
wealthy Jews. Some of the aristocrats were much traveled and
highly educated people. Much traveled and highly educated
Jews were their peers. Intermarriage between the aristocracies
of blood and finance was not rare.

Industrial Workers and the Peasants

The industrial worker represented the new era. If he was
conscious of his special status he joined the Socialist Party
and then he called his fellow worker not proletarian Mr. but
elvtárs, an unusual word, literally translated "principle com-
panion"—companions bound together by the common principles of socialism. The ruling classes considered the Socialists
traitors in those days. They were called *hazátlan bitangok* in
open Parliament—scoundrels without a fatherland. The Socialists appropriated the designation as a badge of honor,
somewhat as the early Christians appropriated the Cross.

And what about the peasant? There were those whom their
fellows called *zsiros paraszt*, fat peasants, who ate well. Many
of them liked to throw their weight around, strutting on the
village street, looking down upon the others with disdain.
The poor peasants were pariahs, who could be knocked about
and addressed by their first names, with the contemptuous
"thou"—*te*. The peasants therefore liked to keep away from
the gentlemen. But contact with the *nadrágos ember*, man in
trousers (many peasants in those days wore flapping wide
pants of white linen), was almost inevitable in the armed
services. If accepted for infantry services, the peasant had
to serve for three years, whereas the term of service of the
more educated person was only one year.

The Economics of Scarcity

Hungary was part of the great Central and Eastern European
peasant belt, and little of the country could not be cultivated.

The land was rich in farm resources. Only 22 per cent of the population lived in urban areas in 1910. How was the land distributed? More than one-half of the landowning population in 1895 owned holdings of less than five *jochs*,* comprising 6.15 per cent of the country's total area. This did not include the lowest level of the peasants. On the highest level, owners of holdings in excess of a thousand *jochs* formed only 0.16 per cent of the owners, while their holdings covered an area of 31.19 per cent. This was a typical picture of the latifundium-ridden land in which there was bound to be a surplus population because of the predominance of large estates.

One could not live on land of less than five acres, especially not in a region of extensive cultivation. (Holland produced two and a half times as much wheat from an acre as Hungary.) Altogether, 87 per cent of the peasants had fewer than ten *jochs*. On the basis of Hungary's 1900 census, not fewer than ten million out of thirteen million agriculturists were landless proletarians. Only 4 per cent of the total had enough land to live decently. The real landless peasants were the farm workers and servants. The former comprised about one-fourth of the total population toward the close of the last century. Some may have had tiny pieces of land, but about 1,500,000 had absolutely nothing.

What made the situation particularly tragic was the fact that the small farmer's plight deteriorated in time, instead of improving. This was due to the competition of overseas grain, to begin with. Then the peasant fell into arrears with his mortgage payment, interest charges were heavy, and the competition of economically stronger estates fatal. Tiny holdings were atomized even more with the population increase. Again the beneficiary of this trend was the large estate. The following few figures tell the story of misery, social injustice, and emigration. They also tell the story of the approaching end of a hardy peasant population that survived the onslaughts of

* One *joch* is a trifle more than one acre—1.07 acre.

Turk and Tatar. In 1895 the total area of landholding of
fewer than 100 *jochs* amounted to 54.6 per cent; in 1913, to
only 45.6 per cent. On the other hand, the corresponding
figures for large estates were 31.2 and 40 per cent.

While millions had nothing of the rich soil, a few had vast
estates. The Esterházy family owned half a million acres; the
Counts Schoenborn had a quarter of a million. Count Mihály
Károlyi—who later distributed his estates among the peasants
—had 186,000, a Count Palffy had 112,000, and a Count Pal-
lavicini had 75,000 acres.

The small peasant could buy land only with the greatest
difficulty, if at all. In certain regions he might have been
working for years in the hope of calling a piece of soil his
own, only to find that his hopes were dashed. This was the
case in areas where the "dead hand" held the land in its rigid
grasp. These mortmain estates belonged to churches, religious
foundations, individuals, family estates, the treasury, or trust
funds. It was this system of entailed land that Kossuth denounced as a "monstrous institution," and monstrous it was
indeed, since no grass ever grew for the peasant in its shadow.
About twenty-five million acres of Hungarian soil were entailed at the turn of the century.

How did the peasants live in this breadbasket? An independent investigation showed in 1910 that the total earnings
of an entire family of five amounted to sixty dollars a year—
three hundred kronen. This was three cents a day per person
for work which during the season lasted *vakulástól vakulásig,*
—from blind darkness to blind darkness.

The fate of the farm worker was even more bitter than that
of the small farmer. He was forced to perform unpaid work
for the lord in many places. While serfdom was no longer
legal, many of its features lingered on. "Discretionary work"
was the name attached to this type of servitude, and that
rendered it legal. The worker in hiring himself out to the
estate owner undertook to perform so many days of unpaid

work. The contract provided in some cases that he must provision the landlord's larder with fresh-killed chickens and eggs. His wife had to serve sometimes as unpaid domestic help for a specified number of days a year; if ill health interfered, the contract stipulated that a certain amount should be deducted from the husband's wages. The average farm servant's annual wages amounted to a cash payment of $16 at the turn of the century in one of western Hungary's more advanced counties, Sopron. These were gross wages, however, out of which the employer was entitled to deduct $6.40 for lodgings, $4.00 for damages caused by the worker, and 60 cents for taxes, leaving a net of $5.00 to $6.00 a year. In later years conditions improved, so that it was calculated that the farm servant actually received $12.80 a year, besides his food computed at $67.

A typical weekday bill of fare for a family of farm workers during the period February 1 to 7, 1911, was reported by an investigator: morning—cabbage with sausage; noon—noodle soup; evening—bread. The Sunday fare was bread and bacon in the morning, stuffed cabbage at noon, and noodle soup in the evening. In poorer districts the farm servants' fare consisted of no more than a piece of bread on weekdays, with some shreds of meat on holidays, and whatever else they might have been able to pick up for themselves. Even during the harvest season, when the worker needed more food so as to have more strength, Count Bereg's farm-servant population received no more than corn bread, potatoes, and vegetables. It is recorded that by the end of the fall many lacked even a little salt. Necessity was turned into virtue by some peasants, who fasted for days, breaking the fast only to eat some crumbs.

Living conditions of the peasant of his district were described by twenty-five-year-old Sándor Csizmadia, himself of peasant origin, charged with inciting to violence in 1895: "I have watched the family life of estate servants, three or four families, sometimes of as many as twenty to twenty-five persons, living in a one-room hut. I have seen men collapsing on the richest soil of the country because of starvation, and I have also seen men being virtually drowned in their fat. Families of the *puszta* [semiarid land] are working for fifteen *krajcár* [less than a dime] from three in the morning till ten at night."

Tuberculosis was called the Hungarian malady, and hunger typhus was endemic in parts of the land in the nineteenth century. Health was impaired by such vitamin-deficiency ailments as pellagra. Insanity induced by hunger was reported in Transylvania and the north Hungarian hills. Half the babies died before the age of five. For every 3,496 persons in rural Hungary there was one physician. Every 1,851 persons had a Roman Catholic priest.

In 1898 the Domestic Service Law provided that one separate room should be built for every family affected by the law. But the legislature allowed ten years for compliance with this provision, and it never set up effective controls. At the Mezőhegyes States Estate, supposed to be a model farm, laborers lived in thatched huts, completely dilapidated, in which one square meter of living space cost half the price of one square meter of the stable. The conservative social-scientist statesman, Gustav Gratz, pointed out that pre-First World War Hungary spent one-third more for race-horse prizes than for sanitation. The peasants spent much of their time in low-ceilinged, smoke-filled, reeking taverns, which were far more desirable than their "homes." Selecting a parochial school at random, an investigator found there was only one child out of 136 who did not know alcohol, and 86 of them daily drank *pálinka*, the Hungarian hard drink, probably because that was one of the few things parents could give them.

Investigating a Hungarian "Middletown," the village of Oros, Béla Bosnyák found that for the six classes of the Roman Catholic and six classes of the Greek Catholic schools, one room and one teacher had to do. The government and influential organizations expressed doubt about the desirability of giving children too much education, presumably on the ground that it would make peasants think and thinking might lead to action. There were many officials in those days who thought that *büdös paraszt*, stinking peasant, was one word. Everything in connection with the peasant was *büdös*. The "public servant" would shout at him: "*Fogd be a büdös pofádat*"—"Shut your stinking mouth." The Chinese laborer lived no worse than some Hungarian peasants, according to an observer. One of the Hungarian magnates—whose name deserves to be forgotten—made the proposal in all seriousness that Chinese should be imported into Hungary because the local wages were "high."

Compounding the Iniquity

Yet conditions were favorable to assure the farmer a better life. Europe's population was increasing by leaps and bounds, and its needs for grain were great. The production of Hungarian wheat did increase between 1848 and 1880, and this increase was due to several causes. The serfs were freed. Serf labor had been inefficient, the work of human beasts of burden with no incentive. The antediluvian wooden plows were largely exchanged for iron ones.

Wheat farming became profitable in modern times when it was done on a large scale. America's open-air bread factories showed the way. Hungary's soil was such that diversified farming would have been possible. The country did indeed have fruit farming, a boon to the peasantry. Truck farming would have been even more profitable, as shown by the success of the independent Bulgarian truck farmers on the outskirts of Budapest and the larger towns. Transformation of wheat land into truck farms would have required either the farmers' cooperative effort or government aid. But the peasants had no capital, nor were they trained in cooperation.

As to the government, it was in the grasp of the land magnates, who stuck to the prevailing pattern.

By 1880 overseas wheat sold cheaper than Hungarian wheat. High food prices raised the general price level, and the cost of industrial production increased. This created favorable conditions for foreign importers. The estate owners of Hungary found it more profitable to increase their acreage than their labor force. They introduced farm machinery, which in turn reduced farm employment. Farming is mentioned in books as a classical example of perfect competition, because the contribution of each producer to the total product forms only a part of the grand total. That was not the case in Hungary, however, where the large operators were able to defy the laws of economics and created conditions that looked like farm monopoly.

The government's taxation system discriminated against the small peasant and favored the lord. The lower the ability of the taxpayer to pay, the higher were his taxes. In the village of Oros, for instance, estates between 500 and 1,000 *jochs* paid taxes at the rate of 1.31 kronen, land between 100 and 500 *jochs* paid 1.49, and less than 100 *jochs* paid 3.76 kronen. This was the result of the system of assessment which worked to the small farmer's disadvantage. The assessing officials were beholden to the magnates' interests. Also, indirect taxes in Hungary amounted to one billion kronen in 1911, against 270 million kronen in direct taxes. Indirect taxes bear more heavily on the poor people because they have to spend nearly all their money on purchases. The tax on sugar rose some 3400 per cent in the four decades up to 1910. Although 1848 freed the peasants, they remained the tax-paying beasts of burden.

Internal colonization might have been a partial answer. Czarist Russia, surely no shining light of progress, experimented with that solution. The land of the Hungarian state and public corporations alone comprised some sixteen million acres, which could have been distributed among the landless peasants and thus a million and a half of them could have obtained a livelihood. Such a move would have increased farm wages and the national income, and would have created a larger domestic market for Hungary's own industries.

In 1903 a minister of agriculture did submit a bill in favor of such colonization to Parliament. To head off land baron opposition, the minister specified that he wanted nothing more than to help the peasants supplement their earnings as employees by cultivating a small plot of their own. It sounded almost as if he had told the employers: "Look here, you can pay low wages, perhaps even lower than now, if you permit these poor devils to dig their own little plots." This is what he said officially: "The creation of labor settlements does not signify that we desire to settle laborers there with a view to turning them into independent farmers." Nothing happened.

If this was the condition of the landowning peasantry, what was the plight of those whom the picturesque Hungarian language calls *nincstelenek*, those who do not have even nothing? Their massed strength might have carried weight if Parliament had been responsive to it, and if it had been considered the legislature's aim to represent the people's will. Parliament, however, in a law of 1876, provided that employers were not subject to prosecution even if they mistreated their employees. Also, the authorities had the right to use force in making farm laborers fulfill their duties under contract.

The First Agrarian Congress—convened by farmers—which opened in Budapest on January 31, 1897, proposed very moderate reforms. It asked that the workday be reduced to twelve hours and that farm workers be protected by minimum daily wages, state employment bureaus, and rural health service. At next harvest time, tens of thousands of farm workers went on strike, whereupon the government drafted strikebreakers on state farms and had thousands of the strikers thrown into jails. Owners thereupon intensified their efforts to introduce underfed Slovaks and Ruthenians from the north as seasonal workers.

In 1898 the Hungarian Parliament passed "A Law Regulating Legal Relations Between Employers and Agricultural Workers," which the peasants dubbed the "Slave Law." It declared combinations of farm workers illegal, and provided punishment for those attempting to found farm labor unions of any kind. The "Slave Law" turned a civil contract into a public act, which the state had the right to enforce.

It was customary for estate agents to visit hunger-ridden farm workers' sections, carrying some food and a little money. The poor wretches they visited were ready to sign away their souls to the devil for a little food. In this case the devil was the agent who offered the farm worker a little food in one hand and the labor contract in the other. The peasant was unable to understand the complicated legal language, if he could read at all. Under normal conditions the farm worker could have pleaded duress or misrepresentation, but not under the Slave Law. He had to live up to the letter of the obligation, and that was not the worst of it. If for some reason he could not or would not do it, the private contract became a public obligation. The government had the right to throw the farmer into jail for nonfulfillment of his contract. If he failed to appear at his place of work he became a "fugitive," just as his forebears had been in serfdom days. The dreaded gendarmes swung into action.

In 1905 a district's workers struck for a daily wage that was the equivalent of a nickel. The gendarmes were augmented by regular army troops and several strikers were killed. Then it was that the suggestion was made to introduce Chinese labor into Hungary. Then it was, too, that an observer remarked: "Coolie ordinances are more liberal than the Hungarian law. The coolie is exempted from work on days of rest, while the Hungarian farm worker has neither religious nor any other holidays. The coolie's workday lasts only ten hours,

while the Hungarian's lasts from sunrise to sunset. . . . Indeed, the Hungarian farm worker has good reason to envy the
coolie!"

Farm servants—household workers—were brought under
even more stringent rules in 1907. The law passed in that year
provided that the standard contract must run for at least
a year and that, barring exceptions, the workers lost the right
to leave their jobs during that period. They were liable to
fine and jail—up to sixty days in the workhouse—if they refused to work. They also rendered themselves liable for
damages caused by negligence and disobedience, which were
determined by the boss. In everything but name, this was
involuntary servitude. Sometimes there were not enough jails
for farm labor, and then barns had to be transformed into
places of detention.

The Hungarian landowners had an ironclad organization,
O.M.G.E., National Hungarian Landowners' Association, not
only a superlobby but also an unofficial government. Preach-
ing patriotism, and calling everybody a "Socialist" (the term
"Communist" was not popularly used then) who disagreed
with its extreme measures, it was indefatigable in bringing
about the social revolution that assumed the shape of mass
emigration.

There were, of course, public-spirited people on the opposite side, who were outspoken in their condemnation of
these conditions. But for them, the conditions themselves
would have gone unnoticed. In the Hungarian Upper House,
Count J. de Mailáth said: "Three out of ten emigrants will
tell you: 'I am leaving this country because there is no justice
here.' Our government is indeed Asiatic." An attorney for
the Hungarian Association of Manufacturers, David Papp,
stated: "Laws such as the Domestic Servants' Act and the
language employed in Parliament in regard to these classes
of people are doing far more damage [from the point of view
of emigration] than the travel agents."

Eventually the government set up a farm employment service and made provisions for farmers to buy tools. It also lent its help to farm workers' co-operatives. The ministry of agriculture established a free legal advice bureau for farm workers.

Hungary had a Parliament, and legislatures operated through the party system. Was there a peasant party in Hungary before World War I? It was then a predominantly peasant country. There was no such party until the beginning of this century, and when one emerged it was little more than a one-man affair. Its name was "Independent Socialist Peasant Party," and its "leader"—and chief follower—was András Achim, who had a seat in Parliament. Achim's program was moderate: universal secret ballot, reform of the public administration, progressive taxation, freedom of speech and press, social legislation for the peasant. He was cautious about land reform and asked merely that estates in excess of ten thousand acres should be distributed among the landless peasants.

Achim was not subtle and he knew it. "More refined people," he said, "may employ subtler ways. The geese of the Capitol of Rome could not utter as lovely sounds as the nightingales, and yet it was the geese that saved eternal Rome. The Romans heeded the warning and did not mind the sound."

Talking about the Hungarians' plight, he said: "The prevailing order is designed for birth, privilege, and wealth. Inferior brains rule the land while competent heads are wasted in foul workshops."

He was denounced as a rabble-rouser and a traitor. His answer was: "The ruling classes have instigated a political hunt against me to keep me—a man of the people—from speaking about the sufferings of the people and the sinful negligence of the ruling classes." He was a violent man and had a violent end: he was murdered, although not for political reasons.

The Industrial Proletariat

Only 16 per cent of the population of Hungary was engaged in industries, transportation, trade, and mining at the turn of the century. The census spoke of half a million industrial units, but that was a grandiloquent statement, since about two-thirds of them employed one worker each. Not more than one-half of one per cent employed more than twenty workers. One-fifth of the industrial enterprises was classified as restaurants and cafés. In 1870 Hungary's industrial population amounted to 776,000, which increased to 992,000 in 1890 and to 1,297,000 in 1910.

Hungary's industries were new and should have been social-minded, since they were not burdened with the heritage of a long tradition. We have the testimony of a shrewd American observer about the plight of the Hungarian industrial worker early in this century. Samuel Gompers, for several decades head of the American Federation of Labor, studied labor conditions in Europe in 1909 and visited Hungary among other countries.

"In few civilized countries," Gompers wrote, "are the trade unions weaker than in Hungary. There are only about 100,000 members." The country, including Croatia, had then about 20,000,000 inhabitants. Gompers went on to point out that, with at least 4,000,000 who under manhood suffrage could guide the state democratically, only 800,000 had the franchise. In the trade unions not one man in twenty had the right to vote. "With regard to landed property," he was told by one of his Hungarian advisers, "we are in the condition of France before her revolution. With regard to child labor, we are in the position of England prior to 1830." The Social Democratic Party, he observed, had not a single member in Parliament. When the railway train of his little group passed a penitentiary, a Hungarian said: "In that building are robbers, murderers, and Socialists."

By way of contrast, American labor's "Grand Old Man" mentioned the fact that a New York hod carrier earned as much per day as a Hungarian one was paid for an entire week. In Hungary's leading industry, milling, wages ran from fifty-five to eighty-five cents a day, which was not bad. Unlike most of the other trades, printing was 95 per cent organized, but it was forbidden to collect strike funds. The union sought to circumvent this injunction by collecting the equivalent of five dollars a year from its members for the subscription of a union newspaper, a modest little sheet worth only a fraction of the sum. The rest of the money was set aside as an unauthorized strike fund.

"Such squalor, such composites of all things to be classed as dirt, such indiscriminate heaping together of human beings," Gompers wrote, "I have never seen elsewhere. . . . Places cost the miserable poor occupants more per square foot of space than were paid by a prosperous artisan in an American city for his home, with all its civilized accommodations."

Information from Hungarian sources presented the following picture. The average weekly wage of the better-paid industrial worker was four dollars a week. Early in this century 40 per cent of the industrial establishments began work at five o'clock in the summer and six in the winter. Less than 6 per cent began their working day at seven-thirty. Quitting time was six in more than 60 per cent of the establishments, while 21 per cent closed at seven in the summer and 13 per cent in the winter.

Official inspectors noted these conditions: "Employers have no understanding of the necessity of employee protection, and the authorities themselves are not strict enough about regulations. . . . In certain places there is not even a toilet. . . . Medical help is inadequate. . . . Authorities do not bother to

inquire into the causes of accidents. . . . Few employers are
humane."

The basic industrial employment act was passed in 1884,
and it forbade the employment of minors under sixteen in
industries injurious to health, and prohibited employers to
work women at night and for four weeks after confinement.
The working day was not to begin before 5:00 A.M. nor end
after 9:00 P.M. Half-hour periods of rest were to be given
workers in the forenoon and afternoon. The lunch period
was one hour. Sickness and accident insurance for workers
was introduced in 1891, in the footsteps of Germany, the
pioneering nation in this field.

Unions were legal on paper but had to be authorized by
the government before they were allowed to operate, and
were placed under strict supervision. Strikes were forbidden
if they were in violation of labor contracts, and unions were
not to give financial aid to strikers. Violence and intimidation
in industrial disputes were punishable offenses. The authorities were invested with the right to supervise union activities.
They could look into their books and attend their meetings.

The laws governing the activities of industrial workers were
less drastic than those relating to farm labor. Hungarian industry was not yet strong, and the ruling landed interests
looked askance at the manufacturers. Status was conferred
upon a person by landholding, and the government was in
the hands of the large estates. Yet the regime could not afford
to liberalize the laws relating to industrial workers too much
for fear of creating an undesirable precedent for farm labor.

The Worker's Way of Life

How did the industrial worker live? On an average he spent
forty cents a week on his lodging, and what a lodging it was!
A French delegate at the Eighth International Congress of
Hygiene and Sanitation in 1896 had to tell his Hungarian

hosts that "among all the large European cities the worst conditions prevailed in Budapest."

The Hungarian capital was one of the most beautiful cities in Europe, if not the most beautiful. The magnificence of some of its public buildings was unsurpassed. Some of the best-dressed people of the Continent thronged its fashionable streets. The Danube Embankment was a dream, and Margareten Island had no peer. But behind this radiant façade misery was rampant. In 1890 one-quarter of the population of the capital lived in cellars. More than 10 per cent of the lodgings had no kitchen, so that the living quarters had to be used for cooking. More than 40 per cent lived in lodgings inhabited by more than five persons per room. At the turn of the century nearly 60 per cent of the Budapest flats consisted of only one room and kitchen, and even two decades later the percentage was 53. Four-room flats were described in official bulletins as "large." It was common practice in Budapest to let beds out for the night to the *ágyrajáró*, bedgoer.

Conditions were worse outside of the capital. For years after World War I there were troglodytes on the outskirts of Budapest, where industrial workers lived in caves. This was, of course, partly due to emergency conditions. In the country's second largest city, Szeged, it was reported at the turn of the century that 72 per cent of the flats had only one room. In the supposedly rich city of Kecskemét, in the heart of the country, the ratio of such flats was 76 per cent, and the respective figures were 81 and 86 per cent in the capital's industrial suburbs, Ujpest and Erzsébetfalva.

A computation shows that the industrial worker's weekly breakfast bill came to thirty-five cents, his lunch—the main meal—to eighty-five cents, and his supper to seventy cents. These expenditures and his rent almost exhausted his weekly wages. He needed money for clothing, the payment of debts and taxes, and transportation, not to speak of entertainment. How did he manage? Perhaps he did not. He may have sup-

plemented his frugal fare by foraging expeditions to rural kins
folk, or his wife and children may have worked. It was a very
hard struggle. Most of the amenities of life which the Western worker takes for granted were not available to the Hungarian. He carried on as long as he could. There were
compensations, of course. The setting of Budapest was exceptionally beautiful, and it cost no money to climb the hills on
Sundays.

Leaving the Native Land

The people themselves, especially the peasants, attempted
to find a solution. One of the most radical ones was known
under the quaint name of *egyke* system. *"Egy"* means "one"
in Hungarian, and *"ke"* is a diminutive. Translated, the word
means "the one little one." In entire districts, parents produced only one child. This was a unique situation in a
Catholic country, so much under the influence of the clergy.
Characteristically, the system spread in regions where the
peasants' economic condition was not the worst.

More important from the national point of view was the
wave of emigration which struck Hungary. The bulk of the
emigrants went to the United States. Immigration statistics
began with three lone Hungarian immigrants in 1871. Three
years later the figure rose to 1347 but dropped down again
to three-figure numbers until 1880, when, with 4364 immigrants, the rush began. If we were to represent immigration
to the United States by a graph, we would now be in the foot-
hills, rising gradually in the next two years, reaching 11,240
in 1883, then 14,798 in the following year. The figures shot
up precipitately to 54,767 in 1900, and then rose tremen-
dously and irrepressibly. The top was reached in 1907, an
all-time Hungarian immigration peak, with 193,460, almost
1 per cent of the total population in one single year—a tremendous loss of blood for Hungary. The grand total of immigrants from Hungary between 1871 and 1913 amounted

to 1,893,647. Only a small per centage of these people returned to Hungary, to buy land and settle there again. The
number of those who returned during the period from 1908 to
1930 was about 161,000.

Certain parts of Hungary were being depopulated, as if the
blight had struck that region. At first the authorities were not
seriously concerned. The emigrants were mainly peasants,
after all. Also their remittances to their Hungarian kinsfolk
ran into high figures. Besides, those who left might have
become troublemakers. But when the emigration assumed
mass proportions, the authorities began to be concerned. "It
is hard to understand," an official publication mourned,
"why workers leave this country, since conditions here are
good."

"It is a sad fact," the Hungarian Chamber of Industry
lamented, "that the population of our country has been
decreasing at an alarming rate during the last few years. . . .
Because of this huge emigration not only are we unable to
develop our industries but even our existing plants are faced
with the possibility of having to shut down."

The effect of the tidal wave of emigration affected the recruiting into the armed services. More thoughtful officials
reflected that the emigrants represented the more enterprising
portion of the population, an additional loss. Also, as the
number of people was being depleted, the labor market sup-
ply-and-demand equation was upset. There were fewer workers, and wages began to rise, slowly but irresistibly. The official
mind fastened itself upon "propaganda" and blamed the
travel agents for the exodus. Laws were passed to keep the
agents away from the people—the old method of curing
cancer with skin salve. It did not work. What would have
happened to Hungary's population problem if the World
War had not broken out? When the war was over the United
States shut the gates to people like the Hungarians, con-

sidered to be an "inferior breed." The Hungarian quota was very small.

The Hungarian Dream

Now the question may be asked: What happened to the Hungarian dream of a free, independent, gallant country in Europe's East pursuing its advanced Western ways? Beginning with the Liberal Party, through the Coalition and the National Party of Work, to the end of the First World War, the Magyar ruling classes pursued a policy which could be called neither progressive nor advanced. It was a class policy for the few and by the few. What was the explanation?

It was the tragedy of pre-World War I Hungary that it lacked the foundations on which the stablest regimes of modern times have been established, a strong middle class generating an intelligent leadership aware of the interlinked interests of the entire nation. Hungary had middle-class individuals, but no middle class as a cohesive unit. The social polarization of Hungary was extreme. We have seen the higher class centering around the landed aristocracy, supremely self-confident, rooted in traditions, considering itself the sole carrier of the national ideals. It was this class that did indeed represent that ideal, the great symbol, the all-pervasive *mystique*.

It would have been so much better for Hungary if she had had a dynasty of her own, such as the Austrians had. Such a dynasty could have afforded to sit back, survey the scene, serve as an umpire, a balancing element, maintaining a kind of balance of power among the social classes. It would have been in the interest of such a dynasty not to let the vested interests of one group grow to enormous proportions, thus upsetting the balance, endangering its position. It was because the House of Austria performed this function in the Austrian part of the Dual Monarchy that it developed far more democratic institutions than the Hungarians, even under the reign of Franz Joseph I, the "last of the Caesars."

It was the function of the gentry to uphold the aristocratic and autocratic traditions. The aristocracy gave the direction and provided the supervision; the gentry transformed
policies into deeds. Facing the monolithic forces of the aristocracy combined with the gentry were the ineffective intellectuals, many of whom were of the Jewish faith.

The ruling classes looked down upon the peasants and
factory workers as the professional "white man" of Mississippi
looked down upon the Negro. When the Hungarian aristocrat
orated about the glories of the nation, he had no vision of
the farm laborer or factory hand. To him, the nation was still
the prerevolutionary bulwark of privilege, which excluded the
great masses of unwashed people.

There was some criticism of these traditional ways, sometimes voiced in the press. However, in order to be tolerated
it had to be both vague and academic. Writers who moved
beyond the dividing line soon found themselves in jail. Worse
than that, they were shunned by the public opinion the ruling classes created, and became social outcasts.

Why were the lines so tautly drawn in Hungary, of all
countries? Again the answer was the problem of nationalities.
There were more non-Magyars than Magyars, and these latter
considered their national ways endangered. The ruling class
was therefore not only "legal" Hungary but the nation in
arms, holding the beleaguered fort against the onslaughts of
the embattled nationalities. Opposing the guard on the national ramparts was tantamount to giving comfort to the foe.
Whoever opposed the bearers of the national ideal opposed
the ideal itself.

The Hungarian ruling classes would have been taken aback
if it had been suggested that they, and not the Socialists,
were *hazátlan bitangok*, outlaws without a fatherland. History
was to show that it was their selfishness and inability to see
any other view that thrust Hungary into the abyss.

CHAPTER 7   THE BEGINNING AND THE END

"THE PIG WAR" was thought to have been a cause of the Great War. Austria-Hungary introduced protective customs duties in 1908 and lowered the quota of hog imports from Serbia. The ostensible object of this measure was the support of domestic hog prices in Hungary. The Serbs felt that the Monarchy was pushing them into a corner, and this feeling stimulated the actions of the "Black Hand"—*Crna Ruka*—a superpatriotic terroristic organization in Serbia.

The historian knows today that the "Pig War" was only one factor, and not a basic one, that precipitated the war. He knows that the basic causes of the World War were far more deeply seated.

This is not the place to go into the details of those causes. It should suffice to say that in the view of many observers, which this book's writer shares, the modern state system is organized anarchy in foreign relations, and as long as this anarchy continues wars are bound to explode, not because people want them but because they do not know how to stop them.

Count Stephen Tisza, Hungary's Prime Minister at the time the war broke out, did not want it. This the world did not know at the time. It may be said that he opposed the war for the wrong reasons, but the fact is that he did oppose it. He did not want it because he feared that additional Slavs in the Dual Monarchy would upset the balance in Hungary's disfavor between its two component parts. During the war he was eager to miss no chance of making peace. He opposed German aspirations for territorial acquisitions and the introduction of unlimited submarine warfare. He was strongly opposed to the German idea of an economic "Mittel Europa."

There were no leading Hungarians in the "War Party" which pressed for war with Serbia. It was headed by Field Marshal Franz Conrad von Hötzendorf, the Chief of Staff, who disliked the Hungarians among other reasons, because they did not share his predilection for a preventive war against Serbia.

Throughout the entire war there were hardly any Magyars in the higher echelons of the army. The only Hungarian to play a leading role in the World War history of the Austro-Hungarian armed services was Nicholas Horthy de Nagybánya, who commanded the fleet toward the end of the war.

Two of the Central European powers—the Austro-Hungarian Monarchy and the Ottoman Empire—were dynastic structures and not national states. In both cases authority rested on the ruling families themselves, not as symbols—as in the case of the European monarchies today—but as the carriers of historic traditions, the incarnations of the peoples' ambitions, and the executors of their wills. The German-Swiss Habsburgs were a-national, since they could not afford to identify themselves with any single group of the large number of national identities over which they ruled. Their German-speaking subjects formed a small minority in the Monarchy. The Turkish Osmanlis were in a similar situation. They ruled over a country in which Arabs, Armenians, Greeks,

Kurds, and many others formed the majority while the Turks were in a minority. The two dynastics were remnants of another age.

The discrepancy between the legacy of the past and the requirements of the present in the Habsburg realm was large indeed. The great Italian patriot, Giuseppe Mazzini, bracketed the Austrian and Turkish empires in the first part of the nineteenth century as "two serpents that paralyze Europe's heart."

Long before the outbreak of the World War, the condition of the Habsburg empire was seen with remarkable perspicacity in unexpected places. There was, for instance, the German writer, K. A. Postl, writing under the pseudonym of Charles Sealfield about American life and adventure, who saw Austria as a "great agglomeration of provinces" that could not long endure. Equally prophetic was the insight of the French statesman and writer, Comte Charles de Montalembert, who thus spoke on the dais of the French Parliament in 1848: "The Austrian Monarchy is a bizarre composition of twenty nations which justice may have sustained but which injustice will push into ruin."

Napoleon III expressed a very strong view on the subject. He called Austria a corpse with which nobody could make a contract. Consistently inconsistent, he made a contract with Austria—which, however, did not help either of them. And there was also Karl Marx expressing a strongly unorthodox view about Austria. He could not have foreseen at the time that Austria's then neighbor, Russia, would become one day the bulwark of Marxism. In 1860 Marx wrote that the only justification for Austria's existence was her resistance to Russia.

Imperial Rebels and Others

There were, however, several members of the House of Austria who were apprehensive that a dynastic state was an an-

achronism in the midst of the modern nation-states. One of
them was Crown Prince Rudolph, promising son of Emperor-
King Franz Joseph I, who did not like the way his father ran
the country and who foresaw the inevitable necessity of
modernizing the monarchy. Political frustration, in the face of
paternal resistance, aggravated the mental condition that led
to the tragic scene of the Mayerling hunting lodge, where his
dead body and that of his young inamorata were found—
victims of an apparent suicide pact.

The next heir to the Austro-Hungarian throne was neither
brilliant nor even pleasant. He was Archduke Franz Ferdinand. Yet he too felt that the Dual Monarchy was a historic
anachronism. He was planning to replace the dualism with
a trialism, under which either Bohemia or the monarchy's
South Slav regions were to join Austria and Hungary as the
third member. It was one of history's tragic paradoxes that
he was murdered by South Slav "patriots" working for the
"Black Hand." His death set off the chain reaction that resulted in the Great War.

The author of this book had a worm's-eye view of the
dissolution of the Austro-Hungarian Monarchy within the
limited purview of the muddy trenches of the Volhynian
battlefront of southwest Russia in June, 1916. A very young
man in those days, a *Kadettaspirant* (warrant officer) in the
Austro-Hungarian army, he was in the first line when the
Russians launched their major project, the Brusilov Offensive,
named after General Aleksey Alekseyevich Brusilov.

At the height of the offensive the author was sent into
the most advanced position of the fighting line, no doubt
because he was the youngest and least-experienced officer.
His task was simply to take his handful of men and save the
Austro-Hungarian Monarchy. This he was perfectly willing
to do, except that his Czech comrades-in-arms had been there
ahead of him, marking each dugout with obvious identifica-
tion marks for enemy attention. The young officer heard only

after the war about the famous statement of Georges Clem-
enceau, the French Premier: "Generals are too stupid to be
entrusted with the conduct of wars." Anticipating this
thought of the French "Tiger," the writer had his own ideas
about the intelligence of Austrian generals. They had broken
up Czech units in the Austro-Hungarian army. The Czechs
had lost their country to the Habsburgs centuries before and
were now trying to regain it by turning against their masters
wherever they could—including the trenches—and helping the
Russians. So the Austrian generals had broken up those Czech
units and "diluted" the Czechs by assigning them to "loyal"
Austrian and Hungarian regiments. Thus they made it sure
that the identifying marks that were to help the Russians
would be distributed all over the battlefields.

This incongruity between the Habsburg dynastic structure
and the national organization of the world was the basic cause
of the tragedy that was to befall the Dual Monarchy in the
war. And it was no coincidence that a similar tragedy was also
to befall the Ottoman Empire.

The rule of the "Last of the Caesars," Franz Joseph I,
was unique not only in his House but also in world history.
When he ascended the throne in 1848 it must have looked
little different in many ways from what it had appeared in
the Middle Ages. Technical sciences were still in their in-
fancy, and the relation of ruling man to serving man was
still medieval. To the Emperor-King the words "By the Grace
of God" were living reality, not an empty phrase.

In the welter of amazing transformations the Emperor-
King witnessed, not the least remarkable was the change in
the character of his own reign. This change was due to the
altered climate of public opinion. It was he who signed the
death warrants of the "Arad martyrs" in 1849, and it was he
who opened the dynasty's gates to the solemn enthronement
of the remains of the two men who had dethroned his own
dynasty and himself: Rákóczi and Kossuth. He had come in

as a sanguine tyrant and went out as a semi-constitutional monarch. This was an even more dramatic contrast than the technical terminal points of his reign—the stagecoach and the airplane.

After a rule of sixty-eight years, Emperor-King Franz Joseph I died on November 21, 1916. He was followed by his grand-nephew, Charles I (1887–1922), Emperor of Austria *(Kaiser Karl)* and Charles IV *(Károly Király)* King of Hungary. Not only in the tenures of office but also in the two monarchs' temperaments, the greatest extremes met. Charles was to rule for only two years. He was a product of the twentieth century, concerned with public opinion, alive to the new forces of nationalism. He was a young man of good will, modest and not quite sure of himself. His critics called him weak. He found the military situation of the Central European powers hopeless, in spite of the fact that in all major theaters of war they were deep in the enemies' lands. The Germans carried almost the sole burden of war on the side of the Central European Alliance, and they showed themselves so superior in the art of warfare that they seemed to belong in a class by themselves. Yet the seeds of destruction were within that towering superiority. The Entente powers possessed far greater economic resources, and that was what counted in the end. Also the Entente nations were not disposed to let military superiority decide the ultimate outcome of the war.

Emperor-King Charles was married to Princess Zita, daughter of Duke Robert of Parma, a branch of the Bourbon family. She was one of eighteen children, belonging to a family that lost its throne of the little Duchy of Parma and associated states in 1859. She had no mind to lose another throne. Zita was a strong-willed, high-spirited young woman who exercised a great influence over her husband. She had an elder brother, Prince Sixtus, who had a French education and was a doctor of law, political science, and economics.

When the war broke out he volunteered for French army service, but was rejected because of a French law that barred members of the House of Bourbon from such service. Thereupon he enlisted in the allied Belgian army, where he advanced to the rank of captain of artillery.

The Austro-Hungarian imperial-royal couple thus had a close relative in the armed forces of an enemy nation.* The young monarchs worked out a plan. They approached the Allied governments, offering them the terms of a separate peace for Austria-Hungary. Unfortunately the parleys got stuck in the rigid mechanism of wartime diplomacy, and eventually they broke down completely. The Allies sought to discredit the young monarchs by publishing their correspondence with Prince Sixtus. This caused dissension between Austrians and Germans but brought the end of the war not one step closer.

King Charles saw that Hungary was politically far behind the times, the only country with a basically Western civilization where the common people had no say in their political destinies. The Entente powers professed to fight for a democratic way of life. Austria knew some phases of political democracy, but not so Hungary, where Allied propaganda might work havoc. The King approached Prime Minister Tisza with the idea of sponsoring legislation about the extension of suffrage in the Hungarian Parliament.

Tisza was the product of his environment. He was not one to change his views on such a vital subject, even though the skies were to fall. He sought to convince the King that war conditions were inauspicious for the measure. Also, he informed him that the Hungarians had such an open and frank nature that they abhorred secrecy even in voting. When the King kept on coming back to this point, Tisza resigned. In 1917 he joined his regiment on the fighting front.

* In addition, the brother of Sixtus, Prince Xavier, was a Belgian army captain.

Meanwhile, there emerged in the Budapest Parliament an antiwar group. Its head was Count Mihály Károlyi (*Károlyi Mihály Gróf*), one of the country's richest landowners and a member of a distinguished old aristocratic family. He was a much-traveled and much-read man, thoroughly impregnated with Western ideals. He detested the king of patriotism Count Tisza and his professed compeers. Count Károlyi was married to Countess Catherine Andrássy (*Andrássy Katus Grófnő*), a member of perhaps the most ancient family, which claimed descent from a conqueror under Chief Árpád. She was a radiantly fetching young woman, with strong sympathies for the democratic ways of the French and English, completely Western-oriented. This aristocratic couple was to play a historic role in Hungary.

King Charles now had an ally in the ranks of the Hungarian aristocracy. The Károlyis felt as strongly as the King that a medieval Hungary in the twentieth century was an anachronism. Count Károlyi was in close touch with a group of Hungarian intellectuals, the best-known member of which was Professor Jászi, the nationality expert, whose name we have already encountered.

Károlyi approved of Jászi's plan for the solution of the Hungarian problem, which, as they saw it, revolved around the nationality question. The Jászi solution was based on the assumption that it was desirable to maintain the Monarchy within its boundaries for several reasons, one of which was economic. It was a natural economic unit. The solution of Jászi was to have Hungary converted into a federation of autonomous nationalities—the only means of maintaining her economic and territorial integrity. Hungary was thus to become an Eastern Switzerland. The Károlyis backed this concept. They also made attempts to establish contact with the Allied countries, which, however, were not any more successful than those of the King and Queen.

Meanwhile the two sides in the war, the Central European powers and the Entente, had dug themselves in on the western front, thoroughly exhausted but determined not to yield. The war had been going on for years and the end did not seem to be in view. This was an appalling war of attrition, each side determined to starve the other into submission. The Allied plan was to cut off food from the Central European Powers. The German plan was to destroy the ships that were taking food to Britain.

How long the deadly clinch would have continued if the United States had not joined the war nobody knows. America joined the Entente in the spring of 1917, and it became evident that the Central Powers were doomed. The war dragged on for months, under its own irresistible momentum. It was Count Tisza himself who made the fatal announcement in open Parliament on October 17, 1918: "We have lost the war!"

King Charles had proclaimed an Austrian federative state, but the monarchy was falling apart. The task of forming a new government was entrusted to Károlyi. Hungary and Czechoslovakia declared their independence. The other nationalities set up national councils, preliminary to taking more definite steps. On November 3 Charles consented to Austria's surrender in the armistice agreement his deputies concluded with the Italian General Armando Diaz. Russia, the other antagonist of the Austro-Hungarian Monarchy, had gone Communist.

There was now no way to halt the onrush of events. Charles and Zita had to pay not for their ancestors' sins, but for the disregard of the historic forces that had brought national states into being. The dynastic state of Austria-Hungary was gone. The other dynastic state, that of the Ottoman Empire, also ended with the termination of the war.

On the day on which the incredibly wasteful war ended, November 11—to be known as "Armistice Day"—Charles relinquished his Austrian throne, and two days later he did the same in regard to Hungary. Five days later the Hungarian People's Republic was proclaimed. Full powers were entrusted to a cabinet of which Károlyi was the Premier. It consisted of members of the Károlyi Party, the Social Democrats, and the Radicals (a non-socialist liberal party, mostly of intellectuals). On January 11, 1919, the Hungarian National Council proclaimed Count Károlyi President of the Republic.

The Károlyi Regime

A leading Hungarian aristocrat had involuntarily paved the way for the Hungarian revolution of 1848—Count Széchenyi. Now again it was an "aristocrat of the aristocrats" who took the lead in the great twentieth-century revolution. The Hungarians were in the habit of heeding their magnates' words, and the aristocratic nature of the leadership on both occasions may have been more than mere coincidence. Was Hungary so deeply steeped in aristocracy that even her most prominent democrats had to be aristocrats?

Not only Mid-Danubia but all of Europe was in turmoil. In Hungary, what was be the fate of the Eastern Switzerland? What would be the nationalities' attitude now that their kinsfolk across the hills were on the winning side? Would they secede from Hungary, or would they remain with her now that she was headed by a man who always was the champion of their rights? Then, what was to be the decision of the masters of the world—no longer dukes and princes as on similar occasions in the past—now assembled in Paris to outline the blueprint of the future? They had proclaimed the rules of the new diplomacy—open covenants openly arrived at. The President of the United States, Woodrow Wilson, who had phrased that famous term, was now closeted in his inaccessible chambers of Paris' Hotel Crillon, protected by bayonets from the approach of the public.

The questions had to be answered by other people. Meanwhile, however, Hungary could start giving the answer to her great domestic question. Hungary was still the land of *latifundia*, large estates, and of the mainmort, the dead hand, a country where a decent peasantry could coax no living out of a rich soil because of property conditions. Károlyi himself was the owner of one of the country's largest estates. He decided to tackle land reform.

The decision of the cabinet was to break up the large estates and distribute the land among the landless peasantry. It was also decided to do away with the iniquitous system of the entail, under which large landholdings had to be bequeathed to the next of kin in a rigidly prescribed way. The maximum holding left with the owners was to be five hundred acres, while the remainder was to be distributed in lots of five to twenty acres, depending upon location and quality of the land. The reform was to be similar to those carried out in the adjacent countries.

"The Hungarian landowners," Károlyi was to write later in his *Memoirs* (Dutton, 1957) "who opposed it [the reform] with frenzied bitterness and pursued me with their hatred for decades, are now well aware—as many have admitted to me—that had it been carried out at that time, it would have meant their salvation."

Károlyi began with the distribution of his own lands. However, there was no time to work out a plan nor to carry out the nationwide land reform. Hungary was struck by a lightning which destroyed the millennial foundations of the country.

The nationalities now gave their answer *à propos* of the proposal of an Eastern Switzerland. They recognized that Károlyi and Professor Jászi were men of good will, their friends, and that the plan had merit. But they did not want it. Remaining with Hungary, they would have shared the fate of a defeated and bankrupt nation which was to be called upon to share the costs of the war. Joining their own kinsmen, where they had countries of their own, they switched from

defeat to victory, and they would get reparations, not pay
them. Also, they recalled the Mid-Danubian adage: "A dog
cannot be turned into bacon." Károlyi and Jászi were fine
men, and so had been Deák and Eötvös. However, these latter
were followed by Count Tisza and the other magnates.
Hungary's nationality policy was bankrupt. The land of the
Magyars was to be dismembered, a work that was to be left
to the peacemakers in Paris.

The peacemakers in Paris were now thinking of making
war on the Soviets, the new danger in the East. White Russian armies supported by them were trying to wipe out the
Communists. In support of this new war they wished to secure
the rear of Romania, adjacent to the Soviets. On March 20,
1919, they ordered the Hungarians to withdraw behind a
"neutral zone" that ran through the heart of Hungary, including both Debrecen and the country's second largest city,
Szeged. The eastern border, which Romania was allowed to
occupy, ran well west of the limits of Transylvania. The
territory thus affected was inhabited by Hungarians.

The Allied dictum should have been rejected, but what
could Count Károlyi do when his "friends" the French and
English treated him in such a way? Also, he was subjected
now to a barrage of criticism on the right and left. What was
to be done?

"At this juncture one person came forward with a new
proposal of how Hungary could be saved, the little Bolshevik
agent, Béla Kun, who said that if he were given the power,
Russia would join forces with Hungary and drive the Romanians back." *

In that desperate situation Károlyi wanted to strengthen
his government by taking in the Communists also. Neither
he nor others thought in those days that Béla Kun was "a
little Communist agent." They did think that the Russians

* *October Fifteenth*, by C. A. Macartney, Edinburgh University Press,
Vol. I, p. 22.

might be of some help in preventing the complete dismemberment of Hungary. In situations like this, one cannot be too
selective about one's friends. Also, Bolshevism in Russia was
too new to be fully known in the West. What happened at
that crucial moment was described by Count Károlyi:

"The Ministers of the Károlyi Party had tendered their
resignation, not having the courage to accept or refuse the
ultimatum. I therefore, proposed that the cabinet should resign, after which I would charge the Social Democrats, in
conjunction with the Communists, to form a new government; this proposal was unanimously accepted. . . . It was
unanimously decided that I should stay at my post." *

Only a strong, homogeneous government backed by organized labor which the Communists could also support would
have the authority to reject the Allies' demands. The plan
failed to work. The Social Democrats went over to the Communists and dropped Károlyi. The Count contended in his
Memoirs that he had never turned power over to the Bolsheviks. The new government took over on March 21, 1919.

The Bolshevik Intermezzo

The Socialists now united with the Communists by forming
the "Socialist Party of Hungary." It became the front of the
Workmen's, Peasants', and Soldiers' Council. Since council
means *soviet* in Russian, Hungary now had a soviet system
to execute the will of the proletarian dictatorship. This was a
copy of the Russian state, including its incantations and
bombastic gibberish.

The nominal head of the state was now an old-line Socialist,
Sándor Garbai. Having obtained that decorative post, he
quickly dropped out of the picture, and the real ruler of the
country was Béla Kun.

Before the war Kun studied law, which in Hungary was the
prescribed path to many posts. Then he turned to journalism,

* *Memoirs of Michael Károlyi*, Dutton, 1957, p. 154.

which he forsook for the sake of politics, and he joined the
Socialist Party in Hungary. He was drafted for military service in the Austro-Hungarian army and was captured by the
Russians. Kun fell under the spell of Lenin, the Communist
leader. When the war was over, Kun was released from cap-
tivity and returned to Hungary, where he started organizing
the Communist Party.

He became a very busy agitator and came into conflict
with the Budapest police under the Károlyi regime. They beat
him up and locked him in a jail. From the prison cell he
stepped right into the limelight of supreme power.

Kun had swallowed the full Soviet Russian program, with
little thought of differences in the needs of gigantic Russia
and tiny Hungary. The standard program was to arm, and
transfer all power, land, and industry to, the proletariat. All
banks, large concerns, and estates, and all private property
above a minimum, were nationalized or, as the Hungarians
put it, "communalized." (For years "communalization" in
Hungarian was used as a synonym for theft.) Business came
to a standstill almost overnight. A truck carrying any kind of
goods on the otherwise busy streets of Budapest was a strange
sight in those days. It was a common sight, on the other
hand, to see very young people with shining new brief cases
getting into chauffeur-driven limousines. They were the
"comrades," the new bureaucrats.

The performance of the government was extremely ama-
teurish. It was said—though it could not be proved—that the
Commissar of Finances (secretary of the treasury) had to be
shown how to endorse a check. Industrial goods were unavail-
able, since nearly all stores were closed. The peasants saw no
point in selling food to cities, since they could buy nothing
for their money. Urban people went to the country to engage
in the most primitive form of trade, barter.

The government members were a motley crew: frustrated
intellectuals, adventurers, Napoleons, and terrorists. Not one

of them knew how to behave in a responsible position. A body of "active revolutionaries" set up an organization with the bloodcurdling title: "Terror Detachment of the Revolutionary Government Council."

Béla Kun thought that the government could be carried on by slogans. As the head of the government, supposedly representing the dictatorial proletariat, he was curiously sentimental. When he had to sign the death warrant of even a common murderer he shed tears. He was ready to help anyone who appealed to him personally, while he was advocating cruel reprisals and ruthless terror. Even though the spokesman of the "proletariat," he was uncommonly flattered when the magnates of yesteryear appealed to him for personal favors, and he could not refuse them anything. Many aristocrats were saved through his personal intervention, including an archduke.

The Communists set up a Red army. Some ex-officers of the Austro-Hungarian Monarchy helped in setting it up, partly because it was in line with their normal work and partly because they thought it would help to save their nation. The army stood its ground against the Czechs in northern Hungary. The Allies in Paris ordered the Budapest Communists to evacuate that territory, and with that strange incongruity that was so baffling to contemporaries, they obeyed.

Meanwhile the forces of anticommunism were gathering strength. A national government was first established in the city of Arad, from where it moved to Szeged. French and British representatives of their country's diplomacy and military forces gave a helping hand to the counterrevolutionary regime. Count Károlyi had never got such a help. The Count and Countess meanwhile had fled the Bolsheviks and were now in an exile that was to last for a quarter of a century.

The counterrevolution was gathering strength. The Communist regime was playing out the nationalist card and was engaged in an armed conflict with the Romanians, who, however, defeated them. The Romanian armed forces were now on their way to the Hungarian capital, whereupon the Communist regime fled. Kun made his way to Vienna, where he found temporary sanctuary in a lunatic asylum. From there he skipped to Russia, where he played an important role in the Comintern, Communist International. During the great Soviet purges of the thirties he dropped out of sight— one of its victims.

How many were the victims of the Red regime? The figures computed by the courts of the succeeding regime indicated 234 victims of the terror itself, while 500 people were killed in battles.

The anti-Semitic excesses that followed the Red terror were explained in some quarters by the large number of Hungarians of the Jewish faith who participated in the Communist regime. "Of the eleven people's commissars," says the article on Hungary in the Encyclopaedia Britannica, "eight were Jews, and the local representatives of the Soviets were also largely Jews; this fact was largely responsible for the subsequent outbreak of anti-Semitism in Hungary." A noted team of French writers, Jérôme and Jean Tharaud, were the authors of a book dealing with the same subject under the revealing title: *When Israel Is King*.

At the same time Hungarians of the Jewish faith were also among the many victims of the Red regime. They were the main losers in the nationalization of the banks, industries, and trade. The Communists were particularly opposed to trade, which they considered "parasitic" and which they all but abolished.

While prewar Hungary had not treated the Jews too badly, they were still a minority and received such treatment. They were kept out of many walks of life, and especially the government. In some of the intellectual Jews particularly, this treatment caused a strong revulsion.

More important than this, the old regime had given no

chance to the middle of the road to develop a program and to try to put it into effect. Only the aristocrats and their gentry satellites had governmental experience. When the old regime was thoroughly discredited, there was nobody qualified to assume the responsibilites of government. Ideological adventurers were quick to fill the vacuum thus created.

The Counterrevolution

Besides the government in Szeged, there was also a government headed for a few days by Julius Peidl, a Socialist. He was succeeded by Stephen Friedrich, who stood on a strictly counterrevolutionary program of retribution for past sins and a return to the main tenets of the old regime.

Friedrich had been on the team of Count Károlyi. He made up for his past record by applying the most opprobrious epithets to the Count. Since the past of Friedrich inspired little confidence and he was little known, he needed the mantle of respectability. In aristocratic-minded Hungary he went directly to the holder of the highest title, Archduke Joseph of the House of Habsburg, who had lived in Hungary as a representative of the House of Austria. The Habsburg was to serve Friedrich as his link with the past, the guarantee of continuity and legitimacy.

This turned out to be a very bad calculation. The states that were now set up on the territory of the former Austro-Hungarian Monarchy, the so-called Succession States, wanted to have nothing to do with Habsburg. They were thinking of the history of the family and not of the good-natured former imperial couple, Charles and Zita, living in Switzerland. The very name of Habsburg was anathema to the Succession States. The Allied great powers spoke for their little friends in Mid-Danubia when they ordered the Archduke to step down. Without this support, Friedrich, a political adventurer, could not maintain himself. The road was now open to the Szeged government.

Hungary now reverted to the habits of the past. The Szeged government drew its strength from the support of such old-line aristocrats as Count Gyula Károlyi (an opponent of Mihály) and Count István Bethlen. Both of them were to become prime ministers in years to come.

Authority had to be backed by physical power, and the Szeged cabinet looked around for ways to establish a national army. The eyes of the counterrevolutionary government fell on Rear Admiral Nicholas Horthy de Nagybánya (1868–1957)—Nagybányai Horthy Miklós—whom they asked to serve as Minister of War and Commander-in-Chief of the Hungarian National Army. This was the beginning of the "Age of Horthy," which was to endure for a quarter of a century.

The Age of Horthy

Horthy belonged to the Hungarian landed gentry, a family with a seventeenth-century patent of nobility and an ancestral mansion on the Hungarian plains. He had started his career as a naval officer in the Austro-Hungarian navy and had his first sea experience in sailing vessels. As a naval attaché of the Monarchy he had an opportunity of seeing much of the work and cultivating valuable friendships. In 1909 he became an aide-de-camp of Emperor-King Franz Joseph, at which post he remained for five years.

During the war Horthy distinguished himself in the Battle of the Otranto Straits, at the entrance to the Adriatic. At the end of the war he was commander of the Austro-Hungarian fleet, and it was his sad task to turn over its units to the victors.

Horthy organized his national army in western Hungary, which was free of Romanian troops of occupation. The Romanians looted the capital thoroughly, and it took some time before the Entente in Paris could induce them to leave Budapest. Finally they left the capital on November 14, 1919, and

retired to the line of the Tisza River. On November 16
Horthy moved into Budapest at the head of his new army.
He sketched in the background of the forthcoming regime
in answer to the mayor's address of welcome: "This city dis-
owned her millennial tradition, dragged the Holy Crown and
the national colors in the dust, and clothed itself in rags. . . .
We shall forgive this misguided city if it turns from the false
gods to the love of our fatherland . . . if it reveres the Holy
Crown once more, if it reveres the Double Cross, the Three
Hills, the Four Rivers—in short, our Hungarian Fatherland
and our Hungarian people." *

The White Terror

The counterrevolution was not yet in full power. The Entente
was anxious to prevent excesses and to see the basis of the
Hungarian government broadened. It sent to Budapest a
mediator in the person of Sir George Clarke, who arranged
a coalition government which included not only politicians
of the old school but also representatives of the Smallholders
and National Democrats, and one Social Democrat. This
government took office on November 24, and it was to act as
a caretaker until elections were held.

However, the moderating influence of the Entente did not
reach far below the top level. "As soon as the field was clear,
more or less unofficial 'bands' had set out over the country,
meting out lynch law to some who, if brought to proper trial,
should have incurred judicial punishment and others whose
fault had been trivial or nonexistent, also to many whose
offense was simply that of belonging to the same race as Kun
and the bulk of his commissars." †

Hungary was ahead of all the rest of the world in introducing a system which later became known under its Italian

* The three hills and four rivers were represented on the old Hungarian
shield, parts of millennial and not of truncated Hungary.
† Macartney, *op. cit.* Vol. I, p. 23.

name of *fascism*. Its substance was worship of the nation and punishment for nonconformism. However, Hungary's fascism was different from those of the other countries, where they aimed also at a certain measure of equalitarianism under the supreme ruler, Il Duce, Der Führer, or El Caudillo. The Hungarian government authorized the internment of any person who "might present a danger to public order," even if not guilty of an indictable offense. Many thousands of persons were interned under this order, including nearly all the more prominent Social Democrats who had not escaped abroad. The Social Democrats thereupon declared that they would abstain from participation in the elections.

During the war there had come into existence an association known as *Ebredő Magyarok*—Awakening Hungarians. They remained dormant, during much of the war but did awaken after Horthy had marched his troops into Budapest. The name of the organization implied that Hungary had not been awake to the "Jewish danger" but was now taking steps to bring it to the country's attention. The Awakening Hungarian was to Hungary what the post–First World War Ku Klux Klan was to the American South.

Several other "patriotic" and secret societies sprang into life under the early Horthy regime. One of the most important ones of these was the MOVE, *Magyar Országos Véderő Egylet*—Hungarian Association of National Defense—which was both counterrevolutionary and anti-Semitic. The official Hungarian statistics, which took no notice of the secret organizations, recorded that 22 patriotic organizations were founded in 1919, not fewer than 101 in 1920, 40 in 1921, and 49 in 1922. Two of the secret societies deserve, however, to be mentioned: the first one because it appears to be the first governmentbacked "racial" organization in postwar Central Europe. It had a revealing name, *Magyar Tudományos Fajvédő Egyesület*—Hungarian Scientific Race-Protecting Society. It was organized on the pattern of the early Hungarian tribes. There were seven leaders, corresponding to the seven Magyar leaders under Árpád the Conqueror. The other organization was of a military nature and was called *Kettős Kereszt Szövetség*—Society of the Double Cross—because of the Cross of Lorraine represented in the Holy Crown. Its aim was to further military education for the recovery of Hungary's lost lands.

Terror swept the country from one end to another. Again, as in the past, the informer was king, the infallible guardian of virtue. Not only the Communists but also the Social Democrats were persecuted. To engage in Communist activities was considered a capital offense. Terrorists in military uniforms constituted drumhead courts executing people, sometimes with no evidence of guilt. When foreign journalists called Horthy's attention to the excesses of these judges, he told them: "They are some of my best officers."

The Hungarian government introduced *numerus clausus* in schools of higher learning. Jewish students were to be admitted to them only in proportion of the Jews to the country's total population. This was iniquitous to the Jews because of their background, and also because they were not employed by the government and in occupations where the authorities' approval was required.

This phase of the Hungarian White terror indirectly affected the rest of the world, and especially the United States. As a result of the Hungarian government's attitude some of the most gifted scholars were forced out of the country.

The Hungarian language has a picturesque word for genius, calling it *lángelme*—flaming mind. Many of the emigrant scientists had "flaming minds," and many of them found their way to the United States. It was some of them who called attention, for instance, to the wartime potentialities of atomic weapons. These ex-Hungarian physicists, mathematicians, and others played a truly historic role in the development of atomic and hydrogen arms. What a strange turn of fate it was that the anti-Semitic laws of Hungary should

have helped the United States to acquire these supreme
weapons!

A Kingdom Without a King

The Hungarian regime was seriously concerned with the problem of legitimacy. It had seized power from the Communists,
but naturally could not recognize that as the source of its
authority. Nor did it want to claim descent from the regime
of the "renegade" Count Károlyi. At the same time, it could
not reach back into the Habsburg era because of the Allied
ukase. How, then, was legitimacy to be safeguarded?

The answer was given by the National Assembly, whose
members had been selected under Allied auspices. First it
decided to sever the union with Austria and to declare that
the Compromise of 1867 was no longer valid. Then it decided
that the king's prerogatives should thenceforth be considered
dormant. But Hungary's government institutions, courts, and
armed services were to be designated as "royal."

On March 1, 1920, Admiral Nicholas Horthy was elected
Regent Governor of Hungary. "Regent" meant one "who
governs a kingdom in the minority, absence, or disability of
the sovereign." His prerogatives were enumerated in detail.
He was *Legfelsőbb Hadúr*—Most Supreme War Lord.* The
declaration of war and conclusion of peace, however, required legislative sanction. He had the right to convene and
dissolve Parliament and to initiate bills. The Regent appointed the ministry. His person was inviolable, and he was
given the title *Főméltóságú*—Serene Highness—just one grade
below Majesty. His residence was the Royal Palace.

What had induced the kingmakers to invest Horthy with
the supreme power? He was known as a dependable conservative, a *solid* man, with no entrenched vested interests. He had
not been in politics and was not the target of political jealousy.

---

* "Hadúr"—war lord—was supposed to have been the name of the
ancient Magyars' war god.

He had the name of a blunt man of arms, an honest man. He was acceptable to the Budapest Allied representatives. He looked distinguished, as a head of state should look, and his family life was impeccable. It is true that he was a Protestant in a predominantly Catholic country, but that was not unusual in Hungary. Besides, his wife was a Catholic. He had been an aide-de-camp of Franz Joseph and was thus a link between old and new.

Nem, Nem, Soha

The Hungarian Peace Treaty was finally signed on June 4, 1920, in the Grand Trianon Palace of Versailles and hence became known as the Treaty of Trianon. Before the war, Hungary, including Croatia, had 125,000 square miles, of which she now lost 71 per cent—89,100 square miles. Also, she lost 60 per cent of her prewar population of 21,000,000. Hungary lost 88 per cent of her timber, 61 per cent of the arable land, 83 per cent of pig-iron production, and 56 per cent of industrial plants. Hungary's territory was now 35,900 square miles, and her population was 7,614,000. Romania received Hungary's Transylvania, a part of the adjacent plains, and part of the rich Banat in the south. Czechoslovakia received all of northern Hungary—Slovakia and Ruthenia. Yugoslavia acquired most of the south of Hungaria, Croatia, Slavonia, part of the Banat, and the fertile Backa. Austria was awarded a slice of western Hungary—Burgenland. Even the Poles and Italians received slivers of Hungary. Besides the nationalities, some three million Hungarians were transferred to foreign rule. Hungary lost her access to the sea. A professional army of 35,000 was all she could keep.

"These losses," said C. A. Macartney in *Hungary and Her Successors* "were proportionately far greater than those inflicted on Germany and Bulgaria." Neighboring Austria, another loser, could at least consider herself part of the great German fatherland. But Hungary, the "orphan nation," stood

all alone in the world, with no kinsfolk anywhere near Danubia. She stood "naked," despoiled of her raiment, that magnificent protective cloak of mountain ranges. The kingdom that
had withstood the Tatar and the Turk, the Habsburg Empire,
and great power jealousies, was now little more than an
agonized carcass on which, Hungarian superpatriots said,
the "vultures" were feasting. And who were these human
vultures? They were the very creatures that had served the
Magyars and upon whom many of them looked down
with the loftiest disdain. They were the Slovaks, of whom the
Magyar adage said: A *tót nem ember*—The Slovak is not human—and they were the Romanians, whom the thoroughbred Magyar never honored with that designation. That would
have implied his recognition of the claim that these people
were descendants of the Romans. Hungarian supernationalists
called the Romanians *Oláh*, corruption of the word "Wlach,"
and often added: *bocskoros oláh*—moccasined Wlach—unable
to afford decent shoes.

The entire country resounded with the defiant motto:
"*Nem, nem, soha*"—No, no, never. It was carved into bronze
and marble, set on hilltop and the Danube banks. More than
that, it was impregnated into millions of minds. These were
the words the entire world was to learn, often the only Magyar words it knew. It became the political program of all
parties, the creed of all Hungarians:

> I believe in one God;
> I believe in one Fatherland;
> I believe in Hungary's resurrection.

How was Hungary to regain the lost land? She had no
army and no armor. What was then the sense of all the talk?
It made Hungary's neighbors close their ranks, formulate
plans of defense, negotiate mutual defense pacts. The Little
Entente of the main beneficiaries of the Treaty of Trianon

came into existence: Czechoslovakia, Romania, Yugoslavia. Was the Hungarian policy realistic?

It was, as Hungarians saw it. Reality must have ideals. All was not lost as long as the principle remained intact.

The Crisis and the King

In the wake of the war and the revolutions, Hungary was visited by an economic crisis. The large estate owners had their money in land; the country was bare of capital. Much of the industrial wealth was held by Hungarians of the Jewish faith, whose future was obscure and who were therefore cautious. Wealthy people transferred their money to foreign countries. Thus came into existence one of the most profitable, although thoroughly unproductive, occupations of the unstable interbellum period, known under its German name as *Schiebung*—shifting—and its hero was the shifter—*Schieber*. Many of them accumulated great wealth and high honors. Meanwhile the Hungarian currency kept wasting away.

The Succession States started building tall turrets of tariff protection around their borders, behind which they were eagerly building their own industries. Before the war Hungary had larger industries than some of her neighbors, and because of the unimpaired size of the country she also had a larger domestic market. Now that market also began to wane, which accentuated the economic crisis.

The country visited by so many plagues was expecting a messianic solution for its woes. Now that the demigods of the Left had failed to provide a solution and the gods of the Right were blundering, a young man in Switzerland was ready to offer himself as the savior.

In the castle of Prangins on Switzerland's Lake Geneva visitors were frequent, and they talked in whispers to the young man and his wife, whom they addressed as "Your Majesties." They spoke of Hungary's misery, the messianic mood of her people, and the two young people's duty to fulfil their mission. He was ex-King Charles and she ex-Queen Zita. In the castle conclaves a plan began to assume shape. The young former monarch derived solace from frequent letters of Regent Governor Horthy. He assured their majesties that he was merely holding their place and would vacate it when circumstances warranted.

Suddenly, and without warning, Charles appeared in Horthy's chambers in the Royal Palace on March 27, 1921, thanked the Regent cordially for having helped him out, and informed him that he now came to perform his royal functions. At the same time, Charles invested Horthy with the Grand Cross of the Military Order of Maria Theresa and conferred upon him the title of Duke of Otranto and Szeged.*

Horthy was as polite as he was categoric. He advised the monarch to leave the country promptly, as the times were not yet ripe for the change. Should a Habsburg restoration occur, he told him plainly, the neighbors would march into Hungary, which was in no position to resist them.

Charles was unprepared for such an answer. He was malleable and weak, prone to heed the latest word he heard. Zita was made of other stuff. If she had been near him the history of the Danube might have taken another turn, but she was not near and Charles was shattered by the refusal. The precious moment which fate sometimes allows for quick rejoinder was gone, and he knew that anything he said would be in vain.

Next day a car with drawn curtains was attached to the Vienna-Zurich Express, and its occupant was a young man who had gone to claim his throne and had been thrown out of his own palace. News spread of the royal fiasco, and as the train stopped at the station of Linz on the Danube, laborers gathered round the curtained car, raising hostile fists.

It was a penitent Charles who was met by a sorrowful Zita

* Otranto was the scene of the famous World War naval engagement, and Szeged was the home of the counterrevolutionary regime.

at the frontier station of Buchs in Switzerland. The Swiss government now considered the ex-royal couple a peril to European security, and the former Allies advised the Swiss to keep a watchful eye on them. The authorities informed Charles and Zita that their permit of sojourn was extended only on condition that they refrained from politics.

Summer came and then the autumn. A bloodless war broke out between Austria and Hungary; its cause, the border region the Allies had deeded to Austria at Hungary's cost. When Vienna wanted to take this strip of land, Hungarian "free corps" resisted. The opposing forces dug themselves in, and some shots were exchanged. On the Hungarian side, Colonel Lehár was an ardent "legitimist," supporter of young King Charles. His envoys had conferred with Charles in Swiss mountain retreats and told him that Horthy's betrayal had aroused the nation and this was the time to come home. His Majesty could count on the colonel's forces, if need be.

Zita was determined to fight, as her religious preoccupations crystallized the issue—a fight between a usurper and the anointed King. This time the decision was for energetic action, well-planned and backed by force. Not even their children knew what they were doing when Zita and Charles motored out of the Swiss castle. Within an hour the occupants of a privately chartered airplane sighted the Danube on their eastward way. The plane landed on an improvised field in western Hungary.

The royal couple spent the night in a loyal aristocrat's house. In three hours they could have reached the capital, but they did not take the train. The local people learned of the sovereigns' dramatic arrival and improvised a torchlight parade. It was only next day that the royal procession got started, and picked up popular ardor as it moved along. By the time they reached Budapest they hoped to have the entire country on their side. The procession took three days. From Budaörs, on the outskirts of the capital, they could see the

Royal Palace on the Danube, and they could also see the trenches their leisurely trip had enabled the Regent's troops to dig.

The country did not rise to the defense of Charles. A few shots were exchanged. Regent Horthy issued a proclamation: "Induced by traitors to their nation, His Majesty took a fateful step. . . ." The second attempt failed to recover the throne for the House of Habsburg. Yugoslavia and Czechoslovakia ordered mobilization. The former King and Queen were guests of the government; they were prisoners. In the monastery of Tihany, overlooking Lake Balaton, the former royal couple occupied two rooms hardly larger than cells. They could pray and look at the enchanting scene at their feet, where precipitous rocks rose out of the lake, but they could not leave the monastery.

What would happen to Charles and Zita? The Swiss government refused to readmit them, insisting they had broken their pledge. The Hungarian government turned to London to provide a minor Saint Helena, and England complied. Before the month of October was over, the destroyer *Glowworm* was on its way to Madeira, their royal exile. In the town of Funchal on that island Charles died of pneumonia the following year.

The Land and Other Reforms

Hungary was now admitted into the comity of nations. The economic rehabilitation of the country was undertaken. A distinguished American lawyer from Boston, Jeremiah Smith, went to Budapest in 1924 as a commissioner of the League of Nations, staying there for two years. Under his guidance Hungary's economic condition was rehabilitated. The government received a League of Nations loan of $50,000,000, the budget was balanced, and the new currency, *pengő*—clinker—replaced the old *korona*.

A large number of new schools were built under Minister

Kuno Klebersberg, especially on the great plains, where the school situation was woeful. Illiteracy, according to government figures, was reduced from 15 per cent when Horthy took over to 4 per cent when the Second World War broke out. Industrialization went on apace. The younger generation in the cities was machine-minded, and the country's technical schools had a good reputation. The capital was further embellished and now attracted a larger number of tourists than ever before.

The unequal distribution of the land, however, continued to be the greatest economic problem of the country. It became even more so when all of Hungary's neighbors started to divide large properties and distributed them among the poorer peasants. The Romanian government distributed about 3,000,000 acres, the Czechs 2,300,000 and the Yugoslavs 2,100,000. These were vast tracts of land in the crowded Danubian world. Of course, the governments in those countries were in position to distribute land which belonged to Hungarian owners.

In 1920 the Hungarian government did introduce a land reform. No two figures as to the extent of this reform agree. Regent Governor Horthy states in his memoirs that about a million acres were distributed under the 1920 act and an additional million was distributed under later land reform acts. These acts were passed in order to counteract the pressure of the agrarian-radical-reform movements, mainly of a Fascist tinge. Also, neither Horthy nor other government sources can give an idea about the nature of the land reform without going into the origin of the land thus distributed and the quality of its soil. Much of the land had belonged to Hungarians of the Jewish faith. Where large estate land was distributed the beneficiaries frequently received inferior tracts, which were liabilities on the owners. In 1930 one-third of the agricultural area was concentrated in about 1500 large tracts, while some 750,000 owners had less than half of the cultivable soil.

Also, the land reform was linked with the ideology of the regime. Those who had displayed military bravery in the war and were of unblemished character were entitled to be admitted into the Military Order of Merit and to use the honorific title of *vitéz*—hero. A hero's standard estate was about sixteen *jochs*, and included a house and stable, two horses, and a cow. The right to inherit such an estate belonged solely to the eldest son. Some three thousand such estates were set up, most of the necessary means of tilling the soil being provided by the state. The object of the government in creating the order of heroes may have been to constitute a reliable praetorian guard for the regime. Besides, this landholding system glorified the military hero's life.

The face of the Hungarian countryside was changed but little as a result of this inadequate distribution of the land. In some respects the peasants were worse off than they had been under the prewar regime. As the Horthy regime settled down, it became more tolerant toward the description of conditions in Hungary, especially if done in books which would not get into peasant hands and therefore could not easily stir up trouble. In the thirties a group of young Hungarian writers went into the villages and farmhouses to investigate conditions. They became known as *falú kutatók*—village explorers—and they wrote up the results of their research in a series of books. The nature of their findings is indicated by the titles of some of the books, such as *The Silent Revolution* —*A Néma Forradalom*—by Imre Kovács, or *The Situation in Tard*—*A Tardi Helyzet*—by Zoltán Szabó. "From the heart of Europe," one of these authors wrote, "you can reach the heart of Asia for the price of a trolley ticket." Another one echoed: "Budapest is an oasis in the wilderness."

In a Hungarian "Middletown," the village of Tard, one of the investigators had the eighth-year pupils of the village school write down what they ate that day. The child of a "wealthy" family, with thirty acres, wrote: "Monday morning I ate grapes, at noon I ate soup, and grapes again in the evening. Tuesday morning: sausage; noon: bacon; evening: milk. Wednesday morning: bread; noon: soup; evening: bread. Sunday morning: grapes; noon: soup; evening: bacon."

The eleven-year-old daughter of a peasant with eight acres wrote: "Bread for Wednesday morning, bread for noon, and noodles for supper. Bread for Thursday breakfast, soup for dinner, and bread for supper. . . . I don't eat meat because we haven't got it." A little boy bragged: "Once I ate an egg and it was very good. I'd like to eat an egg again."

In the best-paid families of agricultural laborers, another investigator found, each member earned less than four cents a day. Wages as low as a cent a day for each family member were found on some rich estates. At harvest times wages went as high as twelve to fifteen cents a day. About 7 per cent of the population was found to live on such a low level.

The author of *The Silent Revolution* quoted government figures for 1930 to show that 0.1 per cent of the landholdings, extending over a thousand *jochs* each, occupied 30 per cent of the land, while 71.5 per cent of the holdings, measuring less than five *jochs* each, occupied 11 per cent of the land. "Out of 4.5 million of agrarian inhabitants, 3.7 million belong to the agrarian proletariat—83 per cent of the farm population." "I hesitate to write this down," wrote the author of the book, "that if we add the 2.2 million urban proletariat, it is seen that close to 6 million souls, two-thirds of the country's total population, are proletarians."

Landowners were shown by the "village explorers" to be absolute rulers on the countryside. A count, to mention just one illustration, prevented the building of a much-needed bridge across the River Tisza, so that he could draw additional profit from the operation of an antediluvian ferry.

How did the peasants react to this situation? The author of *The Silent Revolution* quotes: "Our enemies are not the Serbs, but our own landlords." They spoke with unbounded hatred about those masters. Race suicide was also their answer, the system of *egyke*, not a new institution in the countryside but more widespread than before the war. In those days it still had been possible to escape the horror of an utterly hopeless life by emigrating to the United States, as hundreds of thousands of them did, but now the gates of America were closed. There was a quota of 865 persons a year.

Despair bred semireligious sects in Hungary, some of them nihilistic, professing creeds that denied the right of life. Adherents of the sect of the "Seedless" were landless peasants who turned to the systematic destruction of their kind, practicing complete birth control. They tolerated no vegetation around the house except the symbol of poverty, the acacia tree. The "Starvers' " revival meetings recalled those of the American Deep South. They met closely packed in their houses of worship, where the murmur of their chants rose and fell, broken by the shrieks of the faithful to whom the light was suddenly revealed. Silence fell on the audience as the "seer" took the word, his eyes piercing fathomless mysteries far beyond the thatched roof of the hut. In the gibberish he talked, frenzied emotions could be poured out more easily than in intelligible words. The faithful were the elect, and the candidates were those who had not yet been purged and were awaiting salvation for their sins. They abjured drink, swearing, and carnal love, and were attached to doomsday, the day of fulfillment. The "Tremblers," too, prepared themselves for the final day, and their nocturnal services ended in flagellations. "Devil Chasers," "Whitsun-Waiters," and "Sabbatians" were some of the other sects whose leitmotif was despair.

The Era of Count Bethlen

Hungary's Prime Minister during the full decade 1921–1931 was Count Stephen Bethlen, scion of the great historic family which was "presumably a collateral branch of that which produced the great Transylvanian Princes of the Seventeenth Century." *

Count Bethlen entered parliament as early as 1910, when he was only twenty-seven, and he exhibited a "great native shrewdness and a skill in handling men which was untrammeled by inhibitions, for his guiding characteristic was a profound cynicism which colored his every belief save one: the natural right and duty of Hungary to rule the Danube basin through his own class."

Bethlen was, as Professor Macartney puts it, a conservative in the truest sense of the word. His mind was neither negative nor incapable of recognizing the existence of new conditions. He was far too shrewd not to appreciate when a position had become untenable, in which case he would withdraw to an inner line, as close behind the old one as possible, selecting his new terrain with great technical skill, which reduced the extent of the ground lost to a minimum.

Bethlen saw Hungary's domestic problems in economic terms, as Széchenyi and Kossuth had seen them. What the country needed above all was capital, and the native variety of it was insufficient. The first task facing him, therefore, was to carry out a comprehensive process of consolidation and reconstruction. This process of *Sanierung* did bring in some foreign funds.

Even though Bethlen entertained the Hungarian *grand seigneur's* incomparable disdain for the Social Democratic Party, he realized that the process of organization of the industrial proletariat in the modern world could not be ignored. In the interest of peace and quiet, he came to terms

* Macartney, *op. cit.*, Vol. I, p. 37.

with the Socialists, who were to enjoy the same rights of association and assembly as the other parties. In return for this the Socialists subscribed to the formula that "they regarded the general interest of the country and the nation as identical with their own and objects for which the workers, too, must fight and make sacrifices." In line with this agreement, Bethlen improved the workers' existing social insurance system, shortening the working day and week.

Like his fellow magnates, however, he was not alive to the needs of the *nincstelenek*—the landless peasants. It was during his incumbency that a Hungarian author spoke of the "three million beggars worse off today than forty years before."

Patrons and Clients

In the course of time there had come into being a patron-client relationship between the major powers and the Eastern European countries. France was particularly active in this region. The small countries in the East fitted well into the traditional French policy of a defensive wall against the Germans—who were thought to be the hereditary enemies of the French from the beginning of their history to the end of time—and now against the Soviets. The small countries were to serve as a *cordon sanitaire*, against the Eastern contamination. In turn, the small countries had what they at that time believed to be the protection of a powerful country—France against both the Germans and the Soviets, no less than against Hungarian irredentist aspirations.

It was during the incumbency of Bethlen that the Hungarian franc forgery scandal broke. Large sums of French francs had been forged in Hungary in a crude attempt to flood the international currency market, and thus to reduce the value of the franc and devalue the international position of France. Several prominent Hungarians were involved in the scandal.

The politically articulate Hungarians would have favored

closer links with France. The "Occidental nostalgia" of Hungarian intellectuals and aristocrats was notorious. Because of the role France played in Eastern Europe closer bonds were not feasible. As to the British, there was much private sentiment for Hungary among them, but official Britain considered Mid-Danubia a special concern of France.

Bethlen concluded a pact of friendship with Italy in 1927, his country's first important postwar pact. Hungary obtained the use of a free port at Fiume on the Adriatic. Since the road there lay across Yugoslavia, Budapest established a *modus vivendi* with Belgrade, too.

The Hungarians never thought highly of Italy's role in the First World War. Nominally allies of the Monarchy and Germany when the war began, the Italians had turned against their pact-partners and made common cause with the Entente. At the end of the war Italy was deeply disappointed in the meager spoils she got. She was now a Fascist country, under the guidance of Il Duce, Benito Mussolini, who pursued a dynamic foreign policy the goal of which was to turn the Mediterranean into his country's *mare nostrum*. In the pursuit of his aim, Mussolini attempted to pry open the hinges of France in southeastern Europe. In doing so he made common cause with another disgruntled nation, the Hungarians.

"The Age of Bethlen" was comparatively quiet and for a time it seemed as if peace were to be the fate of man. It was during that regime that most of the countries, including Hungary, signed in 1928 the famous Briand-Kellogg Pact, known also as the Pact of Paris, which outlawed war as an instrument of national policy.

Meanwhile, however, the economic débâcle overwhelmed the United States and began to affect Europe. In Hungary Bethlen, the great success of his age, began to employ high-handed methods in his dealings with Horthy. And he became tired of his job. Eagerly, the Regent accepted his resignation. "The grand old man of Hungary," Bethlen announced his political retirement a few years later, expressing disgust with the politics and public opinion of the day, saying: "Only those who breakfast on Jews, lunch on aristocrats and deal out fortunes not belonging to them are national heroes nowadays. I am no match to them, and it is much to be feared that Bolshevik ideology will strike root in the nation again. I do not see the strong will and clear vision this country needs. This must come from within—not without."

New Forces to the Fore

The "three Counts," Paul Teleki, Bethlen and Gyula Károlyi (Michael's half-brother), had been at the helm for twelve years, and they were followed by Julius Gömbös (1886–1936), the representative of new forces in Hungarian life.

The ancestor's of Gömbös were German-Swabian peasants, and the original family name seems to have been Knöpfle.* The mother of Gömbös did not even speak Hungarian. She appears to have been a Slovak-Hungarian-German mixture. Gömbös was such a Hungarian patriot that he burst into tears when returning to Hungary from a trip. He also shed tears at the sight of the Hungarian *gémes kút*, the well surmounted by a tall pole. He loved the Hungarians passionately and hated the Hungarian Jews, whom he considered "aliens," no matter how long their ancestry. Such frenzied patriotism with his background is, of course, not unusual. Psychologists speak of "compensations" for a feeling of insecurity.

Regent Horthy appointed Gömbös Prime Minister in 1932. After he had come to know him better, this was what Horthy said about his new Premier: "Gömbös' nature was autocratic and the example set by Hitler and Mussolini made a profound impression on him." †

Why did the Regent call Gömbös to the helm? There can

---

* *Gomb*—from which Gömbös is derived—means "button," and so in German does *Knopf*, from which "Knöpfle" is derived.
† *The Admiral Horthy Memoirs*, New York: Robert Speller. 1957, p. 139.

have been only one major motive—because the new Premier
expressed the aspirations of the new Hungarian ruling class
and the new dominant Central European ideology. The landowning magnates had received a body blow when Hungary
was dismembered at the First World War peace conference.
Many of them lost their influence when they lost their land
in regions assigned to other nations, and they were also ad-
versely affected by the currency devaluation.

There was now a new social class in the making, a middle
class, but not quite in the Western sense. A large number
of the members of this class belonged to the bureaucracy.
Some members of it reached managerial posts in industries,
even trade and banking. This class drew much of its ideology
from traditional aristocratic attitudes, and it was extremely
class-conscious, looking down upon the peasants and the industrial proletariat. These were *les nouveaux messieurs* who
were finding their niches alongside the remnants of the aristocracy and were partly replacing it.

It was during the incumbency of Gömbös that Hungary
found herself once again on the brink of war. King Alexander
I of Yugoslavia was to pay an official visit to France. He
arrived at Marseilles on October 9, 1934, and was met by
Louis Barthou, the Foreign Minister of France. They were
being driven through the streets of the harbor city when a
spectator emerged from the crowd, leapt on the running-
board of the car of the King and Minister and fired at them.
The King died instantly, Barthou a few hours later. The
assassin was a Macedonian émigré leagued with Croatian
émigrés from Yugoslavia. He was trampled to death by the
crowd.

Macedonians were waging a campaign of terror against
Yugoslavia, to detach the region they claimed from that
country. They cooperated with Croatian émigrés, who also
wanted to "free" their country from Yugoslavia. The government of Yugoslavia quickly submitted the case to the League

of Nations, making the charge that a camp for terrorists was being maintained within Hungary, at a place called Janka Puszta, not far from the Yugoslav frontier.

It looked for a time as if an armed clash were inevitable. The situation looked ominously like the tragic summer days of 1914, when the assassination of the heir to the Habsburg thrones, precipitated the First World War. Luckily saner counsels prevailed. Yugoslavia had the backing of France; Hungary was supported by Italy and Austria. Before the year was over, the Council of the League of nations adopted a resolution which declared that "certain Hungarian authorities were responsible, at any rate through negligence, for some of the acts having connection with the preparation of the Marseille crime."

The Gömbös government was asked to find and punish these authorities. Also an international convention was to be framed for the repression of conspiracies committed with political or terrorist purpose. The resolution of the Council of the League of Nations was accepted as the settlement of the controversy and the danger of war was removed.

During the Gömbös administration new impetus was given to attempts to revise the Treaty of Trianon. Again the world was to hear the well-known slogan: *Nem, nem, soha!* Never was Hungary to resign herself to the dictates of the so-called peace-makers of Paris. This time, however, Hungary's protest was not merely couched in words. The Gömbös government seems to have reached an agreement with the Mussolini regime under which the latter was to ship some arms to Hungary.

The "Gömbös system" was anti-Semitic for obvious reasons. Hungarians of the Jewish faith held many peak positions of the country's industry and trade. Professional jealousy clothed itself in an ideology which invested it with the appearance of idealism. And Germany was now governed by the Nazis, who believed that most of the evils of the world were associated with the Jews. They had, therefore, a "solution" for it, which they advocated with fanatic zeal. Their doctrine of racial superiority appealed to people who were deficient in positive qualities of prominence—they were not Jews, and that was their supreme virtue.

Gömbös was an admirer of both the Italian dictator, Mussolini, and of the German Führer, Hitler. His admiration for the latter was, however, greater. In those early days, the two dictators were still feeling their way toward co-operation. It is true that Hitler looked upon Mussolini for some time as the pioneer Fascist and respected him for it. Mussolini, on the other hand, did not reciprocate these feelings. He did not relish the idea of Germany executing her plan of absorbing Austria, which would have made Italy the neighbor of an enlarged Teutonic Reich.

Gömbös worked hard to bring the two Fascist leaders closer and to establish a north-south ideological co-operation extending also into the field of foreign affairs. A term which became very famous in years to come was coined by Gömbös: the Rome-Berlin Axis, meaning Italian and German Fascist co-operation.

Under the Gömbös regime the tactics of the Fascist dictators were copied in Hungary: the press was harassed and political freedoms were radically curtailed. In the spring of 1934 Hungary signed the Rome Protocols, which bound her, Italy, and Austria to co-operation, particularly in the economic field.

Looking at it from a historical perspective, the regime of Gömbös was rather barren. Hungary was brought closer to the German Third Reich of the Nazis, which was no help in the days of crucial decisions.

Gömbös had not been at the helm many months when Regent Horthy discovered that he was "no gentleman." It was, however, too late as the Premier was already well entrenched. It was in harness that Prime Minister Gömbös died in the autumn of 1936. The respect in which the German Third Reich held him was attested by the presence of some of its highest dignitaries in his funeral cortege.

The successor of Gömbös was Kálmán Darányi, a Premier of no great importance except that he, too, symbolized the emergence of the new semi-gentry middle class. An electoral law was passed, a complicated one, the aim of which was to convey the impression of freer elections without, however, liberalizing its substance. Another land law was passed, this one even less helpful than its predecessors.

Hungary now became a pawn on the chessboard of the German Third Reich. It had taken the Führer several years before he began to hit his stride, but now the outlines of the new German world order became clearer. The New Order contained a European Doctrine, under which the German Reich Führer possessed the sole right to dispose of the fate of Eastern and Central Europe.

On the one hand, Hungary belonged to the area the Nazis claimed as directly their sphere, and in which other powers were declared *Raumfremd*, "alien to the space." On the other hand, Hungary was considered a fellow victim of the postwar treaty makers. Germany was in full revolt against the Versailles Treaty, imposed upon her by the victors after the war. Hungarians did not permit the Germans or anybody else to forget about the Treaty of Trianon.

And where did the Hungarians rank in the Nazis' racial scale of values, the supreme determinant, the hierarchy of man? The scale was determined not purely by race but also by political interests and convenience. Thus the Japanese, for instance, were classified as "Caucasians," honorary Aryans. The Hungarians far outranked the Slavs, whom the Nazis considered as "slaves" and called *östliche Untermenschen*, members of the Eastern subhuman species. Of course the Hungarians were not considered as Nordics either, and thus they did not stand on the pinnacle of racial values.

To the Third Reich Hungary was important not so much because of her people but because of her location. She was situated in close proximity to the important junction point of East and West, North and South. That region was needed for any operations in the Balkans and also in the Soviet Union. It was therefore a territory which the military-minded German Third Reich had to control.

In trying to control it fully, however, the Nazis had to consider the Hungarian touchiness in matters affecting their nation. Their history was replete with wars against encroachment on their "sacred soil."

The "Jewish Question"

As the Nazis' hold on Germany stiffened, their influence in Hungary increased too. We have seen that the Nazis' principal obsession at the time was with the Jews. They believed that the Jewish question was the very pivot in the determination of the future of Europe—the growth or decline of the West. Hungary's treatment of the Jews did not please them, in spite of the White terror and Julius Gömbös.

Hungary still had a considerable number of Jews occupying more important positions than their coreligionists in any other country on the Continent.* The Nazis knew, too, that some of Hungary's most prominent people had some "Jewish blood" in their veins. Hungarian anti-Semites were later to claim that the Regent's own wife, Mme. Horthy, had a portion of such blood.

Horthy's own "pro-Jewish whims" were noted by Joseph Goebbels, the Third Reich's Minister of Propaganda and Enlightenment. He described both the Regent Governor and his son as *Judenfreund* and *Judendiener*. "Horthy and his family are strongly infected with Jewish blood," ran one of

---

* The Nazis claimed that the Soviet Union was *verjudet*, full of Jews in leading positions. Whatever may have been the case in the Soviets' earlier years, this was no longer the situation after the great Moscow purges.

the Goebbels diary entries, dated May 8, 1943, "and they will continue to struggle against the solution of the Jewish problem. Horthy advances humanitarian arguments which, naturally, have absolutely no validity in the case of the Jews."

These were serious considerations, which entered into the equation of power in Hungary's relations with the Third Reich.

"The New Order" in Operation

In the spring of 1938 Austria was incorporated in the German Reich. In the fall of the same year Czechoslovakia's border-lands, the so-called Sudeten areas, were absorbed. Contrary to the pledge given to Britain and France, the Germans occu-pied the core of the Czech republic, Bohemia and Moravia, in mid-March, 1939. At the behest of a so-called Slovak Diet— Nazi sponsored—Slovakia was declared "independent." In the November 2, 1938, Vienna Award, the Hungarians got back the lower portion of Slovakia, inhabited mainly by Ma-gyars and German-speaking townsmen. They also reacquired the mountainous "Carpathian Russia," also known as Ru-thenia, in the northeast corner of millennial Hungary.

Thus the Treaty of Trianon was completely revised. "*Nem, nem, soha*" seemed to have borne its fruits. Germany and Italy, the so-called Axis partners, constituting themselves a tribunal of international justice in August, 1940, awarded to Hungary the entire upper portion of Transylvania, a compara-tively large region of 17,000 square miles with a population of two and a half million. Next year Hungary was to wrest the Backa from Yugoslavia, the fertile farm land between the rivers Danube and Tisza in the South.

Hungary was thus prepared and partly rewarded for the historic events. The Germans attacked Poland on September 1, 1939, and what was to become the bloodiest war was begun. At first the Hungarians did not join the Germans any more than their Axis partners, the Italians. In a matter of weeks in the spring of 1940 France was subdued. Never had the modern world seen such a superiority in arms and man power as the German Nazis had over their foes. Hitler reminded the Hungarians of their obligation: "He who wants to eat must help roast the meat." The Hungarians still did not want to help with the roasting of the meat.

Why this reluctance? Hitler was not popular in the highest circles in Budapest, even though the reasons for his unpopularity may have been all wrong. His regime did contain some crudely equalitarian features, at least in the professions of its creed. Some members of the Hungarian higher classes considered it outright radical, subversive. Also, Horthy was an aristocrat by training, and he could not overcome his distaste for such upstarts as Hitler, a mere lance corporal in the Bavarian Regiment List during the war, when the Regent himself was in command of the Austro-Hungarian navy.

Then, too, members of the Hungarian ruling classes did have a sense of proportion. They could not see how Britain, and eventually the United States, could afford to have Hitler take over Europe. These Hungarians knew that the god of wars was on the side of the largest oil production, and the Reich was grievously deficient in petroleum, lubricant not merely of the machines of peace but also those of war.

Disregarding Hungary's sovereign right to her own "space," the Germans used it in April, 1941, as their staging area when they thrust into the Balkans. Again it was a superior military performance. One country after another fell, showing that the campaign against France had not been merely a victory over a decadent nation. The South Slavs were certainly not decadent.

Finally, the crucial moment arrived. Germany, the land of the twentieth century Teutonic Knights, was the self-appointed crusader against the Soviets, pagans of the modern world. On June 22, 1941, Operation Barbarossa was unleashed.

The most widely read American commentator on military

affairs arrayed incontrovertible evidence that the Soviet Union
could hold out for not more than three months. The German
armies cut into the monstrously bloated body of the Soviets
as a knife cuts into soft butter. It looked, indeed, as if the
Nazi atmor's performance in France was to be repeated. If
ever, this was the auspicious time for Hungary to join the gay
group of those who were to roast their meat in the flames of
the world conflagration.

Soon after the German attack on Russia, Regent Horthy
was handed one of those letters from Hitler which, as he said
it, he always opened with a "sinking heart." The Nazi leader
called upon him to join the fight by declaring war on the
Soviets. However, the decision of the Hungarian government
was not to do so. Horthy replied that a declaration of war
would have been justified only if there had been a Soviet
provocation. Hungary was copying the Italian government's
wait and see attitude. It was true that the German army was
superb but it was equally true that now both Britain and the
United States were aroused. Horthy and his government remembered what happened in similar circumstances during the
First World War.

However, on June 26, Horthy received the startling news
that Soviet planes had dropped bombs on Kassa and Munkács, two of the recently recovered north Hungarian towns.
Allegedly, marks of a Leningrad armament factory were detected on the fragments of the bombs.

This was provocation indeed and the following day Hungary broadcast this bulletin to the world: "As a result of
repeated air attacks by the Russians upon Hungarian sovereign territory, contrary to international law, Hungary con-
siders herself at war with the Soviet Union."

This version of events was accepted unquestioningly at the
time. Three years later, however, Horthy finally obtained the
information that had been withheld from him in the summer
of 1941. He learned, when the war was nearly over, that he

had been misinformed about the nationality of the planes and bombs at the time of the Kassa and Munkács attacks. The information conveyed to him belatedly was this:

On the day the bombs were dropped on the two cities, the commanding officer at the airfield of Kassa was a colonel of the Air Force, Adam Krudy. He was a witness to the fact that the bombs had been dropped not by Russians but by German planes. He transmitted this information to the Prime Minister at the time, László Bárdossy. By that time, however, Hungary had declared war on Russia, and the Prime Minister let the conscientious officer be informed that it was too late to do anything, and that, besides, he should keep quiet if he did not want to get into trouble. This the officer did, and Horthy himself was not informed of the true state of affairs. It was only at the postwar trials of the war criminals in Nuremberg that the facts were fully disclosed.

Hungary's Participation in the War

Hungary's role in World War II was not very significant. Winston Churchill, Britain's wartime Prime Minister, wrote a detailed history of the Second World War in six large volumes of some thousands of pages. He covered all the phases of the war in all parts of the global conflict. He mentioned Hungary only in passing, and that too only a few times, in all that detailed record. For much of the time the Hungarian army straddled the Dniester River. It came to be called the "Dead Army" and was little more than a whipping boy for the Germans, expendables.

Hitler's apparently irresistible thrust against the Soviets forked out in three directions. One was directed against the heart of the country, Moscow; another swung north against Leningrad; the third slashed out against the main petroleum regions of the Soviets, north of the Caucasus and on the western shores of the Caspian Sea.

The history of the Second World War teaches us that the

crucial moment was late in 1941, when the German juggernaut failed to cut the jugular vein of the Soviets at Moscow.
It also teaches us that history had not taught anything to
Hitler. He did not learn from the example of Napoleon the
Great. Space swallows up the invader in Russia, as long as
the morale of the people holds out. It held out against Napoleon, but did not hold out against the Kaiser in the First
World War. Again, it held out against Hitler, and in this
respect the German leader was the most effective propagan-
dist of the Soviet Communists. Common sense should have
taught him to capitalize on the people's discontent with their
Bolshevik regime. He was so obsessed with his pathological
racial theories that he was unable to give a helping hand to
the Russian people. He treated them as if they were vermin,
setting fire to their villages and towns in a criminal outburst
of sadism which can be compared only with what we know
about the hordes of the Mongols.

The Russian people turned against their invaders. There
were some defectors to the Nazis, but they were only a minority. The people themselves went underground in regions
occupied by the Nazis and then re-emerged as embattled
guerrillas. By the end of 1943 it became obvious that the insanity of Hitler's policies, his failure to reach his goal at the
first try, the cruelty of the Russian winter, and the endless
space of the Soviets had thrown his juggernaut into reverse.

Regent Horthy, whose heart was never in this war, approached Hitler with a new project. Let the Hungarian troops
be turned into a home defense force, drawn up along the
frontiers of their country. They would be far more effective
in braking the Soviets' march. Hitler was obsessed with the
belief that, in spite of the fact that the United States had
now also joined the Allies, the Germans would win the war
if they held out to the end.* His scientists were working on

---

* He was convinced that the Germans had lost the First World War because they failed to hold out long enough.

"secret weapons" which would force the Allies, particularly the British, to their knees.

The German leader did not understand the language of compromise. In answer to Horthy's suggestion, he ordered him into his presence, charged him with disloyalty, and on March 19, 1944, ordered German troops to occupy Hungary, so as to be sure that it did not jump off the Axis battle wagon.

The Regent was now practically a prisoner of the Germans. Yet he still had a certain freedom of movement. It became increasingly obvious to him and the government in Hungary that the German situation was hopeless and that no secret weapon could change the inevitable course of events. Hungary's eastern neighbor, Romania, was in a better position than Hungary, farther removed from the Germans, closer to the advancing Russians. She quickly changed sides and joined the Soviets.

The Hungarian government put out official and private feelers to probe the attitude of the Western Allies. Budapest was dreaming of a Western army of parachute troops descending upon the capital. It did not rule out the possibility of an armed invasion by the Western Allies. But they were trying to pry open the last defensive Nazi lines, while the Russians were rapidly advancing from the east. East or west, they were in the same boat, they were Allies. The West referred the Hungarians to the Russians, and there the matters stood. The Hungarian government was wary of the Kremlin.

The Regent's Proclamation

By the autumn of 1944 it became evident to the Hungarian government that the bitter pill had to be swallowed. The Russians were obviously to be the masters of Southeastern and Eastern Europe, at least up to a point. After long hesitation, Budapest established contact with Moscow. There was no sense in waiting any more. Hungary did not want to be counted as one of the casualties of war. Not even the "miracle" of the secret weapon could now save the Germans.

In spite of German control, Regent Governor Horthy was free enough to work out and have read a proclamation, in which he declared that the war was over for Hungary and that an armistice was to be concluded. The proclamation was broadcast on October 15, 1944:

"I am here informing the representatives of the German Reich that we are concluding a preliminary armistice with our enemies and are ceasing all hostilities against them."

Then he made the government's main points: "Hungary was forced into the war against the Allies by German pressure, which weighed upon us, owing to our geographical position. . . . Today it is obvious to any sober-minded person that the German Reich has lost the war. All governments responsible for the destiny of their countries must draw the appropriate conclusion from this fact, for, as the great German statesman, Bismarck, once said: 'No nation ought to sacrifice itself on the altar of an alliance.' With grief I am forced to state that the German Reich on its part broke the loyalty of an ally toward our country a long time ago. For a considerable time it has thrown formation after formation of the Hungarian armed forces into battle outside the frontiers of the country against my express wish and will. . . . Under cover of the German occupation the Gestapo tackled the Jewish question in a manner incompatible with the dictates of humanity, applying methods it had already employed elsewhere. When war drew near our frontiers and even passed them, the Germans repeatedly promised assistance, yet again they failed to honor their promise. During their retreat they turned the country's sovereign territory over to looting and destruction. . . . Subsequently German aircraft dropped leaflets against the government in office. . . . Trusting in your love of truth, I hope to secure, of one accord with you, the continuity of our nation's life in the future and the realization of our peaceful aims. Commanders of the Hungarian army have received corresponding orders from me. Accordingly, the troops loyal to their oath and following an Order of the Day now issued simultaneously, must obey the commanders appointed by me. I appeal to every honest Hungarian to follow me on this path, beset by sacrifices, that will lead to Hungary's salvation." *

There were no preparations to implement the proclamation, nor did the armed forces stand at the Regent's side in the crucial moment. In an incredible outburst of naïveté, the Hungarian leader believed that the Germans would be swept off their feet by mere words. The proclamation was an embarrassed hodgepodge of unrelated grievances against the Germans. The Regent offered no constructive program—no program whatever—to his nation. He did not call upon it to rise against the Nazi oppressors nor even tell the industrial workers to cease toiling for the Third Reich, so that the tens of thousands of hands in the Csepel factory, in the very suburbs of Budapest, kept on working for the Germans' arsenals of war. Nor did the Magyar army turn against the Hitlerites. Hungary's great opportunity to fight for her freedom was lost.

The following day Horthy withdrew everything he had said. In a counterproclamation, promptly broadcast to all the world, he declared:

"In a difficult hour of Hungarian history, I make known this my decision. In the interest of the successful prosecution of the war and of the inner unity and coherence of the nation, I abdicate from my office and renounce all legal rights accruing from my authority as Regent. At the same time I entrust Ferenc Szálasi with the formation of a cabinet of national concentration. Given at Budapest on the sixteenth day of October, 1944. Horthy, m.p."

A Nazi puppet, Döme Sztojay, former Hungarian Minister accredited to Berlin, had been Hungary's Prime Minister since the country's occupation by the Nazis in mid-March,

* Horthy, op. cit., pp. 259–260.

and he continued at the helm until midsummer. He was then replaced by General G. H. Lakatos and his interim government. General Lakatos had commanded Hungarian troops at the eastern front.

The Germans shipped the former Regent, his wife, daughter-in-law, and small grandson to Schloss Hirschberg, near Weilheim, in Bavaria, where they held them under close guard. The Regent's son, "Niky," in Budapest at the time of troubles, was shipped to the concentration camp at Mauthausen, then to Dachau. At the end of the war he was liberated from there by American units.

The Age of Horthy in Retrospect

When the war was over, Horthy was taken to Nuremberg, where he was called upon to testify in the war criminal trials. The Allies decided not to charge him with war crimes. In consequence, he was released, and moved to the Portuguese seaside resort town of Estoril, where he died on February 9, 1957.

This was then the end of the Age of Horthy, which filled out Hungary's entire interbellum era and overlapped into the war. It was a long regency, a quarter of a century. Although there have been longer regimes in European history, there has been no comparable period into which so many significant events were compressed. Horthy was the very first of Europe's "strong men." His rule outlasted those of Hitler and Mussolini. While these two had violent ends, that of Horthy was serene.

Looking at the various segments of the Age of Horthy, we obtain different pictures of the man and his regime.

The beginning of his reign occurred under the auspices of the new plague of the region—anti-Semitism. Toward the end of his regime, however, he became a protagonist of his country's Jews. His regime, which called itself "royal," eliminated the last vestige of attempt to restore the royal rule. The

Horthy reign was dedicated to the proposition that Hungary would never accept her rump status under the Treaty of Trianon. Yet war for the reconquest of the lost regions was not on the official program of the age. Still, treaty provisions were violated when Hungary built up her armed forces.

Toward the end, Horthy mellowed considerably. His regime did not put the clock back, but it did not advance it much either. In the inevitable course of events, certain improvements took place in the country. Even the common people began to think of themselves a little bit more as human beings. There was some improvement in the condition of the industrial workers, less as a result of a planned policy, more as the unavoidable trend of events themselves. The industrial workers had an organization which could not be entirely disregarded.

On the other hand, the countryside did not fall into line with the advancing times. It was a sad and very backward countryside, in spots badly undernourished, and that in the midst of nature's plenty.

Admiral Horthy was not the "simple sailor man" he liked to appear. He had plenty of cunning, but he was not intellectually complicated; he had only a few simple thoughts and lacked imagination. These may have been some of the reasons that enabled him to fill his place so long to the satisfaction of his "employers," the Hungarian pacemakers.

Those employers were members of a group that usually ran countries, and they are hard to define. In Hungary, as we have seen, they were mainly members of a new type of gentry, still suspicious of industry and commerce but somewhat reconciled to them. In crucial moments the Regent had to defer to the "creative minority," even though he had extensive powers.

In emergency situations Horthy was ineffective. We have seen that he did not want to join the Nazis in their war on Russia but was not strong enough to resist them. Hungary's

location, of course, militated against the implementation
of his own predilections. The Germans could not do without
Hungary's area, and what chance did she have against them?

Time was, however, when Hungary could have entered
world history. It was in the autumn of 1944, when the Nazis
were already reeling under the Soviets' mighty blows. If the
Hungarians had done with the Nazis what they were to do
with the Russians in the autumn of 1956, the war might have
been shortened, countless human lives might have been saved,
and Hungary would have deserved humanity's thanks. Horthy
was not the man to give his nation such leadership.

A Piece of Paper on the Table

Hungary's fate was already decided in October, 1944, at the
time of the Allied Moscow conference. The decision was
made casually, almost absent-mindedly, half-asleep. Yet, even
if the statesmen at the conference had been more awake, it
is doubtful whether their decision could have been different.
In this case, too, Hungary's future was decided by her
geographical location.

In Eastern Europe the Soviets were smashing their way to
victory. They worked their way to the Danube and then onward to the Elbe, which was in the heart of Germany. Was
it to be expected that they would fail to exploit their victory
to the hilt?

The Soviet case could be seen clearly. The Russian frontier
was open to the west, an invitation to invasion. Twice within
one generation the Germans had made war on Russia from
the west. They won the first one, only to lose it against the
Western Allies. The Russians won the second war because
this time they had grown into one of the world's greatest
industrial powers and because, paradoxically, their patriotic
potentialities were fully activated under a professedly international regime. The Nazis helped the Bolsheviks to do this
with Hitler's insane racial superiority theories.

It was not to be assumed that the Soviets were to forget the lessons of history. Now that they had spent so much blood in pushing the Germans to the Elbe, they were not likely to relinquish their hold on a region which possessed the greatest strategic importance from their point of view. It is for this reason that one may almost say that Hungary's cause was not lost at the Moscow conference table, but that it had been lost in 895 when the Magyar horsemen under Árpád descended upon the Hungarian plains.

Let us be witnesses to the casual way in which the representatives of the victorious nations decided the fate of Eastern Europe at Moscow. The event was reported by Winston Churchill in his record of the Second World War.

"The moment was apt for business," Mr. Churchill reports, "so, I said: 'Let's us settle about our affairs in the Balkans. Your armies are in Rumania and Bulgaria. We have interests, missions and agents there. Don't let us get at cross-purposes in small ways. So far as Britain and Russia are concerned, how would it do for you to have ninety per cent predominance in Rumania, for us to have ninety per cent of the say in Greece, and go fifty-fifty about Yugoslavia?' While this was being translated I wrote out on a half-sheet of paper:

"Rumania
    Russia   90%
    the others   10%
Greece
    Great Britain
    (in accord with US) 90%
    Russia   10%
Yugoslavia   50%–50%
Hungary   50%–50%
Bulgaria
    Russia   75%
    The others   25%

"I pushed this across to Stalin, who had by then heard the translation. There was a slight pause. Then he took his blue pencil and made a large tick upon it, and passed it back to us. It was settled in no more time then it takes to set down.

"Of course, we had long and anxiously considered our point and were only dealing with immediate war time arrangements. All larger questions were reserved on both sides for what we then hoped would be a peace table when the war was won.

"After this there was a long silence. The penciled paper lay in the center of the table. At length I said: 'Might it not be thought rather cynical if it seemed we had disposed of these issues so fateful to millions of people in such an offhand manner? Let us burn the paper.' 'No, you keep it,' said Stalin." *

A *Fanatic* and the *Arrow Cross*

The Hungarian government was now entrusted to Major Ferenc Szálasi, leader of a holy-roller type of nationalism. His party was about ten years old; it was five hundred strong in 1935. It was called the "Arrow Cross" and "Hungarist." "By the spring of 1937 all Hungary was humming with his name, the fame whereof had penetrated into distant foreign lands. Frustrated revolutionaries were looking to him as their brightest hope; the authorities were watching him as their most formidable danger. The Germans, going over the form-records of the various Right Radical groups, were noting his name as that on which they should place their next bet. Jews were coming to him secretly with proposals to finance his movement in return for the status of 'honorary Aryan' for themselves." †

Szálasi was neither a good organizer nor a good speaker,

* *The Second World War: Triumph and Tragedy*, by Winston S. Churchill. Boston: Houghton Mifflin, 1953, pp. 227–228. Reprinted by permission.
† Macartney, *op. cit.*, v. I, p. 184.

and nobody understood his ideas completely. How was one to account for his rise?

His family was of Armenian origin; its original name was Salosian, and Szálasi's mother was of mixed Hungarian and Slovak stock. The official name of the party was "Hungarist," and that—not much more—was its entire program: patriotism. Szálasi was the Leader of the Nation. The movement had no organization, not even a list of membership. By Szálasi's own admission it was something of which the dimensions could not be assessed. "It was the soul of that entity the body of which was constituted by the party."

Szálasi had a dream-country, which he called the "Carpathian Danubian Great Fatherland" and sometimes also the "United Lands and the March of Hungaria." It was millennial Hungary on some sort of a federative basis, in which the Magyars were again to play the dominant role. He believed that he had been chosen by a secret force within him and that it was only through the triumph of Hungarism that "the whole organization of Europe will come about." He held that there were three great positive ideologies in the world: Hungarism, Christianity, and Marxism. Marxism must be destroyed; Hungarism must triumph.

Many of Szálasi's followers were peasants, and we have seen how great was the need of a positive program on the countryside. Did the Hungarists offer such a program? They had three of them, each contradicting the other: a program for the extension of viable small holdings; the establishment of a medium holding yeoman type of farming; and the Soviet type of collective, the kolkhoz. The slogan of the party was not any more specific: The Trinity of Soil, Blood, and Work. The Jews were, of course, to be eliminated from Hungary. "Szálasi was serenely indifferent to most practical issues and it is doubtful whether he ever seriously devoted himself to any social or economic detail," says C. A. Macartney. Szálasi did not speak to people, he raved to them, and that was perhaps what they liked, because he had the capacity to evoke fanatic devotion. Into those ravings all kinds of deeper meanings could be read, the revelations of a prophet rather than a mere national leader. Szálasi also attended spiritualist séances.

This was the Prime Minister Hungary had in this fatal hour to save her from destruction. Szálasi was acceptable to the Germans. What the Hungarist–Arrow Cross government did in these months of Hungarian agony belongs in a book on psychiatry. The Soviets were now deep in Hungary, racing toward the capital, held largely by crack German units. The Hungarian government decided that all streets in Budapest which were called after Jews should be renamed. Up to the last minute freight cars badly needed by the government for the prosecution of the war were filled with Jews to be shipped to German extermination camps. Boys of twelve and teen-agers carried rifles and shot down anybody whom they suspected of being Jews. In a frenzy of murder Arrow Cross men lined up Jews—women and children too—along the Danube banks so that their bodies should topple into the river, saving the inconvenience of digging graves. On January 18 all Pest was in Soviet hands, but Buda was still holding out. The Hungarian government fled into western Hungary, taking along the Holy Crown and the crown jewels. Wherever it stopped, it constituted itself a bloody assize and executed the few prominent people who dared to raise their voices against this Walpurgis Night madness. Buda was lost to the Soviets on February 13. On March 22 the Hungarian Parliament, meeting in western Hungary, passed an act authorizing Christians married to Jews to divorce their partners.

Meanwhile a new government was constituted in Debrecen with the aid of the Soviets. It was a coalition government, in which the parties of the Smallholders, National Peasants, Social Democrats, Communists, and various bourgeois groups were represented. The new Prime Minister was General Béla Miklós, former head of Horthy's military chancellery and commander of the First Army. "Legitimacy" evidently played its role, even in these tragic days.

Szálasi was eventually captured in the West, delivered to the Hungarian government, tried, and executed.

Again, as in the First World War, Hungary had been on the losing side. In the autumn of 1946 there was a peace conference at Paris, at which Hungary was again reduced to her "Trianon" size. An epoch ended and a new era began. Was it to begin an alleviation of the sufferings of the much-tried country?

And what were Hungary's immediate wartime losses? About 100,000 were the military losses; some 220,000 Hungarians of the Jewish faith killed (out of a total estimated 400,000). The material losses of Hungary amounted to 40 per cent of the national income. The loss in the engineering industry was estimated at 40 per cent; textiles, 13 per cent; iron and steel, 12 per cent. Eighty-nine per cent of all the railway cars, 90 per cent of the railway bridges, and 69 per cent of the locomotives were destroyed—appalling losses for such a small country.

CHAPTER 8

A FATAL SPACE AND ITS CONSEQUENCES

THE SWATH OF NATIONS stretching across Eastern Europe from the Baltic to the Aegean could properly be called *espace fatal*, fatal space, and Hungary's current position can be seen only against this background. In two world wars within one generation that belt of land played its fatal part, and what came to be known as "cold war" also began in the same area.

The heart of this region is Danubia, but its most explosive part is the Balkans. This entire belt is the great divide between East and West. Most of the area belongs to the Soviet sphere, the region of the "satellite" states. The very topography of the region must be considered a *casus belli*. Why is this area such a trouble center? Because much of it is mountainous— the Balkans lie to the south of Hungary—and because it is peripheral. The region was peripheral to the great empires of the past, too—Roman, Eastern Roman, Ottoman, French, English, German. The Social character of the region was formed in the early Middle Ages when Asia's nomads fled the desiccation of their grazing grounds and wandered toward the fabulous realms of Europe's west. Many of them could never reach their goal, as early comers had settled the western lands. Those who came late were forced to remain in the East, fighting with their neighbors, treading on one another's toes.

The rest of Europe was settled by strong groups which crystallized into nations. These mighty states developed gravitational pulls, as do celestial bodies, while the smaller countries fell into the orbits of greater powers, and were absorbed by them or were allowed to exist as satellites.

Sometimes the great powers agreed to divide the loot in preference to entering the lists. The empires of Russia and Austria and the Kingdom of Prussia, for instance, partitioned Poland at the conference table in the late eighteenth century, instead of going to war. When the Ottoman Empire fell into decay, the rapacious powers sought to establish a balance among themselves so as to remove the danger of war. In the nineteenth century Great Britain's long-range policy was to contain Russia, which, having extended all the way across the Siberian wilderness to the Pacific shores, wanted to obtain warm-water ports in Europe.

Then Germany, another "giant that was late," wanted to attach this region to its orbit. Before World War I the Reich's *Drang nach Osten* pointed toward Turkey and the Persian Gulf. Southeastern Europe fitted admirably into the German scheme. Here was a large territory with great potential strength that could be turned into a profitable colonial region at the very back door of the Reich—Africa in Europe. Under Hitler a similar eastward drive pointed to the Ukraine, breadbasket of the Old World, and toward the oil treasury of the Caucasus.

Southeastern Europe with its large Slavic population centers had been for centuries one of Russia's ports of entry into world politics and trade. It was also the battleground for rivalries with the Habsburgs, with Germany, with England,

and in the twentieth century it served as a staging area of Russia's foes. As the Second World War ended, the Red Army swept into the region in the wake of Germany's cataclysmic collapse, providing Moscow with a unique opportunity for fulfilling long-standing ambitions.

The Western Allies had no thought of ceding this region to the Kremlin. In their view, the Eastern European countries were to remain free to find their way to true democracy. This view was incorporated in the peace treaties the victorious Allies framed. The postwar world saw the realization of another aim.

"The Salami Technique"

In Hungary there was now an Allied Control Commission, which authorized six political parties in 1945, the year in which a general election was fought. In Hungary's millennial history this was the first time when national elections were really free. Their outcome was that the Independent Smallholders emerged with 245 seats, the Social Democrats with 69, the Communists with 70, the National Peasants with 23, and the Democratic Party with only 2. The four major parties formed a coalition. The Soviet army remained in Hungary, ostensibly for the purpose of keeping open its supply line to the eastern part of Austria, assigned to the Soviets by inter-Allied agreement. Under the protection of Soviet arms the Communists in Hungary began to assert themselves. The Soviets were now also predominant in the Allied Control Commission.

Leader of the Communists was Mátyás Rákosi. He had originally wanted to become a consular official of the old Austro-Hungarian Monarchy but ran into difficulties, probably because of his Jewish origin. His family name had been Roth. During the First World War he served as a soldier in the Austro-Hungarian army, was taken prisoner by the Russians, met Lenin, and became a fanatic Communist.

Returning to Hungary after World War I, he was made a commissar in the short-lived government of Béla Kun. He managed to escape from the country before Horthy's police caught up with him, fled to Russia, and became secretary of the Communist International. In 1925 he sneaked back to Hungary in order to set up the Communist Party again, was arrested, and was tried for his life. He escaped death, probably because of international interest in his case, and was sentenced to eight and one-half years in one of Europe's worst jails. He spent much of that time in solitary confinement. At the expiration of his term he was rearrested and placed on trial for "mass murder, conspiracy, and treason," which he had allegedly committed as a member of the Kun cabinet fifteen years before. This time he was sentenced to life, but was released in 1940, when relations between the Soviet Union and Germany, and her satellites—Hungary was one of them— appeared to be good. Rákosi went to Russia again. He returned to Hungary in the wake of the victorious Soviet army. He became Secretary General of the Communist Party in Hungary, besides being Vice Premier in the government.

Rákosi held that he and his Communist colleagues had the edge over non-Communist politicians in that they had working experience with government problems in the Soviet Union. Other Hungarian leaders, he maintained, could not match this experience. He expressed this view to H. F. Arthur Schoenfeld, former American Minister to Hungary. "There was some truth in the Rákosi statement," the American diplomat commented in an article in *Foreign Affairs.* "The Communist leaders were energetic and able men; and it was apparent that they intended to fill the administrative vacuum, with or without the backing of the electorate."

In his surprisingly frank way, Rákosi once explained what he called his "salami technique." The Communists would slice the majority and then devour each slice separately. In May 1947 the head of the anti-Communist section of the

Smallholders' Party, Prime Minister Ferenc Nagy, was ousted. On August 31, 1947, new elections were called, in which the Communists practiced disfranchisement and other abuses. The Smallholders' vote was whittled down. The Communist Party polled 22 per cent of the votes—only 5 per cent more than in the previous election.

Rákosi now started to eliminate the mandates of opposition members of Parliament, and also the parties themselves, one by one—the salami technique. The Smallholders' Party was played into the hands of weak sisters, and the Social Democratic Party was merged with the Communists under the name of "Hungarian Workers' Party." All the existing parties were now formed into the "Independent People's Front," and new elections took place on May 15, 1949. It was a May-day picnic, at which the voters were presented with a single ticket. The voters who favored the Front returned the list to the election committee, while the voters who wanted to change the ballot had to enter the polling booth. The People's Front obtained 95.6 per cent of the votes. The salami slicer had done its work. The "Republic of Workers and Working Peasants" was proclaimed on August 20, 1949, the same day the new constitution was also proclaimed. This was Hungary's historic national holiday, St. Stephen's Day.

Under the new constitution supreme power was vested in Parliament—the Hungarian dream. However, parliamentary functions were exercised between legislative session by a Presidential Council of twenty-one—and "council" in Russian means "soviet." This, then, was the Hungarian reality. The Council was empowered to dissolve government bodies and annul legislation if it "infringed on the Constitution or was detrimental to the working people's interests." The constitution also provided a guarantee of private property, but only "if it did not violate the public interest." The chief means of production, natural resources, banking, and transport were turned over to the state.

National Brainwashing

Number two man among the Communists in Hungary was Ernő Gerő, who was once called the "bridge builder" because of his effective part in rebuilding the Danube bridges of Budapest after the Second World War. He and his Russian-trained Hungarian team performed remarkable feats in repairing the country's railway service.

The Communists were handicapped in filling less prominent posts. For a generation Hungary had been under a violently anti-Bolshevik regime, imbued with a strong dislike of the Kremlin ways. The cadres were absent. In an attempt to solve this problem the leaders drew up a three-point program of training. First, promising youth were indoctrinated, given careers in party work, and helped to acquire vested interests in the success of the cause. For a time at least, it appeared as if the dogmatic creed and simple solutions of Bolshevism appealed to some young people who were disillusioned by the violently anti-Communist Fascist failures. Second, specialists were subjected to intensive courses of political training to remove the effect of previous indoctrination. Finally, the lower echelons were often recruited among the ex-Nazis.

The dreaded State Security Authority, AVO, *Államvédelmi Osztály*, was set up, with its nocturnal knocks on the door. Undesirable members of society were banished to remote villages and placed in concentration camps. Prominent people suspected of cherishing thoughts of their own were frequently bludgeoned to death by the political police. Then there were the so-called Peoples' Courts—in reality political courts—for those who failed to co-operate. A dedicated Communist, László Rajk, was condemned and executed in October, 1949, for no other reason than his desire to see communism flourish more like a native product than a mere Russian transplantation.

Hungary was flooded with Soviet propaganda. The stage, the screen, literature, and all media of art were Sovietized. Magyar history was deprecated while Russian history was glorified. All over Hungary there were monuments to the "great Joseph Stalin" and the "Soviet liberators." The Hungarian soldiers were dressed in Russian-type uniforms. The Soviet star was displayed everywhere. Rákosi assured a meeting of the Hungarian Academy of Sciences as far back as February, 1952, that communism was firmly in the saddle and the opposition parties were mere wrecks.

The Communist regime encountered one of its greatest obstacles in the Prince Primate of Hungary, Cardinal Joseph Mindszenty. The only firmly established nation-wide organization was the Catholic Church, and the village priest was a power. Cardinal Mindszenty opposed the Communist program and particularly its policy of education and land reform. On charges of treason and illegal monetary transactions, he was arrested in 1948, and he pleaded guilty at a show trial. How these confessions were obtained remained a mystery. He was sentenced to jail. Eventually he was confined to enforced residence in Felsőpetény. He was liberated by freedom fighters and reappeared in Budapest during the revolution of the autumn of 1956. After it had been crushed, he found sanctuary in the United States Embassy.

The Hungarian Working People's Party—Communists—continued to be the power in Hungary, in spite of the Hungarian People's Independence Front, which included also the Smallholders, the National Peasant Party, the Trade Union Federation, the Association of Working Peasants, the Democratic Women's Association, and the National Youth Organization.

After Stalin's death in March, 1953, the reign of terror in Hungary, too, began to abate. On July 4, 1953, the arch-Stalinist, Mátyás Rákosi, stepped down as Prime Minister and was succeeded by Imre Nagy, a national Communist. Who was this Imre Nagy, about whom we shall hear more in connection with the Hungarian uprising in the autumn of 1956?

He was a member of a sternly Calvinist family, of peasant stock. In his youth he was a locksmith's apprentice. In World War I he served in the Austro-Hungarian army as a foot soldier, and was captured by the Russians. It was in Russia that he joined the Communists. He fought on their side in the civil war, then returned to Hungary just in time to see communism at the helm. At the age of twenty-two he played a minor role in the Communist government.

After the collapse of the Kun regime in 1919 he submerged in the underground and carried on clandestine work for a decade—a courageous undertaking, since the penalty of such activity was death. Finally he fled to the Soviet Union, where he adopted Russian citizenship. For fifteen years he stayed in Russia, then returned to Hungary with the victorious Soviet army.

He became speaker of the Parliament and was a member of the Central Committee of his party. He reached the summit in 1953. Even though Nagy was a Communist, he was not quite a conventional one. He was in the habit of discussing politics frankly. Later he wrote in a book *(Imre Nagy on Communism)* about his philosophy:

"Russian communism cannot be copied. Communism's way in the Soviets was due to historical, social, and economic reasons; conditions peculiar to Russia have governed its direction, development, and pace. It is wrong to hold and to teach that the Russian variety of communism can be realized everywhere, as, for instance, in Hungary." (The author's translation from the Hungarian original.)

Nagy held that a political line in Hungary could be realized by taking the historic development of the country into account, and that would mean neither international communism nor even a national one, but "Hungarian socialism."

Nagy rejected force as a means of the realization of this ideal, and he stressed the importance of persuasion. He also rejected rigid theses and dogmatic precepts. He evaluated the possibility of the coexistence of the capitalist and Communist systems from a higher strategic point of view, and found it was not only possible but also highly desirable. However, he did not want to co-operate with capitalism merely for the purpose of gaining time to crush it. He visualized coexistence in terms of giving both sides their chance to compare and compete. Let socialism prove its superiority and then capitalism would have no power to stand against it, no matter how desperately it fought the new idea.

Nagy as Prime Minister took an "unorthodox" stand against the "orthodox" ones. The great issue was heavy vs. consumer industry. The orthodox promoted the former, their opponents the latter. Heavy industry looked toward the future, while people at present had to live under the regime of austerity. Consumer industry, on the other hand, envisaged the present and the "better life." Imre Nagy was a consumer-industry man, and living standards in Hungary did improve slightly during his incumbency. He also liberalized the policy of the government toward farm collectivization and relaxed the pressure on the peasantry to join collectives. The political police was restrained, the terror less ubiquitous, fear less pervasive.

While elsewhere in the Soviet satellite realm Stalinism was beating a retreat, in Hungary it made another attempt to come back. In April 1955 Nagy was ousted from his party offices and the premiership. It was charged that he "put the brakes on Socialist construction, industrialization and especially the expansion of heavy industry . . . obstructed the development of the collective farm movement, . . . tried to push the party into the background."

While his disgrace was complete, Hungary and the world were to hear about him again. He was followed again by Rákosi—a "new Rákosi"—who kept on denouncing Stalinism, of which he had been the foremost exponent in Hungary, denouncing the cult of personality—the cult of Rákosi. He went even further, at the behest of the Kremlin, no doubt. He declared that László Rajk, the national Communist, who was hanged in 1949, was innocent. Yet, it was he who had him hanged. Rajk's body was reburied in the midst of the pomp of a national funeral.

In an orgy of self-abasement, Rákosi admitted many mistakes, announced the imminent release of several captive left Socialists, apologized to Yugoslavia's Marshal Tito for past misdeeds and denounced many features of his own policy. Meanwhile, he held onto power with all his waning might.

Economic Problems

We have to turn back now to the early post–World War II days to consider the country's economic problems. The period began with a currency catastrophe for which there is no parallel in history. The nominal value of the Hungarian pengő was 17.5 cents, but its value declined rapidly after the war—not an unusual phenomenon after lost wars. This decline, however, was most unusual. It gathered momentum at such a rate that the high-speed printing presses could not keep step with it. The value of the currency became so astronomical that it could not be expressed in words. Attempts were made to pay the workers in "calories" of food instead of money. On August 1, 1946, however, a new monetary unit was created, the forint. One forint was to equal 400,000 quadrillion pengős, 400,000,000,000,000,000,000,000,000,000.*

Germany's post–World War I and II currencies also declined, but to nowhere near this extent. Yet the Reich's physical destruction during World War II was greater than Hungary's. What accounted for this fantastic decline?

* This tremendous amount was worth 4.75 cents on the tourist market at the end of 1957. The official value of the forint was 8.5 cents. Never have so many figures meant so little.

Possibly the Hungarian currency was encouraged to lose its value as part of the Communist policy of wiping out the moneyed classes.

After the currency reform, the Communists of Hungary turned to the basic problems of production. They believed that planned economy was as superior to laissez-faire as the tractor was to the wooden plow. They also held to the view that they were bound to win the fight between capitalism and communism.

Hungarian agriculture was extensive rather than intensive, and in the period 1931 to 1935 one acre on the *Alföld*—plains—produced only 17.5 bushels, against 425 bushels to the Danish acre. Yet Denmark's unimproved soil was inferior.

The great farm problem of all southeastern Europe was monoculture, the cultivation of one main crop. As there are banana and coffee republics in Latin America, so there were pork kingdoms and corn monarchies in this area. Raising one crop was simple because the small-farm peasant could do it. It required hardly any capital, provided work for all the members of the family and kept famine from the peasant's door. Should that one crop fail, however, it was ruinous.

Communist Hungary's agrarian policy, therefore, envisaged a change to multiculture, and especially to the more profitable stock raising. Truck farming and horticulture were to come into their own. Irrigation and drainage were to regain the semiarid steppe and marsh land. Mechanization and fertilization were to be drawn into service to enable the peasant to better his lot while improving his soil. The agrarian Five-Year Plan began in Hungary in 1949, and it provided for an over-all increase of output by 27 per cent, while that of the farms owned directly by the state was to rise by 80 per cent. New crops, such as cotton, were to be introduced in the south.

Hungary's great economic problem was, as we have seen, the preponderance of large estates and the existence of a wretched farm proletariat. Already under the coalition gov-

ernment after World War II, in which the Smallholders had
an important role, Hungary distributed land among 640,000
families, each of which received six to eight acres. Greatest
beneficiaries were the farm hands and former estate servants.
Building lots to go with the land were assigned to 300,000
families. Even so, some 20,000 farm families received no land,
because there was not enough of it. Also, the allocations were
sometimes very small.

The small holdings were very often unprofitable, since they
did not lend themselves to mechanized cultivation. The Communists urged that co-operatives and collectives should solve
this problem, but the very name of "collective" was enough
to scare peasants out of their wits. They were passionately
attached to that cruel land and preferred to live poorly as
owners rather than to live better on a collective farm.

In Hungary the peasants were encouraged at first to enter
co-operative farm organizations, in which they would retain
their separate holdings while pooling their resources for more
efficient management. The National Co-operative Center,
MOSZK, boasted of 2400 farm members three years after the
war. It had its own processing industries, which it acquired
with the expropriated large estates. A multitude of benefits
were conferred on the co-operatives, such as cheap seeds,
higher prices from government purchasing agents, and tax
remissions. The rich peasants, kulaks, on the other hand, were
subjected to higher taxes and driven from political life. Later
the government urged the peasants to join the collectives, in
which individual property rights were submerged in those of
the entire membership. At the height of the collective period
about 35 per cent of the country's cultivated land was in
kolkhozi. After the death of Stalin and during the premiership of Imre Nagy the collective farms decreased to 12 per
cent of the cultivated land.

Irrigation made great progress. In 1949 only some 65,000
acres were under irrigation, as compared with 455,000 acres

at the end of 1954. Much land was transferred from grains to commercial crops, including 282,000 acres to cotton in the middle fifties.

"Industrial Agrarian"

Hungary was to be transformed "from an agrarian industrial country into an industrial agrarian country," according to the Five-Year Plan that went into effect on January 1, 1950. The plan made provision for a five-year investment of 35 billion forints, of which fully one-half was earmarked for industries and less than 20 per cent for agriculture. The rest was set aside for housing, communications, and cultural and social aims.

The industries were nationalized. The first nationalization law—under the coalition government—was passed in 1946, and applied only to the largest enterprises, such as the Ganz-Danubius, Bauxite, Rima-Murányi, machine, metallurgical, and steel factories. Two years later a far more drastic step was taken, when all industries employing more than a hundred persons were taken over by the state. Since most of the plants were small, this meant some 80 per cent of the total. Even more radical was the third step, in December, 1949, when all firms employing more than five persons were nationalized, leaving only the small handicraft industries in private hands. The restrictions on private ownership were further tightened subsequently.

In Hungary, too, as in the Soviet Union, the accent was on the heavy industries. The 1955 budget, for instance, provided 35 per cent of the total investment for such heavy industries as machine building, while only 8 per cent went into such consumer industries as shoes and clothing. The pace of industrialization was forced, as it was in Russia, at the expense of the people's current living standards. This was in expectation of "better things" in the future, when the full effect of the increase in heavy industrial production would be felt. While this may have made sense in the Soviet Union, a vast country with underdeveloped industries and a sense of urgency in the face of international conflicts, it made absolutely no sense in Hungary, which was fairly well industrialized for her size and location and which, naturally, had no great-power role to play.

As in the Soviet Union, the Communist industrial revolution made possible the shifting of the locale. In Russia its center of gravity had been shifted toward the east. A large measure of shifting of the locale took place also in Hungary. There the general direction of the transfer was toward the east, northeast, and south. The city of Debrecen was to be turned into a major industrial center. Another industrial city was to be Miskolc, on the road to Russia. At the town of Dunapentele, renamed Sztalinváros, on the Danube to the south of the capital, a large industrial combine of steel, coal, and coke was built.

The reasons advanced for this change were numerous. The Hungarian capital was said to be overindustrialized, while the rest of the country was underindustrialized. Industries with their higher wages were to compensate the peasants who had not been able to get a piece of land.

How did the industrial workers fare? They were supposed to be the elite of the country, "front soldiers" in the battle for industrialization. Also, they were expected to take an active part in the life of the party. They were subjected to continuous indoctrination at and away from work. Their activity was represented to them as a social service for the noblest of all causes, communism. They had to put in unremunerated extra work—"socialist emulation." All means of propaganda were employed to glorify the "advance guard" in the great battle of production and to abash the "rear guard," the laggards. A vast speed-up system was thus instituted with no extra cost to the state. And what was the result? Production did not keep step with the plan. The workers, unhappy, gradually became mutinous. They were the first to heed the call to rise against their masters—the Communist bureaucrats.

THE SITUATION IN Hungary in the autumn of 1956 was this:

The prewar aristocracy and gentry were gone—dispersed around the world, or reduced to the performance of lowly work. The old army was gone too, but it took some time before the influence of the Catholic Church could be reduced. Industry, trade, and finance were now in the government's hands.

The foundation of the regime was a combination of industrial and agricultural toilers—at least on paper. The regime was particularly determined to indoctrinate the factory workers and students. This was a round-the-clock job—speeches, lectures, discussions, study groups. The framework was the Marxist-Leninist-Stalinist social, political, and economic philosophy. After the death of Stalin it was changed to Marxism-Leninism.

Real political power was in the hands of the Hungarian Working People's Party, pseudonym for the Communists. First Secretary of the Central Committee was Ernő Gerő, a Muscovite Communist.

The Disgruntled Toilers

The impression one gained in Hungary in those days was that of a tired and disgruntled country. The industrial "toiler" had to work for long hours to earn enough money for a shoddy piece of clothing. Such luxuries as a refrigerator or a car were beyond the boldest dreams even of the "advance guard" workers. The speed-up system, disguised as Socialist emulation, did not fool anybody. The fringe benefits, such as paid vacations and social insurance, were considerable, but not enough to compensate for the extra work.

The peasants were also represented as real "heroes" of labor. The magnate was gone, to be sure, and the fat peasant, the kulak, was the special butt of the regime. Social security was introduced to the countryside. Yet the peasants appeared to be sullen. Most of them did not like the co-operatives or the collectives.

Because of the emphasis on industries, Hungary's prewar exportable food surplus had dwindled, and the country—part of the European breadbasket—had to import food. There was no shortage of food in the country as a whole, but it was costly.

The foundation of the regime was the bureaucracy, a thin layer, headed by the party and government chieftains. There were some fanatic Communists among the bureaucrats, dedicated individuals, but the majority of them were sycophants. A large number of them had been linked to the Arrow Cross, the wartime extreme right wing. The Communists could not afford to be selective because no European country was as deeply steeped in anticommunism as Hungary, the nation that had already experienced it after World War I. Hungary's interbellum regime was a crusade against bolshevism.

Strengthening the foundation of the regime was the AVO, the political police. Its members were among the best-paid public officials in the country. Not a few of them were on the

Fascist side during the war, and still others were the *condot-tieri* type, who would serve anybody who paid them.

Then there was the Hungarian army, which could be built up to a strength of 65,000 personnel under the peace treaty and which was also entitled to have a force of ninety aircraft. However, the army was not up to its treaty strength—a sign of weakness that not enough young men could be found to stand up for the regime.

The seeds of the Hungarian revolution of 1956 can be traced back to the Magyars' descent into the plains in the year of 895. The Magyar conquerors of those days faced a Slavic foe. Subsequently the Magyars were much in contact with the Slavs. The writer of this book remembers his history teacher in a Budapest secondary school, who told his class that it was the Hungarians' great mission to keep the North and South Slavs apart. Why this was a desirable aim, he did not explain —it was taken as a fact of history. Then the Hungarians had their traumatic experience with the Russians in 1849, when the armies of Czar Nicholas I crushed the hopes of an independent country. To generations of Hungarian school children the Russians appeared as incarnations of the Devil.

Not to be forgotten as a cause of fear is Hungary's location. There is that speck of land in the vastness of the Eurasian continent, the entire top of which is filled out with Russia. Tiny Hungary found solace in a compensating sense of superiority. Many Hungarians looked down upon the Russians—those "Asian barbarians."

The writer recalls his own prejudice when he was taken prisoner by the Russians in the First World War. With foreboding he faced the prospect of meeting with the "abominable Russians," and he could not help sharing the view of his fellow prisoners that Russia still lived in a medieval stage. Was life in Russia to be even more dangerous than in the trenches? In the prisoners' minds the Russians were subject to many epidemics because of their unsanitary ways. Great was the prisoners' surprise when they saw that Russian life was not that primitive.

When the Russian troops swept into Hungary at the end of World War II, fears were not allayed. The first-line soldiers behaved correctly, to be sure, but the waves of uniformed men that followed them were beyond description. Most of the occupation troops seemed to have come from deep Asia, and many of them appeared to be authentic primitives. Countless tales were told about their strange ways. This was the period of large-scale looting and raping. These soldiers were particularly eager to get hold of wrist watches. When some time later a monument was erected in the most conspicuous place of Budapest to the "Soviet liberator," the irreverent people of the capital maintained that it was in memory of the "Unknown Wrist Watch Snatcher."

In the wake of the Red Army came the red rulers, and they made themselves unpopular with their demands on the despoiled country. Hungary was to deliver goods to the Soviets to the value of 200 million dollars. An additional 70 million dollars' worth was to go to the Yugoslavs, and 30 million dollars' worth to the Czechs.

Another method was employed to squeeze the country dry. Several special mixed companies were organized to liquidate former German, or allegedly German, assets. These companies were concerned primarily with the exploitation of oil and natural gas, bauxite and aluminum, air transport and shipping. The stock holdings of the Soviets ranged from 33 to 50 per cent, and hence a goodly proportion of the proceeds left Hungary for good. Budapest jokesters said that in some such cases the arrangement was truly fifty-fifty, as for instance in connection with Danubian navigation. The Russians had the right to navigate the river lengthwise, while the Hungarians acquired the right to navigate it sidewise.

The Hungarians could not forget that their number one

leader, Rákosi, had acquired Russian citizenship and was married to a Russian wife.*

Writers and Revolution

In 1956 it was again the writers who struck off the revolutionary spark. It will be recalled that the early-nineteenth-century Hungarian renaissance was sparked by authors. Hungary's greatest poet, Petőfi, some years later stirred the Hungarians to a high pitch of patriotism on March 15, 1848, with his poem: "Arise, Hungarian, the fatherland is calling." It was a literary organization named after him, the Petőfi Circle, which called upon the Hungarians to arise in the autumn of 1956.

Under the Stalin-Rákosi rule the writers were expected to observe the stringent rules of "proletarian realism," glorifying the regime. Since everything was perfect, there was nothing to criticize. Criticism was equated with the bourgeois regime, and that was reaction. The punishment of reactionary sentiments was great.

Now members of the Petőfi Circle began to state the view that it was not only the writer's prerogative, but his obligation, to criticize the world as long as it was not perfect, and it would never be that. A man was an author because he was more perceptive than others. As one of the well-known authors, Julius Hay, wrote in June, 1956: "It is the writer's prerogative to tell the truth, to criticize anybody and anything." And another author wrote: "Don't tell me it is worse in Africa. I live in Europe, my skin is white, but who will embrace me to make me feel that I am human?"

---

* It struck many Hungarians as ludicrous that Rákosi should pose as a Magyar superman, this pudgy little man with a polished skull. Yet his picture was everywhere, shining pate and all; his name was everywhere; and he was built up as a superman, the fountainhead of all wisdom.

"Szervusz, Lengyel!"

The scene now shifted to Poland. Again the familiar greeting was heard in Hungary: "Hello, Pole!"—*szervusz, lengyel*. For centuries Poles and Hungarians were bulwarks of Western culture. Generations earlier the Poles had lost their country and the Hungarians their freedom. During Hungary's war of independence, it will be recalled, the Poles played leading roles.

Between the two twentieth-century wars Poland and Hungary formed segments of the same *cordon sanitaire* which the Western world set up against the Soviet Union. After the Second World War it was the Soviet army that drove out the Germans from the two countries. In both countries the Communists established camouflaged governments, the United Workers' Party in Poland and the Hungarian Working People's Party in Hungary. Both nations had their Stalinist periods.

After Stalinism had been denounced in Moscow by the new Soviet leaders, it was the Poles who first took their cue. In Poland, too, the Stalinist regime had been concentrating on heavy industries, at the cost of such consumer goods as shoes and clothing. It was said there, too, that a nation was as strong as its heavy industries which produced machines and articles of war. It was only in the "heroic age" of industry-building that living standards were low, but they were bound to rise when the promise was fulfilled.

In Poland, as in Hungary, the workers were subjected to the party officials' pressures to produce more at the same wages and to listen to more indoctrination—brainwashing. A food-surplus country in normal times, Poland had become a food-deficiency country, just like Hungary. The Poles became shabbier and gloomier as the years went on, and their living standards declined.

On June 28, 1956, the bitterness accumulating in Poland

erupted in a bloody strike in Poznan. The workers staged a
mass walkout. At the same time a procession of some fifty
thousand people was formed and demanded freedom. The
demonstrators called for the departure of the Soviet troops
from their country and for free elections. There was a clash
with the armed forces and the police, in the course of which
more than fifty people were killed and a couple of hundred
were wounded. This was a bad omen indeed for the rulers of
the satellite countries on the Soviets' western peripheries.

The warning was understood because another month had
not elapsed before Hungary's Communist leader, Mátyás
Rákosi, made the dramatic statement:

"I request the Central Committee to relieve me of my post
of the First Secretary and of my membership in the Politbureau. One of my reasons for this request is that I am in my
sixty-fifth year. For two years I have been suffering from an
illness which hinders me from discharging the work devolving
upon the First Secretary of the Central Committee."

Rákosi was promptly replaced by Ernő Gerő, who wrote
the same day in *Szabad Nép—Free People*—the party journal:

"It would be a great mistake to draw no lesson from the
Poznan provocation. . . . The enemy says that its aim is to
stir up 'Hungarian Poznans.' . . . Hungry pigs dream of
acorns."

Gerő seems to be determined to draw all the wrong conclusions from the Poznan demonstrations.

In Poland, meanwhile, the crisis continued. The people
were clamoring for the return of the anti-Stalinist national
Communist Wladislaw Gomulka, who had been kept isolated
and under house arrest for years. The people were also
clamoring that the Soviet army stationed in Poland should
be withdrawn. Instead of that, the Soviet troops were marching upon the capital, with the idea of crushing the spirit of
revolt. It was only at the last minute that the Soviet units
were recalled and the people had their way. On October 21

Gomulka became First Secretary of the United Workers' Party—the key position in the country—and the dissidents won.

Poles visiting Hungary in those days were received with more than customary cordiality. Children greeted them with the friendly words: *"Szervusz, lengyel."*

Students and the Workers

The appointment of Gomulka seems to have touched off the chain reaction of events in Hungary. On October 22 a number of student meetings took place in Budapest, the most important of which was held at the Building Industry Technological University, where the students adopted a list of sixteen demands.

The substance of these demands was the following:

1.) Immediate withdrawal of all Soviet troops; 2.) election of new leaders of the Hungarian Workers' Party; 3.) government to be headed by Imre Nagy; 4.) trial of leading Stalinists; 5.) general elections; 6.) re-examination of Hungarian-Soviet and Hungarian-Yugoslav political, economic, and intellectual relations; 7.) reorganization of Hungarian economy with an eye to the vital interests of the Hungarian people; 8.) information about and free sale of uranium; 9.) revision of industrial norms and wages; 10.) new basis for peasant food delivery system; 11.) re-examination of trials and repatriation of deportees from Soviet Union; 12.) complete freedom of opinion and its expression; 13.) removal of Stalin statues; 14.) reintroduction of the old Hungarian Kossuth coat-of-arms; 15.) solidarity with Poland; 16.) freedom for youth organization.

The traditions of 1848, when the March 15 revolution began with the proclamation of the Twelve Demands, had a strong hold on the generation of 1956. On the same day the Petőfi Circle published its Ten Points, on the following day the Youth Group of the Hungarian Workers' (Communist) Party proclaimed its own Ten Points, and on October 28 the

Revolutionary Committee of the Hungarian Intellectuals published its Ten Points.

The Hungarians Writers' Union proposed to express its
solidarity on October 23 by laying a wreath at the statue of
General Bem, the 1848–1849 war of independence Hero, who
was of Polish origin. The students decided to organize a
silent demonstration of sympathy on the same occasion.*

The demonstration at the Bem statue took place, and there
was another demonstration at the monument of Sándor
Petőfi, the war of independence bard, and his famous poem,
"Arise, Hungarian," was recited with fervor. The crowd then
moved to Parliament Square where it called for Imre Nagy,
whom they wanted to be the new Prime Minister. This was a
revolution, therefore, which wanted to have a national Communist, Nagy, at the head of the government.

On this October 23 Nagy addressed the demonstrators from
the balcony of Parliament Building. "There had so far been
nothing to suggest," the United Nations report noted, "that
the demonstration would end in any other way than the
crowd's returning home."

However, an episode at 8:00 P.M. greatly embittered the
people. The First Secretary of the Central Committee of the
party, Ernő Gerő, had returned that morning from a visit to
Marshal Tito, and the public was eagerly awaiting a speech
which he was to broadcast at that time. The general hope was
that he would take account of the popular demand voiced by
the students and make some conciliatory announcement.
What did Gerő say?

"Of course we want a social democracy and not a bourgeois
democracy. In accord with our party and our convictions, our
working class and other people are jealously guarding the
achievements of our People's Democracy, and they will not

* *Report of the Special Committee on the Problem of Hungary*, United
Nations General Assembly; Official Records: Eleventh Session. Supplement
No. 18 (A/3592), New York, 1957, pp. 5–6.

permit anyone to touch them. We shall defend these achievements under all circumstances from whichever quarter they
may be threatened. . . ."

And so on throughout the entire address. It was all the old
gibberish, the usual incantations, and not a word about reforms or what had happened in Poland. The tone of the address angered the people. It is possible that even a more
perceptive speech might not have changed the turn of events,
but it is certain that this broadcast was of no help. The anger
of the crowd now turned against the most obvious symbol of
the old regime, the monument to Stalin. They moved on it,
overturned it, and demolished it.

The First Shots

On the same evening a large body of students, reinforced by
others, moved on the Radio Building of the capital in an
attempt to have their demands broadcast, and they sent a
delegation into the building in order to negotiate with the
director. Time went on, but the delegates did not return.
A rumor spread—an unsubstantiated one—that a member of
the delegation had been shot.

The Radio Building was guarded by the dreaded and hated
political police, *Állãmvédelmi Osztály*—AVO *—the State
Security Authority. As the crowd was getting larger, it began
to press against the gate. The AVO seems to have become
panicky. It began to throw tear gas bombs from the upper
windows. The time was now nine o'clock in the evening.
Thereupon the crowd became more excited, and a shot rang
out. It was followed by others. The AVO men had opened
fire on the crowd, killing a number of people and wounding
others. "Insofar as any moment can be selected as the turning point," says the United Nations report, "which changed
a peaceable demonstration into a violent uprising, it would be
this moment."

* Also known as *Állãmvédelmi Hatóság*—AVH.

To the south of Budapest, on the Danubian island of Csepel, tens of thousands of workers of large steel and industrial combines learned about these events. They seized trucks and drove into Budapest. By that time the capital was in an uproar, as fighters suddenly emerged from nowhere. Soldiers and the police joined the insurgents and supplied the Csepel workers with arms. The wrath of the crowd was directed first against the AVO men, many of whom were flushed out of their hiding places, hanged, sometimes by their heels, and lynched in other ways.

In the capital the first few days of the uprising were marked by the transfer of power from the Communist bureaucracy to Revolutionary and Workers' Councils, the UN report states. There were Revolutionary Councils in the army, government departments, professional groups, radio, and telegraph. The most influential of these bodies was the Transdanubian National Council, representing the people of western Hungary. Using the free radio station of Győr, this Council demanded that Hungary should denounce the Warsaw Treaty of "mutual assistance" among the Soviets and their satellites and proclaim her neutrality. The emergence of the Councils throughout the nation "represented the first practical step to restore order and to reorganize the Hungarian economy on a Socialist basis, but without rigid party control or the apparatus of terror."

A Crucial Day

October 25 was another crucial day in the revolution. On that day Soviet tanks guarding the Parliament building opened fire on demonstrators in support of the AVO. Many people lost their lives. Who brought in the Russians? It was thought at the time that it may have been Imre Nagy, but this was denied later. It was only months later that György Marosán, Hungarian Minister of War, stated that it was he who had called in Soviet troops against the Hungarian insurgents.*

Meanwhile Gerő resigned and János Kádár became the First Secretary of the Central Committee of the Party. Imre Nagy formed a government on October 27, into which he invited both Communist and non-Communist ministers. Several Stalinists were also retained. The Central Committee of the party now announced that the government would start negotiations for the immediate withdrawal of Soviet forces.†

The street battles in Budapest continued. The revolutionaries were on one side, representing several strata of society, mostly, however, students and industrial workers, of nearly all ages from twelve up, Catholics, Protestants, and Jews. The remaining members of the Hungarian political police and the Soviet tanks were on the other side. The heavy tanks encountered serious resistance in the narrow streets, exposed to "Molotov cocktails," loosely corked bottles filled with gasoline, which exploded when hurled against the tanks. Soviet mechanized forces were also hampered by lack of food and insufficient infantry support.

In a matter of days the Communist Party disintegrated, revealing its lack of popular support. Nagy meanwhile was making radio broadcasts, telling the people to go home, but his voice was drowned out. He seems to have lost his grip on the people. A few days before he appeared to be the miracle worker, and now he himself was awaiting a miracle which never came.

On October 28 the government announced the dissolution of the political police. Meanwhile, however, the matter got completely out of hand. Since there was no central revolutionary authority, no arrangement between the insurgents and the government was possible. On October 30 Cardinal Mindszenty was liberated from his confinement. "My sons," he told

---

* *The New York Times,* July 31, 1957.

† There was a report also that Nagy had formed his government on October 24.

his deliverers, "I shall carry on where I left off eight years ago." But eight years ago he was against land reform, and the Hungarian peasants certainly would not have stood for the return to old times. He might have been able to stop the fighting if he had found the right word.

The carnage continued until October 28, particularly at the strategic points of Budapest. It seemed as if the insurgents had won. The new First Secretary of the party, János Kádár, announced that a reformed party was in the making. It was set up eventually under the name of "Hungarian Socialist Workers' Party." It would defend the cause of socialism and democracy "not by slavishly imitating foreign examples, but by taking a road suitable to the economic and historic characteristics of our country. . . . We do not want to be dependent any longer, we do not want our country to become a battlefield."

Meanwhile, certain sidelights of the insurrection came into view. The London *Observer* reported that "the Budapest rising must have been the cleanest revolution in history." The reporter of this English paper saw large boxes in the main thoroughfares bearing notices: "Give to those who remain alive!" They were filled with hundred-forint notes. The boxes were unguarded and emptied periodically by small boys. Nobody else touched them, and they were still there after the battle.

Yugoslav journalists, traveling up to Budapest when the fighting was at its worst, found bucolic scenes in the Hungarian countryside. A score of young couples were whirling happily to the tune of a gypsy band in a restaurant in the city of Kecskemét, some fifty miles southeast of Budapest.

The Tragedy

The interest of the insurgents, meanwhile, was concentrated mainly on the immediate withdrawal of Soviet troops from Hungary. Diplomatic negotiation was of no avail, as the hand of Prime Minister Nagy was forced. The railroaders proclaimed a strike until the Russian troops were out of the country. One of the principal leaders of the army insurgents, Paul Maléter, was designated Deputy Minister of Defense. Subsequently, he went over to the freedom fighters and became the hero of the revolution. His defense of the strategically located Kilian barracks in Budapest invited international attention.

The Workers' and Revolutionary Councils' clamor for immediate action swelled. On November 1 Nagy assumed direct responsibility for the conduct of foreign affairs, and he told the Soviet Ambassador of information he had received about the entry of new Russian units into the country. He also told him that this was a violation of the Warsaw Treaty, of which both Hungary and the Soviets were signatories, and which provided the undertaking of the parties "to refrain in their international relations from the threat or use of force." *
Nagy told the Ambassador that the Soviet troop movement into Hungary was a violation of the Treaty, and unless these forces were withdrawn forthwith he would denounce it.

In reply, the Ambassador stated that the Red troops had crossed the border only to relieve the fighting men and to protect Russian civilians in Hungary. The Soviet government was ready, he stated, to negotiate the partial withdrawal of Soviet troops, and he suggested that two delegations be appointed to discuss the political and technical problems.

At 2:00 P.M. Premier Nagy told the Ambassador that, according to word he had just received, fresh Soviet troops had crossed the Hungarian frontier within the last three hours. As a result, he further declared Hungary was withdrawing from the Warsaw Pact, to take effect immediately.

Two hours passed, and then the Hungarian Council of Ministers took the most momentous decision of the revolu-

* Warsaw Treaty, May 14, 1955, "of Friendship, Co-operation and Mutual Assistance."

tionary period. It proclaimed Hungary's neutrality. At the same time it requested the United Nations to place the question of Hungarian neutrality on the agenda of the General Assembly. It also asked the United Nations for assistance.*

This was the text of the Hungarian note:

"Reliable reports have reached the Government of the Hungarian People's Republic that further Soviet units are entering into Hungary. The President of the Council of Ministers in his capacity as Minister of Foreign Affairs summoned Yuri V. Andropov, Ambassador Extraordinary and Plenipotentiary of the Soviet Union to Hungary, and expressed his strongest protest against the entry of further Soviet troops into Hungary. He demanded the instant and immediate withdrawal of these Soviet forces.

"He informed the Soviet Ambassador that the Hungarian Government immediately repudiates the Warsaw Treaty and, at the same time, declares Hungary's neutrality and turns to the United Nations and requests the help of the four great powers in defending the country's neutrality. The Government of the Hungarian People's Republic made the declaration of neutrality on November 1, 1956. Therefore I request Your Excellency promptly to put on the agenda of the forthcoming General Assembly of the United Nations the question of Hungary's neutrality and the defense of this neutrality by the four great powers."

The four great powers—unspecified in the message—must have been the United States, Great Britain, France, and the Soviet Union. Compliance with this request would have meant three members of the North Atlantic Treaty Alliance moving into Hungary, diplomatically or otherwise, facing the

---

* The student of history is bound to recall that famous scene in the Calvinist church of Debrecen on April 14, 1849, when Kossuth dethroned the Habsburgs. The decision of the Council of Ministers in Budapest on November 1, 1957, dethroned the Soviet rulers in Hungary. However, both dethronements failed to take effect.

Soviet Union. At 7:45 P.M. Prime Minister Nagy broadcast this declaration of neutrality to the Hungarian people and to the rest of the world.

The following day Radio Moscow accused "counterrevolutionary gangs" of having caused chaotic conditions in Hungary. In Budapest, at the same time, Cardinal Mindszenty joined Nagy in making an appeal for help to the West. "While news came in of the massing of Soviet armored forces," the United Nations special report recorded, "negotiations continued for the withdrawal of Soviet troops from Hungary. By the afternoon of November 3 agreement appeared to be near and only certain technical details of the withdrawal remained to be settled. . . . The Hungarian negotiators attended a banquet given in their honor by the Soviet military representatives at Tököl. It was nearly midnight when the party was interrupted by the arrival of General Serov, Chief of the Soviet Security Police, who entered the room accompanied by NKVD officers and ordered the arrest of the Hungarian delegation."

Several Revolutionary Councils reported to the Hungarian government during the night that Soviet forces in battle formation were advancing and asked urgently for permission to oppose them by force of arms. It was estimated that some 2500 Soviet tanks and 1000 supporting vehicles were in Hungary by November 3. All strategic centers, airfields, railways, and highways had been brought under control of Russian troops. Premier Nagy believed that a successful outcome of the negotiations for the Soviet troops' withdrawal was still to be expected, and he gave specific instructions not to open fire. The insurgents, however, did open fire. Nagy now announced over Radio Budapest that the Soviet troops had attacked the capital with the intent of overthrowing the legal government. He declared that it remained at its post and that Hungarian troops were in combat.

Meanwhile an announcement had been made over the

radio outside of Budapest that four members of the Nagy government, including János Kádár, had left his cabinet and formed the "Hungarian Revolutionary Worker-Peasant Government." Kádár had been considered one of the "national Communists," and he had been jailed by the Stalinist regime in Hungary.

The head of this new body was Kádár himself, and he announced over the radio:

"We were prompted to take this responsible step by the realization that within the Nagy government, which became impotent under reactionary pressure, we could do nothing against the counterrevolutionary danger menacing our People's Republic of the workers and peasants.

"Respected champions of the working class have been murdered . . . and many highly esteemed sons of the peasantry have been exterminated. . . . We have decided to fight with all our strength against the threatening danger of Fascism and its murderous gangs."

There were now two rival governments in Hungary. The one headed by Nagy was a coalition cabinet, national Communists predominating, and it had just broken with the Soviet by declaring Hungary's neutrality. The other government was headed by Kádár. Soon there was to be only one of them, headed by János Kádár, the Soviets' choice.

Kádár started his life the hard way, as an apprentice locksmith, no bed of roses in Hungary. An ambitious young man, he fell under the influence of the Socialist young workers' movement and gradually edged his way toward communism, outlawed during the Horthy regime. He was found out and jailed for two and a half years. During the Second World War he became popular among the anti-Nazis in Hungary because of his courage. He joined the leader of the Communist underground, László Rajk.

There were few Communists of leadership timber in Hungary after World War II and Kádár rose high as a member of the Politbureau, apex of the party hierarchy, and deputy secretary general. However, he was not considered a "Muscovite" thoroughbred, and had one of his feet in the "red-white-and-green" group, so called because of the Hungarian tricolor flag.

When Rákosi lashed out against this group, Kádár followed him and turned against his former idol, Rajk, who was then sentenced to death and executed. Yet Kádár had been unable to buy himself immunity from prosecution. In 1951 charges similar to those preferred against Rajk were brought against him: espionage, treason and Titoism. The political police went to work on him; his fingernails were torn out and he spent three nightmare years in solitary confinement. But he did not break, so he could not be turned into the villain of a show trial.

He was released during the 1953 "thaw," when Imre Nagy headed the government. Kádár served as the party secretary of an important Budapest district. In July, 1956, he took the lead in the revolt against Rákosi, the Stalinist boss. Rákosi had demanded that some four hundred writers and intellectuals should be arrested in order to head off a revolutionary wave. In an open meeting of the Communist Central Committee in Budapest, Kádár told Rákosi that the country had had more than enough of him. Rákosi resigned. It was believed that Kádár had mounted the offensive against him at the behest of the Kremlin, determined to get rid of the "last Stalinist."

During the 1956 autumn uprising, Kádár first joined Imre Nagy, then, suddenly, turned against him and went over to the Russians. His counter-government announced over the radio station of Dunapentele (it had been Sztalinváros): "Treacherous occupation forces have attacked Budapest and several other cities. The battle is on in Pécs, Székesfehérvár, Dunaföldvár and Veszprém. Hungarian soldiers are fighting as one man against the invaders and will continue fighting for the sacred cause of the Hungarian revolution to their last drop of blood. The situation is serious but not hopeless."

The main battles were fought on the arterial roads and at the approaches to Budapest. In order to slow down the Russian tanks' advance, barricades were hastily thrown up. Fighting side by side, units of the army and freedom fighters, equipped principally with light arms, resisted the advancing tanks. The freedom fighters were transmitting their desperate appeal to the outside world. The writers, who felt a special responsibility for the success of the revolution, made their broadcasts both in the capital and in Dunapentele. An unidentified radio pleaded: "Civilized people of the world, listen and come to our aid, not with declaration but with force—arms and soldiers. Do not forget that there is no other way to halt the wild onslaught of Bolshevism. Your turn will come when we perish. . . . Save our souls! Save our souls!"

Addressing the UN, Radio Dunapentele, one of the most active stations, pleaded at noon: "We beseech the United Nations to send immediate help. We ask for parachute troops to be dropped in western Hungary."

An unidentified free radio pleaded an hour later: "Peoples of Europe whom we helped for centuries to withstand the barbarous attacks from Asia, listen to the tolling of the Hungarian bells which warn of disaster. . . . Civilized people of the world, we implore you to help us in the name of justice, freedom, and morality. . . . Our ship is sinking, the light is falling, and the shadows are growing darker every hour over the Hungarian soil. Listen to the cry, civilized peoples of the world, and extend your fraternal hand."

The Soviet armored units broke through the defenses, acquired control of the strategic Danube bridges, of the Parliament building, of the central telephone exchange which covered the entire country, and of other vital services. Late in the evening of November 4, the government of Nagy was gone, and the government of János Kádár was at the helm. "The events of the day," it announced, "have led to the complete dispersal of the reactionary forces."

The following day the Home Service of Radio Budapest announced: "We are dealing the last blows to the counter-revolutionary forces." Some of the insurgent groups were still fighting, and the Free Radio Rákóczi stated: "We are not Fascists and we can prove this to the world." A few minutes later the appeal was broadcast: "Can the world let a small country lose its liberty—the freedom of a country which had maintained it with great loss of blood through a thousand years? Why are only the interests of the great powers important? Why can't you hear the call of our murdered women and children?"

Late on November 6 the government-controlled Radio Miskolc reported that "Fascist bandits" were still fighting, destroying railroad equipment and stations. A weak voice was heard on the seventh over Radio Rákóczi: "Please forward this appeal to President Eisenhower. . . . We are asking for immediate armed help." Even Radio Budapest, which minimized the battles, admitted that resistance in the capital continued. The Moscow and satellite radios spoke about the "Fascist counterrevolutionaries and bandits." Sporadic fights flared up in Csepel and Dunapentele, centers of the heavy industries. There were guerrilla fights around the uranium and coal mines, and in the rugged hills of the Bakony in Trans-Danubia. Former Premier Nagy found sanctuary in the Yugoslav Embassy in Budapest. He stayed there for a few days. He left it in the belief that he had the Hungarian government's safe-conduct pledge to go to his home. However, as he left the Embassy, he was apprehended by Soviet agents and taken to an undisclosed place.

Resistance to the Kádár regime continued as the industrial workers refused to return to their plants. Emigré newspapers reported that the Hungarian government sought to starve the resisters into submission. This it did by holding up food shipments from abroad at the Austrian frontier. The Kádár government claimed that foreign relief was merely a cloak for the shipments of arms. As a result of the workers' resistance, production continued at an extremely low level. Daily coal output, for instance, was down to 3500 tons from the normal 75,000 to 80,000 tons—less than one-twentieth of the standard.

The foreign press reported mass arrests by the Soviet and the Budapest authorities. Eyewitnesses who had made good their escape reported that trainloads of deportees were on their way out of the country, headed toward Russia. A year after the revolution reports spoke about large groups of Hungarian deportees in the Central Asian republics of the Soviets. These people were allegedly working on the newly opened Soviet "virgin lands." The United Nations special report on the problem of Hungary stated: "No accurate figures exist regarding the number of Hungarian citizens deported, but these certainly run into thousands." * And the most important loss—human lives? Neutral observers estimated the loss at 25,000 people; the Hungarian government admitted 2,700 deaths.

Disarming the Opposition

The stand of the János Kádár government toward the opposition was ambivalent. On the one hand, it claimed that "the armed insurrection that occurred in Hungary between October 23 and November 4, 1956, was designed to overthrow by violence the constitutional and social order of the Hungarian republic and to restore the old Horthyite Fascist regime which was directed against the social progress of the Hungarian people." †

* See below additional information disclosed at the Special Session of the General Assembly of the United Nations held in New York in September, 1957.

† Statement by Peter Mod, Hungarian delegate to the United Nations General Assembly, made on September 10, 1957.

On the other hand, the government blamed the "Rákosi-Gerő clique" for having ignored Hungary's special conditions and "slavishly" applied Soviet methods to the solution of Hungarian problems.

The economic situation with which the Kádár government was faced was disastrous. We have seen that the Communist governments of Hungary had forced the tempo of the heavy industries at the cost of the consumer industries and farming. The prices of general goods, as a consequence, had risen sharply. Hungarian living standards in 1956 had been lower than in 1937. Whereas in 1937 it took the work of ten hours to buy the food requirements of an average family for one week, the corresponding figure for 1956 was seventeen hours.*

On top of this, there was the great material damage suffered during the revolution and the lost man-hours due to the strike epidemic. Obviously, it was not enough to place the blame for these conditions upon the already heavily overladen shoulders of "Western imperialists" and "Horthyite Fascists."

The condition of Hungary after the revolution was such that only the quickest financial aid could help. Hungary's neighbor, Poland, was in negotiation with the United States in regard to such aid, but in the case of Hungary this was out of the question. There was only the Soviet Union to which the Kádár government could turn. Negotiations were carried on in the latter part of March, 1957, on a high level, indicating the urgency of the problem. Finally an arrangement was reached. The Soviet Union undertook to send Hungary a billion rubles' worth of goods (about 100 million dollars in real purchasing power), which included food and vital industrial raw materials to get the Hungarian plants going. The shipments covered, among others, wheat and fodder grain, iron ore and coal, oil, and a long list of minerals and metals indispensable for industrial production. The Soviet government also granted Hungary long-term loans and canceled a

* "Der Spiegel," August 21, 1957.

part of the country's previous indebtedness. In return, the Soviets were to receive Hungarian capital goods, such as boats and cranes.

The most important change in the economic management in the country was the change in the ratio of heavy capital goods to consumer articles. The postrevolutionary accent was on the production of the latter, clothes and shoes among many others. The new Three-Year Plan, beginning in 1958, projected a balance between capital outlay for investments and the manufacture of consumption goods. Housing received priority in the list of investments.

The economic planning of the country was subjected to additional changes. Private enterprise was given a chance to stage a modest comeback. Not more than a year after the revolution it was calculated that private business in Hungary— outside of agriculture—accounted for about 10 per cent of the national income. The Hungarian countryside had never been completely sovietized. In the autumn of 1957 more than three-fourths of the cultivated land—78 per cent—was in private hands, and only about ten per cent of the land remained fully collectivized. The rest is in State experimental farms. The Hungarian peasantry evidently had stood its ground even in the face of the strongest Communist pressure.

Private trading also was liberalized in the wake of the revolution. The remaining small businesses were exempted from further nationalization. Private businessmen now won the right to engage help. The limit was one employee and one apprentice, apart from family members. Further liberalization of private trading was contemplated, making it possible to engage three employees and two apprentices. Loans up to the equivalent of one thousand dollars were made available by the Hungarian government for the launching of private business. When the large-scale nationalization of private trade began in 1950 there were 40,000 to 50,000 stores in private hands. In mid–1957 their number was 13,000—on the increase, and over 50 per cent more than in the previous year. Of course most of the increase was in small stores. The official position was now that certain types of trade were not worth while for the state to handle, and that it served public convenience in many areas to open private shops.*

Wage increases were decreed on all levels in order to keep the "industrial toilers" quiet. Unpaid overtime was not ground out of the workers in the name of "Socialist emulation." Endless hours of indoctrination yielded to propaganda in a less time-consuming way. Tax rates were being reduced. Prices, on the other hand, rose on many items, as a result of material destruction and lost man-hours. Still, workers' wages were higher than before the uprising because there had been no increases in the cost of basic necessities.†

On the other hand, police terror was as extensive as under Rákosi, but it was more discreet. Corruption was rampant. Hungary was covered by the gloom of hopelessness.

Budapest "Galgenhumor"

During more than a generation, Budapest, famous for its serenity in happier times, had witnessed terrors of several hues, Black, Red, and White, Nazi occupation, Soviet "liberation," the Rákosi reign of terror, and the revolution. During all these years the "Queen City of the Danube" had been disfigured, suffering great damage in human lives and material values. It retained one traditional trait, however—a sense of humor, which Hungary's famous playwrights, headed by Franz Molnár, author of *Liliom, The Swan,* and many other plays, had made known throughout the world. In days of adversity that humor assumed a grim trait, *Galgenhumor*, as the Germans put it picturesquely, "the humor of the gallows." Dictators and conquerors came and went, but the humor of the capital city remained. The revolution was crushed, but its spirit re-

* AP dispatch from Budapest in *The New York Times*, September 8, 1957.
† *The New York Times*, October 10, 1957.

mained, as shown in these few samples of the humor of Budapest:

"Wanted!" said the posters pasted clandestinely on the walls of the houses. "Wanted! A Hungarian Prime Minister. Qualifications: a criminal record and Russian nationality. Character and backbone unnecessary."

And here was another one, in reference to the Communist allegation that the revolutionaries were agents of the old aristocratic regime:

"Warning: 10,000,000 Fascists are at large in Hungary. For the most part they are former Cardinals, aristocrats, and Horthyite officers,* who for the last ten years have disguised themselves as Csepel Island workers."

After the revolution many Csepel Island workers greeted one another: "How are you, Prince Tailor?" "And how are you, Archduke János Smith?"

Hungary Before the United Nations

Before the revolution was crushed, the United Nations debated the Hungarian question. On November 4, 1956, the General Assembly voted to condemn the Soviet action in Hungary. The vote was 50 to 8, only members of the Soviet bloc being in the opposition. However, 15 members abstained, consisting mainly of the so-called Arab-Asian bloc members, also Finland and Yugoslavia.

On September 10, 1957, a special session of the General Assembly was called to deal with the problem on the basis of the Report of the Special Committee on the Problem of Hungary, published the previous summer.

The chief delegate of the United States to the United Nations, Henry Cabot Lodge, stated on September 10 that the number of the Soviet troops in Hungary at that time was 68,000, as compared with 25,000 the year before. He further stated that all the 300 workers of a factory in Miskolc, one

* Hungary's population at the time was ten million.

of the revolutionary strongholds, had been sent to Russia for
a "study visit" but had not returned. The Hungarian government had taken punitive action against 1768 individuals between November, 1956, and August, 1957. The list of these
individuals was drawn entirely from Hungarian Communist
sources—newspapers and radio broadcasts. Budapest government sources revealed fifty-one death sentences and
twenty-three executions; also twenty-nine sentences of life
imprisonment.

In the early morning hours of September 14, 1957, the
General Assembly adopted a resolution condemning the
Soviet Union's armed intervention in Hungary and its con-
tinued defiance of the earlier Assembly resolution.

The September 14 resolution designated the former Foreign
Minister of Thailand, Prince Wan Waithayakon, as the Assembly's representative to try to obtain compliance with the
resolution. This time the vote was 60 in favor and 10 against
the resolution, with 10 abstentions. Yugoslavia voted against
it. The abstainers were again some members of the Asian-
Arab bloc, the most important of which was India, and the
Soviets' small neighbor, Finland.

The resolution found:

"That the USSR, in violation of the UN Charter, has de-
prived Hungary of her liberty and political independence and
the Hungarian people of the exercise of their fundamental
human rights;

"The present Hungarian regime has been imposed upon
the Hungarian people by the armed intervention of the USSR;

"The USSR has carried on mass deportations of Hungarian
citizens to the USSR;

"The USSR has violated its obligations under the Geneva
Convention of 1949;

"The present authorities in Hungary have violated the
human rights and freedom guaranteed by the Treaty of Peace
with Hungary."

The resolution condemned these acts and called upon the USSR and the authorities in Hungary to desist from repressive measures against the Hungarian people.

On Jan. 27, 1958, a footnote to the history of the Hungarian revolution was written. Kádár resigned as Premier but remained as the first secretary of the party. He was replaced by 72-year-old Ferenc Munnich, a faithful Muscovite. The government was not expected to change its course.

An Appraisal of the Revolution

The Hungarian revolution of 1956 was unique. A small nation rose against one of the superpowers. The Hungarians did their battling with little more than rifles in their hands. Seldom has Western public opinion been aroused to such a pitch of excitement as during the Hungarian uprising, and no contemporary event has received comparable attention. More copy was filed about Hungary, more pictures shown, more radio and television programs produced, more books printed— sometimes in a remarkably short time—than about any other current event.

Superlatives of the most purple hue were evoked. The Hungarian revolution was described as "the greatest," "the most awe-inspiring," and "the most inspirational event of the century." The Hungarian refugees—of whom there were nearly 200,000 *—were received as immortal fighters for human freedom. This was especially so at the beginning of the great exodus. The gates of countries long bolted to Hungarians were thrown wide open with amazing speed. The free world could not do enough for the "freedom fighters."

The world had known Hungary only superficially, as a small nation somewhere in eastern Europe, in the neighborhood of the fairy-tale countries of "Ruritania" and "Carpa-

* The Hungarian frontiers were wide open during a period of chaos, which enabled these thousands to escape.

thia," a nation with an attractive capital, beautiful women, fiery music, spiced food, heady wine—in other words, a Hungarian rhapsody.

Suddenly the world learned that there was far more than that to the Hungarians—that they were an exceptionally courageous little people, who had the pluck to do what no other nation had dared to undertake. And what did the world know about the Hungarians' real life? It knew next to nothing about their history, background, traditions, way of life, national traits—nothing that might have enabled the world to sate its curiosity about this phenomenal event.

Was the unparalleled interest in Hungary's revolution due only to the admiration the world gave to the freedom fighters, or was it due partly to a mixture of extraneous factors? How much was it due to the strategy of the cold war? Was this not the propitious time for the free world to marshal its ingenuity to crush the Soviets in the war of propaganda? The West had appeared to be on the verge of losing the war of words, largely because of the ineptitude of its leadership. Here was the supreme chance to destroy the Soviets with the atom bombs and hydrogen explosions of publicity. Many of the publications could not have been published without governmental aid.

The observer can only wish that all the countries of the Western world had entered the lists on behalf of Hungary with immaculate hands. Still, the interest of the world was greatly focused, no matter what extraneous issues may have been involved. Because of that interest, thinking people also wanted to know more about the motives, the background, and the aims of the Hungarians.

A Spontaneous Uprising

The Soviet Union was quick to enter the arena with its heavy propaganda weapons. It made the charge that the

Hungarian revolution was really not that; it was a "counter-revolution" stage-managed from abroad. It blamed "Fascists" and "imperialists" for the blood that flowed in Budapest's streets. It pointed an accusing finger especially at the United States. It was that country, it said, that financed the "propaganda balloons" which at one time were said to have covered the skies of the satellite countries. It was Radio Free Europe, with the backing of the American government, which stirred up the Hungarians to revolt. Congress appropriated hundreds of millions of dollars, Moscow said, to foment subversion in the Communist countries. American arms were used by the "counterrevolutionaries."

Moscow also charged that "Horthyite Fascists" rushed into the country at the time of the troubles, and that this was with the connivance of Austria and of the United States.

What was the truth of these charges? The Special Committee of the United Nations on the Problem of Hungary went thoroughly into an examination of them, and it found unanimously that there was "no evidence whatsoever to suggest that any political personality associated with the pre-war regime exerted the slightest influence on events." The Committee found that what took place in Hungary in October and November, 1956, was a spontaneous national uprising that developed from "long-standing grievances which had caused resentment among the people." One of these grievances was the inferior status of Hungary in relation to the Soviet Union. The system under which the Hungarian people were governed was reinforced by "the weapon of terror" wielded by the secret police and "a complex network of agents and informers permeating the whole of Hungarian society." Soviet pressure was resented in other respects also. "From the stifling of free speech to the adoption of a Soviet-style uniform for the Hungarian army, an alien influence existed in all walks of life." Hungarians felt no personal animosity toward individual Soviet soldiers, the report noted, "but these armed forces were symbols of something which annoyed a proud people and fed the desire to be free."

As to the "Fascist" and "Horthyite agents," it was true that a considerable number of the most extreme types of Fascist, the Arrow Cross partisans, remained in the German Republic hoping for the day they could return to their country. However, when the revolution broke out, the Austrian government laid down a barrage against the possible return of undesirable elements to Hungary. Since the frontier was wide open in those days and every inch of the border could not be policed, it would have been almost a miracle if a few of these people had not sneaked back. However, if they did— and this is not established authentically—they played no role in the revolution.*

The Revolutionary Paradox

Since the revolution was not prepared, it had no central leadership. Leaders arose within the groups as the uprising gathered momentum. The revolutionary vanguard consisted of students and industrial workers, backed by soldiers. The largest single occupation group in Hungary, the peasantry, played a very minor role. And here lies a paradox. The people who bore the brunt of the fighting were the ones who had been exposed to the largest doses of Communist propaganda, the industrial workers and students.

Under the Communist regime the industrial proletariat was represented as the advance guard, "power elite," crusaders for the realization of the happy toilers' new fatherland. Their indoctrination was a ceaseless process, employing saturation techniques, so that no interstices should be left in their minds for independent thought.

Even more was this true of the university students. Chil-

* *The Truth About Hungary*, Facts and Eyewitnesses' Accounts, Moscow: Foreign Language Publishing House, 1957, presented the Soviet case. It is an undocumented and unconvincing book, containing the usual double talk. It cannot be taken seriously.

dren of Hungary's "historic classes" were excluded from the schools of higher learning. Admission was open to those of the former lower classes, peasants and industrial workers. In the schools, too, the students were impregnated with the Marxist-Leninist ideology, so that it should be their only living reality. First their minds were purged of old ideas and kept clean of contaminating bourgeois influence. The Soviet Union was represented to them as the incarnation of man's noblest ambitions, a happy land of carefree people, in full control of their destinies. The capitalist world, on the other hand, was shown to them as a land of deep darkness where wage slaves were chained to heartless machines in constant fear of losing their crumb of bread. The soldiers, of course, received double portions of all this propaganda.

What was the explanation of the phenomenon, then, that the advance guard of the regime, the grand army of the brain-washed people, was also in the forefront of the fighters for freedom?

There were several explanations, and these included the traditions of the country—a thousand years against a mere decade of Communist indoctrination—and the history of the country itself. It was also the Catholic Church, the only nation-wide organization to cultivate personal relations with the people before the war. The Catholic Church in Hungary was a fighting institution, with a long history of resistance to the "pagans"—Turks and Mongols—and the "schismatic" church of the East. It was a well-served bulwark.

The explanation was also the distaste for the Russians and their global empire encompassing the entire top of the Old World—the distaste of a tiny country in the crushing presence of an overwhelming vastness. Part of the explanation was the post–First World War Communist regime of Béla Kun with all its incredible bungling, which left a bitter taste in millions of mouths. It was also the anti-Communist indoctrination of an entire generation between the two World Wars.

Also the Communist "pie in the sky" did not appeal to articulate people. Students and industrial workers like to dress decently, but that was not possible under the regime. While working harder than ever, the country was sliding downhill at an accelerated rate.

The attempts of the Communists to denationalize Hungary hit the most heavily indoctrinated people with the greatest force. Those Russian uniforms, the ubiquitous Soviet stars, the Stalin statues, the glorification of Russian history, were so many stabs to patriotic Hungarians.

The Communist technique of supersaturation was also part of the explanation—the law of diminishing returns. Not only did the excess bubble over, but also the normal substance evaporated. The crude methods of the Soviets boomeranged against the Hungarians, a sophisticated people that have to be shown, not only told. The Soviets oversold themselves. Then, too, let us not forget that Eastern Europe is part of the world's anti-Semitic belt, and many of the leading Hungarian Stalinists were Hungarians with Jewish backgrounds, even though they did not practice their religion. The industrial workers, specifically, were resentful of the speed-up system operated at their cost.

The Communist regime elevated the industrial workers and students into the caste of a "new aristocracy," but only on paper. Now they did act as the new aristocracy, the new "gentry," bearers of the old national ideals, proponents of historical ideologies and aversions. Their great aversion was the Soviet.

Peasants in the Rear

It is strange to record, but it must be said that the peasants did not pull their weight in the Hungarian revolution. The brunt of the fight was borne by Budapest. There was also heavy fighting in the larger industrial centers, such as Győr, Miskolc, and Dunapentele. There, too, it was the industrial workers who did the fighting. The peasants remained comparatively quiet.

Technical reasons provide a part of the explanation. The revolution was spontaneous, and it had no national headquarters or central leadership. It acquired organization as it moved ahead. Villages and farmhouses do not lend themselves to organization under such conditions. They are too widely scattered and too individualistic. But Hungary had seen peasant revolts, and there were no signs even of a *jacquerie* in the land during the revolution.

There was a basic reason for this restraint. We have seen how the peasants lived in Hungary up to the end of the Second World War—the majority of them wretchedly poor and oppressed. Then came the end of the war, and for the first time in the history of the country the estates were distributed. The land reform was effected not by the Communists, to be sure, but by a coalition government in which the Smallholders had numerical preponderance. However, it was the Communists who claimed credit. Whoever was responsible for the reform, there were no magnates now on the Hungarian countryside, not even too many *zsiros parasztok*, fat peasants, kulaks. Many peasants helped the revolutionaries with free food, but on the whole they decided to sit out the revolution.

Why Not the Polish Solution?

It will be recalled that Wladislaw Gomulka, Poland's leading non-Stalinist Communist, had been denounced for "nationalist deviation" and had lived under house arrest for years. Then, a few days before the outbreak of the Hungarian revolution, he was accepted by the Soviet Union as the First Secretary of the United Workers' Party (Communists) in Poland. This was accomplished without any bloodshed in Warsaw.

After the success of the bloodless Gomulka revolution, human freedoms were quickly restored in Poland and attempts were made to readjust the country's economic system to its true requirements. Poland at the same time adhered to the Warsaw Treaty of "mutual help" among the satellites and the USSR. Gomulka quickly turned to the West for help and received some aid. The Poles thus obtained many of the things the Hungarians wanted. Why not the Hungarians? Why no "Gomulka solution" for them?

The answer may be provided by the chronicle of the revolution as recorded in the UN Report of the Special Committee on the Problem of Hungary. It registered the fact that at 4:00 P.M. on November 1 the government of Imre Nagy adopted a Declaration of Neutrality, and that at five it invited the Soviet Ambassador to its meeting, informed him of its decision, and conveyed the news to the other diplomatic heads, asking for the "aid of the four great powers in defense of Hungary's neutrality."

Three of these four great powers were members of the North Atlantic Treaty Organization—the United States, the United Kingdom, and France—which the Soviet Union considered its *bête noire*. Inviting them into Hungary must have been regarded by the USSR in the same way as the United States would view an invitation of the Soviet Union and Communist China into Mexico to guarantee her neutrality. The USSR would have been in a minority of one against three. Also, as the report of the United Nations stated, Imre Nagy merely acquainted the Soviet Ambassador in Budapest with a *fait accompli*, without any preliminary negotiations with him. This must have riled the Russians even more.

The Hungarian situation, in this connection, also calls for a comparison with that of Austria. For years after the Second World War the USSR had occupied a part of that country. Vienna herself had been under a four-power occupation, including the Russians. In May, 1955, the Soviets signed the Austrian State Treaty, under which the Russian forces of occupation were withdrawn from the capital and from the

Russian-held zone. Under the same treaty Austria was to become a neutral country, although she acquired the right to
build up her armed forces for defense and internal security.
If the USSR reconciled itself to Austrian neutrality, why
not to Hungarian neutrality too?

The locations of the two countries may provide part of
the explanation. Hungary is directly contiguous to the Soviet
Union, while Austria is not. Austria never called in the United
States, Britain, and France to guarantee her neutrality. It was
in the Soviets' interest to relinquish an outpost which was
expensive to man in peace and hard to hold in war. It was
also in Austria's interest—and the Kremlin knew this—to remain neutral. That was a desirable solution for a small country wanting to lead an independent life. Austria could have
armed herself fully only with great power aid, and she had
enough of that when she was armed by Germany. In the case
of Austrian neutrality, then, both Vienna and Moscow took
calculated risks.

The situation in Hungary would have been different. First,
there was Nagy's blunder in asking the guarantee of the four
great powers. Then, Hungarian neutrality gained under such
conditions would have been wrung from the USSR, not
granted by it of its free accord. Russia did not know whether
the other satellites were not crouching in those history-filled
moments, waiting for their chance to break loose. She could
not afford to lose face. And indeed the Hungarian revolution
did not spread, as the Kremlin lion tamer kept the unruly
beasts on their perches. The satellite empire did not dis-
integrate.

Another theory of why the Soviets shunned the "Gomulka
solution" in Hungary and chose a violent method was suggested subsequently by the Prime Minister of India, who was
well informed on these matters. Speaking in the Lok Sabha
(House of Commons of India) on July 23, 1957, Jawaharlal
Nehru said: "It was a great misfortune for Hungary that this

[revolution] coincided with the Anglo-French intervention in Egypt because both these things coming together raised the tempo of the world situation and the temperature was high, no doubt. There was grave danger in the minds of many people and many governments that war was coming. Because of that, many things were done which, perhaps, normally would not have been done." *

The Role of the Radio

The Soviets charged that Radio Free Europe and other Western radios, particularly American, were inviting the Hungarians to revolution. They produced no evidence in support of this contention. However, the German press was uneasy about the role of Radio Free Europe. At a press conference on January 25, 1957, Chancellor Konrad Adenauer of the Budesrepublik referred to an investigation of his government into the activities of Radio Free Europe. This is what he said:

"Investigation has shown that assertions which appeared in the press, that Radio Free Europe promised the Hungarians assistance by the West—armed assistance by the West—are not consistent with the facts. However, remarks were also made [on the radio] which were liable to cause misinterpretation. But a discussion, an exchange of views, took place which also resulted in personnel changes, and I believe the matter can be considered settled for the time being."

The report of the United Nations had this to say about the broadcasts:

"In a tense atmosphere, such as that prevailing in Hun-

---

* "Foreign Affairs Record," Ministry of External Affairs, Delhi. Debate for Grants of the External Affairs Ministry. July 1957, vol. III, No. 7, p. 149. (The Anglo-French intervention referred to was the two nations' action in the Suez Canal area in the autumn of 1956, coincident with the Hungarian uprising. It has been suggested in other quarters, too, that the Soviets turned from a contemplated "soft" action in Hungary, à la Gomulka, to a tough one because the Middle Eastern events indicated the possibility of an impending conflict between East and West. As events turned out, the United States and the Soviet Union acted in accord on this issue, although for different reasons.)

gary during these critical weeks, optimistic and encouraging broadcasts, which paid tribute to the uprising, were welcomed. The generally hopeful tone of such broadcasts may well have been over-emphasised in the process of passing from mouth to mouth what various speakers were alleged to have said. The attitude of the Hungarian people towards foreign broadcasting was perhaps best summed up by the student referred to above, who said: 'It was our only hope, and we tried to console ourselves with it.' It would appear that certain broadcasts by Radio Free Europe helped to create the impression that support might be forthcoming for the Hungarians. The Committee feels that in such circumstances the greatest restraint and circumspection are called for in international broadcasting." *

The observer may add that Hungarians were prone to be carried away by their feelings and to regard daydreams as realities. In the revolutionary ecstasy, hopes were easily exchanged for assumed pledges. The Western radios were working around the clock and countless words were uttered—countless words had to be uttered—not all of which were well weighed. Sometimes the tone of voice, the mere intonation, may have indicated that there was more in the *sous-entendu* than in what was said. Both the United Nations Special Committee and Chancellor Adenauer indicated that more care should have been exercised.

Anti-Semitism During the Revolution?

In view of the fact that Hungary is situated in the anti-Semitic belt of Europe and that several of the Stalinists had Jewish backgrounds, what was the attitude toward the Jews? One should recall, though, that Jews were the ones who suffered most from the Stalinists because so many of them were in trade and banking, considered "parasitic" occupations by the Bolsheviks. Also, it should be recalled that some of

* *Report, op. cit.*, par. 131, p. 18.

the most prominent writers who were the spiritual fathers of
the revolution had Jewish backgrounds.

The fighters themselves represented the entire cross-section
of urban society, and there were among them Catholics, Protestants, and Jews. The writer of this book was told about
incidents when one of the fighters would make an anti-Semitic
remark, only to be silenced by others:

"This is not what we are fighting for."

As the days went on the number of anti-Semitic incidents
increased.

"There was enough anti-Semitism to present a danger
signal in a country which recently had gone through several
years of Jew hating," wrote an eyewitness, "and which had
maintained an official anti-Semitic policy since 1919. During
the fifth and sixth days I saw four people attacked and beaten
because they may have been Jews." *

Even more disturbing signs of anti-Semitism appeared as
the hoped-for foreign intervention failed to materialize. Anti-
Semitic posters appeared. One of the slogans that disfigured
the walls of Budapest was a reference to the extermination
camp of Auschwitz, where millions of Jews were cremated
alive during the Second World War by Nazis. This was the
slogan:

"*Itzig, most nem viszünk Auschwitzig.*"—"Itzig †, this time
we won't take you as far as Auschwitz."

At first the Hungarian revolutionaries expected aid from
the United States, and they knew that America did not
condone anti-Semitism. During the war the German Nazis
and their Hungarian allies represented the United States as
verjudet—under Jewish influence. Anti-Semitic inclinations
had therefore to be restrained. When the foreign aid failed
to materialize, most of the outbursts occurred. Perhaps they

---

* "Marginal Characters," by Leslie B. Bain, *The Reporter*, November 15,
1956; quoted in *The Hungarian Revolution*, Praeger, 1957.

† A pejorative appellation of the Jews.

were just the expressions of bitter disappointment. Even so,
they were not so numerous as to indicate a decided trend.

What About the United Nations?

Whenever the Hungarian revolutionaries thought of salva-
tion, they were thinking of the United States and the United
Nations. "Where is the United Nations?" they would ask.
"Why does it not help us? This is aggression." What type
of help did the insurgents want? The help of armed forces?
But the United Nations had no such forces at its disposal.
The General Assembly was in session, and it passed resolu-
tions condemning the Soviet Union. Of what help was it?

The Hungarians were not different from other people in
assigning competencies to the United Nations which it did
not possess. They did not know that the United Nations was
not yet what the people of the world were hoping at its in-
ception that it would become: an autonomous world organization, following the conscience and interests of all mankind.
They did not know that the UN was merely an instrument
which could be activated by a state of mind—and that was
not there yet.

The United Nations went into action in Korea because
the United States considered it a territory of strategic importance for its own security. The UN took no action in
Kashmir, apart from offering its services for mediation. Nor
did it take decisive action in Palestine, or later in Guatemala
or in Algeria. The Hungarian revolutionaries were knocking
in vain at the UN gates.

And the United States? Could it have forced the hand of
the UN? Events were to show that it did not even attempt
to do so. Was it because the government of the United States
considered Hungary as falling within the Soviets' sphere of influence? Certainly not officially. The condemnations of Soviet
action in Hungary were initiated in America. What about our
unofficial attitude?

At the time of the Hungarian revolution, responsible correspondents of responsible American newspapers reported from Washington that had there been an armed Communist revolution in France or Italy, where the Communists were very important and where the United States had armed forces, countries which are important North Atlantic Treaty Organization pivots, American units stationed in those countries would not have been able to look on if their aid had been invoked by the governments of those countries. We may be sure that they would not have acted brutally. But were those correspondents right?

After the Hungarian revolution was over, the United States government could have issued a basic declaration, a new doctrine. It did so: the Eisenhower Doctrine. The United States government undertook to send aid—including military aid—to Middle East countries threatened by the invasion of "international communism," in case those nations invoked American help. No American doctrine covered the Eastern European satellite area. Did this mean that the situation was accepted, that we would keep on protesting through and outside of the United Nations—measures for the record? Certainly the Hungarian freedom fighters were not familiar with the complicated ways of diplomacy.

The Twilight and a Glimmer

Hungary's case can be compared with that of England, in reverse. While Britain has had all the protection of nature that she needed, Hungary has been in every conqueror's way. Name any major conflict for the last thousand years and you will find this little country in the melée. Was it the locusts of the *Völkerwanderung*, the Tatars, Turks or Habsburgs— they all breached those impressive-looking mountain defenses of millennial Hungary. Then came the voracious Habsburgs, with their dynastic wars. *Pax Habsburgica* in Hungary was short and fitful. Even the Grande Armée of Napoleon did not overlook Hungary.

Pax Britannica extended to the Mid-Danube region, too, and Hungary was able to bask in the sun of a short-lived Golden Age. The revolver shot at Sarajevo gave the starting signal for the Marathon race of frenzied great powers and it has not ended yet. An overconfident Italy attempted to take Hungary under the wings of a rejuvenated eagle. Then came Hitler with his New Order under the dispensation of which Hungary was to remain a peasant country. The "thousand year" Reich of the Nazi chieftain lasted for less than a decade in Hungary. Then came the Soviets.

Until the arrival of the Soviets, Hungary appeared to have been situated in the very midst of a power vacuum—a region which lacked the physical strength to defend itself against the encroachments of major powers. Nations in a power vacuum are deficient in the substance of effective sovereignty in foreign affairs. Hungary shared this deficiency with her neighbors on the north, to the Baltic, and on the south, to the Adriatic, the Aegean and the Mediterranean. Particularly, she shared this fate with the Poles.

The Soviets, however, appeared to have filled out the power vacuum with their tremendous presence, an uninterrupted mass of land from Central Europe to the farthest reaches of the Pacific, almost contiguous with the western peripheries of the Western Hemisphere. This looked, indeed, like the realization of the *Pax Sovietica*.

Today, months after the Hungarian uprising of the autumn of 1956, what the Soviets can offer Hungary is not peace but naked force. Bayonets alone do not fill out a power vacuum and nothing but bayonets was available to fill it. The Soviets know where the Hungarians would stand in a major crisis among the great powers and that, surely, must be a restraining influence on them. That power vacuum is there again, that

twilight zone, those tragic peripheries, against which imperial
ambitions have been rising in tidal waves.

If the Hungarians were able to express their will freely
which side would they chose? Before answering this question
let it be said that they learned a lot from the outcome of
their uprising and from subsequent events. They are no longer
as romantic as they were before, believing that they could
remain in possession of their liberated land unaided. They
have learned that there is no such thing as sovereign equality
for small countries. There is only sovereign unequality. They
know, too, that they would need strong foreign backing. But
they have learned that the backing of the United Nations
would be no stronger than the influence of the dominant
group within the UN.

If a completely free plebiscite were held in Hungary, very
few votes, if any, would be cast for the Soviets. They would
get very few votes even from so-called Communists. The
Hungarians' aversion to the Russian is traditional and deep-
rooted. To them Russia has always appeared as the land of
darkness, *Ex Oriente Nox*. This refers, of course, to Russia's
political and social institutions, not to her artists, musicians
and writers. Russia in her Soviet form has been even more
repugnant to the Hungarians.

How would the United States fare in such a plebiscite?
America occupies a special position in the Hungarians' affec-
tions and that has not been changed basically even by widespread disillusionment over official American action at the
time of the uprising. There are few Hungarian families without bonds to Americans—an uncle, a cousin. America therefore is not merely a great power but also a family affair. Also,
America is something that poor people need to feast their
eyes upon, a fable and, even more than that, a dream. The
United States in Hungarian eyes is compounded of more
fiction than reality. There are very few Hungarians who would
not vote for the United States.

Who will ask the Hungarians to vote? Such a plebiscite does not appear to be in the cards as yet. But the field is wide open to our indoctrination assault, Hungarian ears are eager to hear. We need more imagination and intelligence in our approach than we have displayed in the past, a more accentuated and more graduated approach, not all black and white. Above all, we need the deeply human voice which Hungarians still hope is the real voice of America.

Within Hungary herself there are bound to be symptoms of a chronic Time of Troubles. We have seen in our survey of Hungarian history what was the composition of the country's "creative minority" throughout the centuries. That minority consisted of strong and mostly ruthless men, the landed aristocracy and, more recently, an upper middle-class gentry, imbued with the ideology of the historic nobility. Hungary's location between east and west, between the gravitational pulls of opposing great powers, had much to do with this. The country was a perennial battlefield where strong hands were needed in order to offer resistance to endless encroachments. This necessitated the creation of a nation in arms, a certain measure of regimentation and self-confident leadership. The aristocratic leaders were very far from ideal, but they were a leadership.

The Communists in Hungary demolished the old leadership. Not only is the aristocracy gone, but gone also are the gentry. From a historic point of view these developments would have been welcome if the new rulers had succeeded in establishing new foundations—on a more democratic basis. They did set out to build new foundations, an industrial proletariat and a student body. However, the new rulers sought to impregnate the new social strata with ideas that were unacceptable not only to them but also to the entire country.

Today the Hungarians say that while they are in favor of some form of socialism, they are wholeheartedly opposed to communism. By socialism they mean political democracy, a larger degree of social democracy and a hybrid type of economy. They want to retain the desirable features of a partly planned economy, which they consider essential in the case of a country with far more limited resources than the great western powers. At the same time, they also want a certain leeway for the expression of the venturesome individualistic type of production.

Hungarians are today, perhaps, the best qualified people to express valid opinions about the nature and feasibility of communism, as it was interpreted by their so-called Communists. It was not communism at all, they say, if thereby was meant the communal planning and execution of a society-centered way of life. It was arrant Russian imperialism. From the Hungarian point of view, it was not only an absurdity but also a monstrosity because it ran counter to those global movements which cannot be deflected from their ways any more than the sun and stars.

The Communists wanted to denationalize them and to submerge their national feelings in a vast regional Soviet loyalty. This was patently absurd. This is *the* age of nationalism. There are few corners of the world where it has not become the dominant force. Perhaps the world will move toward higher integration in the future—but not yet. Then, and then only, may the prophecy be fulfilled: "Before going out forever, the flame leaps up once more, and the political explosions of our century are nothing more than the climactic blaze that precedes the extinction of virulent nationalism." *

The Communists in Hungary were not able to prepare the foundations of a new "power elite" because they were unable to provide them with the economic incentives that serve as bonds between groups and ideals. The industrial proletariat

* *The Coming Caesars,* by Amaury de Riencourt. New York: Coward-McCann, Inc., 1957, p. 319.

was very poorly off under the Communist regime, with no stake in its continuation, and with no ultimate goal. As to the students, they were certainly not beholden to the idea of working a professional man's treadmill merely for the sake of an elusive idea the practicability of which was never apprehended.

The poor peasants were better off under the Communist regime but they could not serve as foundations of the regime because of the very nature of their work and location. The work was such as to keep even the ambitious from devoting endless hours to extracurricular activities, especially as the farms and villages are widely scattered.

For the first time in a long history, therefore, Hungarians have no "power elite," except for the few professional politicians and their henchmen. What will hold the country together? Fear of the Russian guns, for the time being. How long can such a situation last?

The answer will not be given by the Hungarians or any other satellites. The Hungarian problem is a part of the much larger problem of the cold war. How strong is Russia? Her collapse has been predicted for forty years. How strong is the western alliance? Especially, how strong are such pivots as Italy and France? Are the people right who maintain that this war of attrition between the two giants cannot go on much longer without bankrupting both of them? Are those right who say that the entire cold war idea is absurd since the two giants cannot overwhelm each other with the force of arms? Who knows?

Thus when facing the future there are only questions, no answers, except, perhaps, one. No war has lasted forever, nor can it last forever, hot or cold. No country has unlimited resources to provide itself with all the fantastic weapons modern technology forces upon it. Sooner or later the question of the power vacuum, of which Hungary is a part, will begin to haunt the world. What can be done with that vacuum?

While the writer of these lines does not claim to know the answer, he does know that Hungary did have a Golden Age, even though it was a short-lived one. It was when she formed part of a large economic unit. The late Austro-Hungarian Empire may have been a political monstrosity, but it was an economic necessity. Its economic success shows the way to an ideal solution of the "Hungarian problem" as well as of the problems of the other small countries on the margins of eastern and central Europe. This region is inhabited by some hundred million people, with all kinds of different backgrounds. They are a very unhappy people, who have been kicked around and bruised in this tragic twilight zone.

Western Europe is preparing to set up a "common market" area, within which its members will be able to trade with one another freely, without the obstructions of tariff walls and multi-currency complications. Western Europe already has a Coal and Iron Community, for the production and distribution of those basic communities on a cooperative basis.

If ever there was a region that needed a coal and iron community, a common market and economic cooperation on all levels, it is Eastern Europe. All these small countries in the twilight zone are interdependent, economically insufficient when standing alone but wonderfully complete when working together. Such a community under Soviet thumbs would be worse than useless. But is it a dream to expect that, as all wars, even this cold war will end in time? Is it not possible that this eastern European twilight zone, of which Hungary is a part, may become a strong force, a kind of neutral zone? There is a precedent for this, on the periphery of this zone, and the name of that precedent is Austria. Today she is one of the most prosperous countries of Europe, going her own way. Hers may not be a bad precedent.

Only within the framework of such a larger settlement

can the Hungarian problem be solved. Unless we show sufficient courage to face the irrefutable facts the day may be
not distant when, in Byron's words, "the precious porcelain
of human clay" may be shattered.

OTHER READING

THE FOLLOWING READINGS represent a selection of the more representative books. Those who read Hungarian are referred to the writings of Henrik Marczali and Gyula Szekfű, the most assiduous toilers in the field. Material about Hungary is included also in books on Central Europe and Southeast Europe. A large number of books has been published about Lajos Kossuth, the leader of the mid-nineteenth-century revolution, and about the 1956 uprising.

Apponyi, Albert Grof, and others. *Justice for Hungary*. London, Longmans, Green & Co., 1928.
Bandholtz, Harry Hill. *An Undiplomatic Diary*. New York, Columbia University Press, 1933.
Bethlen, István Gróf. *The Treaty of Trianon and the European Peace*. London, Longmans, Green & Co., 1934.
Brabourne, Cecil Marcus Knatchbull-Hugessen. *The Political Evolution of the Nation*. London, The National Review Office, 1908.
Eckhart, Ferencz. *A Short History of the Hungarian People*. London, G. Richards, 1931.
Glaise-Horstenau, Edmund von. *The Collapse of the Austro-Hungarian Empire*. London, J. M. Dent and Sons, 1930.
Goergey, Arthur. *My Life and Acts in Hungary in the Years 1848 and 1849*. New York, Harper and Brothers, 1852.
Graham, Malbone W., Jr. *The Governments of Central Europe*. New York, Henry Holt and Co., 1924.
Horthy, Nicholas. *The Admiral Horthy Memoirs*. New York, Robert Speller and Sons, 1957.
Jászi, Oszkár. *The Dissolution of the Habsburg Monarchy*. Chicago, University of Chicago Press, 1929.

————. *Revolution and Counter-Revolution in Hungary.* London, P. S. Kin and Son, 1924.

Kállay, Miklós. *Hungarian Premier.* New York, Columbia University Press, 1954.

Károlyi, Mihály. *Memoirs of Michael Karolyi.* New York, E. P. Dutton & Co., 1957.

Kornis, Gyula. *Education in Hungary.* New York, Columbia University Press, 1932.

Kosáry, Dominic G. *A History of Hungry.* Cleveland, The Benjamin Franklin Bibliophile Society, 1941.

Lengyel, Emil. *Americans from Hungary.* Philadelphia, J. B. Lippincott Co., 1948.

Lukinich, Imre. *A History of Hungary in Biographical Sketches.* Simpkin, Marshall, 1937.

Macartney, Carlile Aylmer. *Hungary.* London, E. Benn, 1934.

————. *Hungary and Her Successors.* Oxford, Oxford University Press, 1937.

————. *October Fifteenth.* Two volumes. Edinburgh, Edinburgh University Press, 1956.

Marczali, Henrik. *Hungary in the Eighteenth Century.* Cambridge, Cambridge University Press, 1910.

Mende, Tibor. *Hungary.* London, Macdonald & Co., 1944.

Mikes, George. *The Hungarian Revolution.* London, André Deutsch, 1957.

Montgomery, John Flournoy. *Hungary, the Unwilling Satellite.* New York, Devin-Adair Co., 1947.

Nagy, Ferenc. *The Struggle Behind the Iron Curtain.* New York, The Macmillan Company, 1948.

Padover, Saul Kussiel. *The Revolutionary Emperor, Joseph the Second.* London, J. Cape, 1934.

Paloczi Horváth, Gyorgy. *In Darkest Hungary.* London, Victor Gollancz, 1944.

Pribram, Alfred Francis. *The Secret Treaties of Austria-Hungary, 1879–1914.* Two volumes. Cambridge, Cambridge University Press.

Redlich, Joseph. *Emperor Francis Joseph of Austria.* New York, The Macmillan Co., 1929.

Rutter, Owen. *Regent of Hungary.* London, Rich and Cowan, 1939.

Seton-Watson, Robert William. *Racial Problems in Hungary.* London, A. Constable, 1908.

Teleki, Pál Gróf. *The Evolution of Hungary and its Place in European History.* New York, The Macmillan Company, 1923.

Vámbéry, Armin. *The Story of Hungary.* New York, G. P. Putnam's Sons, 1889.

Yolland, A. B. *Hungary.* London, T. C. & E. C. Jack, 1917.

INDEX